The Millennial Money Masterplan

How Millennials (and anyone else
for that matter) can achieve
True Financial Freedom
in 10 years or less

Matthew Smith

First published in Great Britain by Springtime Books

© Matthew Smith, 2021

ISBN: 978-1-8381746-3-7

Designed by Upshot
upshotdesign.co.uk

Disclaimer

Although every care has been taken, the author cannot take any responsibility for any actions taken or omitted to be taken as a result of this book. Financial and tax rules can and do change and if you are in doubt you should seek personal advice from a qualified financial planner.

Praise for The Millennial Money Masterplan

"An insightful and engaging piece of work! Matthew has distilled these pearls of wisdom, acquired through years of advising high net worth families, into a few practical steps for everyone. The ideas in this book will not only save you tons of money, they'll save you a lot of headaches and help you build a financial future that many people can only dream of."

Abraham Okusanya
CEO, Timeline

"Finally, a book that talks directly to the group of people who've in some ways been left high and dry by conventional financial education and money lessons passed down by their parents. The millennial generation does have a financial challenge and the first step in tackling this challenge is becoming wise around their money and habits. This book pulls no punches and is an essential resource for anyone wanting to take control of their financial future."

Andy Hart
Founder, Humans Under Management

"This is an inspiring book about money – and life. Written in a no-holds-barred, down-to-earth, life is not a rehearsal way, it will inspire you to take action – NOW! Pay attention to what young Matt has to say, before it's too late!"

Paul Armson
CEO, Inspiring Advisers and author of
Enough? How Much Money Do You Need For The Rest of Your Life?

"People say that Millennials are different to 'normal' people! Turns out that is both correct and incorrect. In this amazing book, Matt Smith shares with us how to understand what is important and how to achieve it. While written for Millennials I would urge parents to read this book to better understand what their children are thinking and how to help them achieve what they want in life."

David Batchelor
MD, Wills & Trusts

To Katherine

For never giving up on me. For supporting me and
believing in my battles, no matter how tall the odds.
For letting me be free. For your love, kindness and
support – forever and always.

To Amy

For being the sunshine that lights up my days.
In many ways this book is for you in the hope you
see that you too can be free.

Acknowledgements

This book, like all of my professional endeavours and business exploits, would not have been possible without the love, support, encouragement and counsel of my wife, Katherine. When we married in 2013, we said for better, for worse, for richer, for poorer, in sickness and in health. I think it's fair to say I've tested all of those vows (especially the 'in sickness' one) to the limit. If nothing else our married life has been eventful – definitely not boring – and through it all Katherine has been there for me, unwavering in her selfless care and affection.

I would also like to thank my daughter, Amy, for that wonderful smile and for those delightful observations about the world around us that only a child could have. I hope one day this book will guide you in your financial life. That you can follow in my footsteps and find *your* freedom, whatever that means for you.

To my mum, dad and brother. Thank you for a wonderful upbringing and family life. Thank you for all the advice and guidance over the years which, although I might not have known it at the time, has had the most profound impact on how I live my life today. I love you all dearly.

To Graham, Alex, John & Jay. Thank you for being the best friends that any guy could wish for. For always making it feel like it used to, even if we've not seen each other for years on end.

This book would not be anywhere near as polished or refined without the input of my editor and writing mentor, Jo Parfitt. There have been times I have wanted to scream and shout when receiving yet another volley of comments, criticisms and amendments to make, but the book you hold in your hands is so much better for it. Thank you for your patience and counsel as this book has grown from an idea to something I hope can be much, much more than that.

David Scarlett deserves a special mention for being my long-suffering business coach and mentor. David, you helped me to see the art of the possible before I was even aware of the term. You helped me to believe in myself and believe in my business. I'm not sure I would be where I am today if not for your guidance and support in this journey we call business and life.

Dan Sullivan and Strategic Coach have been a huge part of my entrepreneurial journey, and the support of my wider workshop group has been invaluable.

I would also like to thank the Internet entrepreneurs I've been following from afar for years now. People who I've never met personally, but have had a huge influence on my life and business. People like Brendon Burchard, Amy Porterfield, Michelle Schroeder-Gardner, Grant Sabatier and many more.

My team in Buckingham Gate have been instrumental in creating the fantastic business we have today. Their hard work and dedication have led us to achieve things we could only dream about a few years ago. You are all amazing. Thank you for believing in me and believing in our mission.

Finally, I would like to thank my wonderful clients in my businesses, both online and offline. I say this at every annual conference and every online event (in fact, every opportunity!) but it's because of you I get to do what I love every single day – I am not sure many people in this world get to say that. I will forever be in your debt.

Contents

PART 1
The Essential Lessons

PART 2
The 6-Step Process to Prepare
You To Achieve True Financial Freedom

PART 3
The Hallowed Ground – Passive Income

Important Terms

True Financial Freedom

A world where money works for you, not against you. Where you do not have to worry about money ever again. Where money is your slave and not your master.

A world where you do what you want to do when you want to do it, not what you have to do when you are told to do it. Where you work because you love it, not because you need the money.

A world where money creates joy and empowerment, not anxiety and stress. Where money is not a ball and chain, but a positive force for change in your life.

NB. You will notice many references to financial freedom in the book. Let me be clear right from the off: there's a difference between financial freedom and True Financial Freedom. There are a lot of people who have financial freedom – that is, they have the money to do what they want to do. But despite having that money, they might not have the time to enjoy it, or even enjoy what they are doing to earn it – not really freedom at all in my book.

True Financial Freedom, on the other hand, means you have enough Passive Income to live life totally on your terms. You have enough income being generated while you sleep to do what you want to do, where you want to do it, when you want to do it. This is your Perfect Life. It might involve work that you want to do, it might not, but True Financial Freedom should never be reliant on work to generate income.

Freedom Figure

The amount of capital or the monthly income that you need in order to achieve True Financial Freedom in your life.

Freedom Fund

The bank accounts, savings and investment products where you will save and invest to accumulate your Freedom Figure.

Foreword

I first met Matthew when he was wading through some desperately exhausting and demoralising months businesswise and that threatened to run into years. This harsh truth makes the narrative and advice you're about to read all the more impressive.

That meeting took place not long after his near-death experience. An experience which, looking back, gave that 26-year-old the perspective and wisdom of someone easily 20 years older.

When you couple that wisdom with a mind and heart that refuses to give up – refuses to be cowered by impossible odds; well, you have a combustion of gifts that is nigh on unstoppable.

Add to that a creative streak that sees wonder and opportunity in the most difficult situations and you have someone who has a voice worth hearing. You also have someone who has gathered around him a young, vibrant team building a role-model of a business, which demands serious professional skill.

With all of that glorious, praiseworthy talk, it's time I raised a serious question about Matthew. And it's this:

"Where on earth was the 'Matthew' in my life, when I was in my 20s?"

Because I know what it's like to lose everything. Everything!

I know what it feels like to be walking the uglier streets of London, terrified that I'd not find a place to sleep before the cold, wet night descended. Jobless. Homeless. Months of self-inflicted embarrassment, misery and hopelessness.

Yet, here I am today.

Showing business leaders how to build inspiring businesses, and so transform their world. Teaching undergrads and graduates courses in philosophy, religion and leadership skills. Leading, writing, coaching, blogging, podcasting, and creating educational programmes.

Totally debt-free. Enjoying life – in spite of lingering post-Covid symptoms. Married to a ridiculously wise being, whom I adore. Engaging constantly with our five talented adult children: each making their unique mark in the world.

How did that massive change come about? It happened because I was 'rescued' by people like Matthew!

I was fortunate enough to start mixing with people who saw the world through eyes undimmed by the doom-laden media (or the half-baked stories from social media today).

I was fortunate to be taught basic principles of Financial Freedom by those same people. Not just that, but a more selfless and caring way of living. These people shaped my life to the depths of my core.

I was so influenced by what I learned that I eventually became a financial planner myself, ultimately advising successful business leaders. In doing so, I vowed I would help others avoid the mindsets and short-sighted habits that brought me (literally) to my knees.

What I love about this book is that it lays before you what really works. It just does.

I love what author and leader Nancy Kline says about shaping our future: *"The quality of everything we do – everything – depends on the quality of the thinking we do first."*

The principles and practices you're about to encounter can reshape *your* thinking. With that thinking, you'll have the chance to build different habits. And with those habits will come a different financial destiny.

They'll help you overcome the darkest of times in your financial life. They'll help you to think for yourself: in a way that will astound and revitalise your belief in your human capacity to invent your own future.

Time and time again, I've seen young (and not so young) people rise from dire circumstances – because of the truths you're about to learn in this timely book. I've seen them rise – literally – from the gutter. Then go on to shape their world.

This book explains fundamental truths that will reshape the way you think about money.

It will start you playing a long-term financial game that avoids the short-sighted mentality we pick up when leaving secondary education. It will help you understand how wealthy – even rich – folk think. You'll find that's probably not like most of the folk you might associate with today!

It will show you step-by-step processes to powerfully shift your mindsets and emotions about how money truly works.

Thankfully, it will help you see – and avoid – some pitfalls that consumed me in my earlier years.

My hope is that you don't just see this as a 'quick read'.
My hope is that you'll recognise when gold-dust is held in your hands.
My hope is that this becomes a workbook to your financial future.

**Matthew might not have been there to help my thinking in my 20s.
But he's here – right now – for you.**

Take this opportunity – this Millennial Money Masterplan – while you can.

David J Scarlett
Author of *The Soul Millionaire* and *The Flight of the Soul Millionaire*
The Soul Millionaire, www.soulmillionaire.com

Preface

It was May 2018 when I wrote the opening line of this book. I was sitting on the train (I tend to write in transit) and staring out of the window when an idea came to me: what if I could start a movement to help Millennials reach True Financial Freedom?

The clients I work with in my Financial Planning practice have already, in most cases, reached their Freedom Figure. If not, they are generally pretty close. I love working with these people and helping them solve the puzzles and complexities that significant wealth brings.

But what about their children and grandchildren? What about the millions of people who aren't already wealthy, but who'd certainly like to be? There's a huge Millennial generation that needs guidance on how to reach True Financial Freedom, but they probably don't have the wealth to pay for a professional Financial Planner. Could I help them? How?

Once this idea popped into my head, I just couldn't let it go!

The world in 2018 looked very different from the world today. Around a decade earlier, we had the Global Financial Crisis – so big and so profound it has its own acronym, the GFC! Until recently the GFC was still talked about in news programmes, blogs, magazines, and in pubs and bars the world over. Even though it happened well over 10 years ago, that's how much of an impact it had on people. Little did we know at the time that just two short years later another crisis would strike – one that would impact not just our finances, but our lives and health too.

The GFC caused huge, sometimes irreparable damage to the financial fortunes of many people. But it's widely accepted that younger people took the lion's share of pain. It's been reported that the GFC caused more harm to Millennials' job prospects, career progression, wealth accumulation and housing ambitions than other generations – simply because they had less to begin with.[1]

You see, those people who had wealth at the beginning of the crisis would have seen a *temporary* decline in that wealth, which quickly recovered. For those people who already had stock market and property investments, they suffered for all of about two years. The FTSE 100 (the leading index of large company shares in the UK) fell by around 42% between May 2008 and March 2009 – it was totally devastating some might say. But it had recovered almost all of those losses just 13 months later by April 2010.[2] The property market recovered within three or four years too in most parts of the country.

What's really telling, though, is what happened after that recovery – after the losses of the GFC were recouped. Well... stock markets and property prices continued to surge, making those people who were wealthy before the crisis even wealthier. The moral of the story: those people who had significant wealth before the crisis often became even richer afterwards.

Now, please don't misunderstand me. In my mind, there's nothing wrong with this. I'm not a Robin Hood-type character who believes we should take wealth away from the rich for some mass re-distribution (although everyone should, of course, pay their fair share). Despite the very rare exceptional story of people being born into money or winning the lottery, most wealthy people I know got there the hard way. They worked for what they have – very hard. They sacrificed and made wise financial decisions in order to accumulate what they have today. I believe they *deserve* to be wealthy. And one of the great rewards of accumulating wealth is the opportunity to grow even wealthier.

But what about those people who *didn't* already have wealth at the beginning of the crisis – predominantly the Millennial generation? Well... for them life was made harder. As businesses cut wages and even jobs to survive, those people on the receiving end were made worse off. It meant they couldn't save money for a property deposit to have their own home, let alone save money into a pension or make investments for their future.

The challenge here is that, if people can't afford to buy their own home, they tend to rent one. Their landlord will generally be someone who is wealthy (someone who owns rental properties) and so the gap gets wider. The people who are already wealthy become wealthier still by receiving income from those losing wealth in rental payments.

What's more, the price of property and investments rose higher than before the crisis because of a spectacular recovery. So we end up with a catch-22. Millennials have less income and therefore less ability to accumulate wealth while, at the same time, the assets they are saving to buy (houses, investments, etc.) have risen in price. It doesn't sound like a story with a happy ending.

Again, this is not to attack those in a fortunate financial position, but to acknowledge the challenges that younger people face when starting out on the financial ladder.

Come 2018, when I first put pen to paper, there was some light at the end of the tunnel. Things were starting to look up. The economy had recovered to a greater or lesser extent and people's incomes had risen. Would you believe, there were even positive catch-ups in the media with Millennials 10 years on from the GFC to see how they were doing – and many of them were doing fairly well.

There were stories about how Millennials had started businesses, created new and innovative ways to earn income and re-trained into much more rewarding and fulfilling careers. All the while they were *living* more – more travel, more experiences, more time with friends and family.

As I sat there on the train on that sunny, May 2018 morning, I thought to myself, *perhaps things are actually looking up for Millennials? Perhaps they don't need this book? Perhaps I will be wasting my time?*

Then... COVID happened.

The world was plunged into an enforced economic and social recession the likes of which have never been seen before. The GFC was described at the time as an 'unprecedented' financial crash, but the COVID-crash quickly blew those records out of the water – and they were not the kind of records we ever thought would be broken.

Stock markets fell at the fastest rate in living memory. People were made redundant, furloughed and lost their income at a devastating pace. The UK economy lost nearly 20% of its value in three months![3]

Young people once again seem to be taking the brunt of the damage. The BBC reported that half of 16 to 24-year-old workers were furloughed, compared to only 25% of those over the age of 45. The unemployment rate for those in the 16–24 bracket rapidly increased to 13.1% compared to 4.1% for the population as a whole. At the same time, online graduate job vacancies fell by an astonishing 60%.[4]

And what happened to those people who were already wealthy at the beginning of the crisis? You guessed it: they got wealthier. Stock markets around the world recovered within weeks this time, going on to break new records in some cases. UK property prices boomed as people looked for more space as they escaped the cities. So, once again, it's the young facing the toughest time as the world recovers from what has been the most severe economic shock ever recorded.

With everything going on in the world right now it'd be easy to just give up. Every five minutes it seems there's another news story about the devastating economic consequences of this pandemic on young people (and older people too, of course) or another story about a business going bust, people losing their jobs, their homes and their livelihoods. In fact, you might say the media is painting a picture of complete and total desolation. All of this before we even come on to the obvious health impact of the crisis, which I'm sure has touched everyone in one way or another.

I'm telling you *not* to give up just yet.

People felt the same back in 2008. There was a sense the world was coming to an end and we all might as well give up and go home.

But out of that adversity was born a new breed of Millennials. There were many who stood up, who fought on through the pain, who triumphed against it all. These Millennials have created new businesses, new income streams, new lives for themselves – and all during one of the most challenging decades on record for young people's economic prospects.

As we come out of the COVID-crisis, you have a choice. Will you be one of the people who just gives up? Who thinks to themselves, *why even bother?* Or will you be one of those who fights, who innovates, who takes control of their own destiny?

Someone said to me this book had been made redundant by the COVID-crash. That Millennials are in such dire economic circumstances the possibility of True Financial Freedom doesn't even register. That they're worrying about how to make ends meet at the end of the month, or where to find a new job.

While these concerns exist for many, I don't buy into the narrative. I believe despite the current circumstances we find ourselves in that Millennials envision a better life. They want financial security and they want to live a life they can love.

I believe the Millennial Money Masterplan you hold in your hands was relevant in 2018 and is *more* relevant now than ever before. No matter where you're starting from, no matter your current position, no matter how hopeless things seem right now, I promise that you can get to where you want to be. I know it because I've been there. I've been through a near-death experience. I've been through dire economic times. I've been on the verge of giving up. But there's light at the other end of that tunnel and, believe me, when you emerge on the other side, the view is breathtaking.

So, buckle up – you're in for one heck of a journey!

---

1 www.businessinsider.com/millennials-financially-behind-great-recession-wealth-2020-6
2 www.londonstockexchange.com/indices/ftse-100?lang=en
3 www.bbc.com/news/business-53918568
4 www.bbc.com/news/explainers-54005156

How To Use This Book

The most important thing you need to do when you read this book is not take offence.

In the following pages I generalise about Millennials and Baby Boomers, but please don't be upset. Consider my flippancy to be a kind of shorthand for a mindset – and not a judgement.

What I'm Talking About When I Talk About Baby Boomers and Millennials

First off, I'm a Millennial. I belong to what is, in my view, one of the most exciting generations of all time. We have grown up with the most amazing opportunities in life and have taken full advantage of them all. As a group, we are changing the world and the way we do things both in our society and in the way we work. We are even thinking about colonising other planets (OK, so Elon Musk is not technically a Millennial, but close enough in my book).

Most of my clients are Baby Boomers and I love working with them. They are the reason my business exists, and I would not be writing this book were it not for the lessons they've taught me. They are, in my view, one of the most resilient, disciplined generations ever to have lived. They've adapted and thrived in a world that's changed almost beyond recognition since they were children.

In order to write this book, it's been necessary to make generalisations and assumptions about these generational groups.

When I make these generalisations please know they are backed up by large-scale studies from reputable sources (the UK's Office for National Statistics, for example) and are designed to represent the experience and position of each generation as a whole.

Of course, there will be exceptions to the general rule. **In fact, the purpose of this book is to make *you* an exception to the general rule.**

Learning From Each Other

Throughout this book, I will look at the strengths of each generation, but also their weaknesses. This is not to criticise, but rather study what each generation can learn from another.

I truly believe the Boomers have a lot to teach Millennials about how to save and accumulate wealth. I also believe that Millennials have a lot to teach Boomers about how to spend and enjoy money (but that's the subject for a different book entirely).

Case Studies of Success

As we go through the book, not only will I give you all the theory, tools and resources you need to make this happen in your own life, I will also walk you through some simple case studies to show how other people have made it happen too. Some of these case studies feature what I call *micro-celebrities.* These will almost certainly be people you've never heard of before, but can have millions of followers in their niche markets. Although these case studies are great, some people might be a little put off that they don't feature 'normal people'. Now first off, let me be clear: everyone starts off as a *normal* person. Nobody is born more 'special' than anyone else. Most 'special people' started off normal and worked super hard at something to get to where they are today.

Just to make sure you feel all of this is believable, though, I will also include some case studies of my own clients. These are definitely 'normal people' (although very special in my mind), and they are certainly not celebrities, micro or otherwise.

These stories have all been reproduced with the permission of those who feature in them. However, to protect the privacy of those who have kindly shared their experiences, the names and specific details have been changed slightly to protect their anonymity. (The stories are all 100% real-life experiences, but James might become Jeremy and Barclays might become HSBC – just to maintain privacy.)

Deceptively Simple

The vast majority of the recommendations in this book are deceptively simple. I have not reinvented the wheel or discovered how to turn water into money. The advice in this book is a distillation of decades of work in the personal Financial Planning and FIRE (Financial Independence Retire Early) communities.

You might be tempted to think the ideas that follow are too simple. You might be tempted to think, *if it's this easy, why doesn't everyone do it?* Now, just to be clear, I didn't say easy, I said 'simple'. There's no doubt that the methods for personal financial success are straightforward to understand. You don't need to have a finance degree or be a maths professor to put these tips into practice.

Despite the simplicity of many of the strategies you'll find in this book, most people don't put them into action. It makes no sense when you think about it (*why would people not implement simple things to improve their own financial life?*) but it's still true – most people are just not doing this stuff. I hope in reading this book you can become an exception to the rule.

I can't take credit for all the systems you find in the following pages, because I didn't invent them. In fact, many of the methods I recommend are so logical, so commonsensical, so in tune with human nature, that I'm not sure anyone knows who invented them. Some of these strategies are probably as old as money itself.

What I have done here is package all these tips, tricks, methods, systems and strategies into an easy-to-follow book that will guide you towards True Financial Freedom. This book will tackle concepts step-by-step so you can follow along and watch improvements happening in your life from the moment you begin.

What I am saying is: please don't equate the simplicity of these ideas with their ability to radically change your life. The simplest things are often the best, and that is very true when it comes to personal finance. The beauty of True Financial Freedom comes from the simplicity of the strategies you need to get there.

While the methods I prescribe are simple to understand and easy to implement, you will need some commitment, hard work and dedication to make this work for you.

Now, as I Was Saying, About This Book...

With that out of the way, let me briefly explain how the book is laid out.

The text is divided into three PARTS and in each I use the analogy of a journey up a mountain to explain the Journey to True Financial Freedom.

PART 1 contains the vital groundwork you need to start your Journey to True Financial Freedom. It will highlight some universal truths you need to know, understand and internalise to be successful.

It also contains little-known secrets that will become vital companions on your Journey. This part of the book is mainly about **mindset** and **preparation** – how you need to *think* if your Journey to True Financial Freedom is going to be successful.

Consider this part of the book like the research you need to do before you even leave your house to head to the mountain. These are the things you need to read, comprehend and prepare for before you even set off.

PART 2 walks you along the path to the base of the mountain, step by step. Please note that this is a long Journey – it's a trip in itself just reaching base camp and the hardest part of the route, the mountain itself, still remains ahead.

But this section contains huge insight and actionable steps to lay the groundwork for you to achieve True Financial Freedom in your own life. This part of the book is about **action** – what you need to *do* to make True Financial Freedom a reality.

PART 3 begins at the bottom of the mountain as you begin the climb to the peak. This is always the hardest part of any mountain journey, but also the most rewarding. When you reach the top, you will notice things you didn't see before. You can look out over the vista and appreciate the world in new ways. That is the power of True Financial Freedom!

Do This First – Read

I would suggest in the first instance, you read the whole book cover to cover. Don't stop, don't do any of the tasks or homework, just read.

Once you have read through the book the first time, I guarantee you will have a different perspective on True Financial Freedom and how you can get there.

Do This Next – Roll up Your Sleeves

Now read it again. Yes, you read that correctly. Please read the whole book a second time, starting inevitably with *PART 1* in full. This time I recommend that you take your time and complete all the tasks, in order, and then take some more time to read the resources at the end of each chapter.

Now, this may seem like hard work (reading the book twice) and it is. But I can promise you'll get a lot more out of it the second time. When I read any books on personal or business development, I always use this strategy because it works every time. The first read-through I call the *leisure read* – just read through at your own pace and enjoy it. The second is the *action read* – this time, you must take action and implement what you learn.

And Then This – Back to Reading Again

PART 2 is split into sections that I call *Steps*. This is the practical stuff you need to do to help you on your Journey to True Financial Freedom.

Re-visit *PART 2* as many times as necessary throughout your Journey. You will need to. The content of this book is the distillation of over a decade of trial and error, of blood, sweat and tears, of success and failure and the lessons that come from this experience.

PART 3 is all about the final part of the Journey. You can only begin this section once you're ready, once you've read and implemented all the learning that comes beforehand.

This Journey takes time. Some people will get there faster than others, but know this: if you truly commit to creating a life of True Financial Freedom, you will get there.

It'll need hard work and dedication, there'll be times where you feel like turning back, but you *will* get there.

So, without further ado, let the Journey begin.

Introduction

The world is broken. We live in a time where Baby Boomers have accumulated vast amounts of wealth in property and assets, while their Millennial children struggle to make ends meet, let alone buy a property or save for a pension.

Millennials vs Boomers

Those aged 16–34 in the UK make up around 30% of the total population, yet have only 14% of the total wealth. Those aged 65 or over similarly make up around 30% of the population, yet have 36% of the total wealth – 2.5x more![1]

This problem will be exacerbated over the years to come because Millennials are renting properties in proportions that haven't been seen since before the Second World War. Private rented housing has grown almost twofold over the past decade.[2]

||||||||||||||||||||||||||||||||||||||||||||||||||||||||||||||||||||||||||||||||||||||||||

FACT Over 30% of Millennials now expect to rent a home for their whole lives![3]

||||||||||||||||||||||||||||||||||||||||||||||||||||||||||||||||||||||||||||||||||||||||||

Common sense financial advice has always been to buy a property as soon as you can because anything paid in rent is dead money. Sound as this advice may be, Millennials are not able to save the deposit required to get on the property ladder, consigning them to rent for years or even decades to come.

And who are they renting from? You guessed it: the Boomers. As a result, this wealth divide is only set to grow over the coming decade or two. Millennials will continue to pay rent to the Boomers, making the Boomers' pots larger and larger, while the Millennials continue to struggle to pay the rent each month (let alone save anything for the future). According to the UK Ministry of Housing, Communities & Local Government, the Boomers are expected to acquire even more rental properties, pushing house prices up further and continuing the cycle.[4]

A Bleak Millennial Future

This issue has emerged in the years since the turn of the millennium and is one that governments and policy makers have yet to fully take hold of. But just imagine the world 30 or 40 years from now when most Millennials *should* be retiring.

The problem is that none of them have any savings to retire for the next five minutes, let alone what could be five decades. (Yes, rising life expectancy means if you're 30 today, you might plan for a 50-year retirement.)

During their 20s and 30s Millennials were too busy enjoying life and/or struggling to make ends meet to really think about saving for the future. They just got by and enjoyed life where they could, taking holidays and experiencing the world as and when the opportunity presented itself.

During their 40s and 50s – when previous generations were waving goodbye to children and the real saving started – they were still struggling to pay rent. They never did manage to save a deposit and there's little hope of them doing so now because they have two children (born when the parents were in their mid-30s – evidence suggests Millennials are having children a lot later in life).[5]

As they enter their 60s and 70s, now the children have left home (if they can afford to that is), finally some saving can start. But it's too late: not only do they not own a home, so they're *still* paying rent, but they're saving so late in life there's no time for the power of compounding (where interest earned on money then earns more interest) to work its magic. As a result, they have to keep working to make ends meet.

As they move into their 80s and 90s (yes – reaching the age of 90 will be commonplace by the time we Millennials get there), their health starts to fail. They're no longer able to work and so they have to retire, but they have very little to retire on. They are reliant on the state pension or social security (if these even exist by then) and have to cut back on everything (food and heating included) just to get by.

Does this sound like a future you want a part in? I didn't think so.

The other big issue we have is the media making this all much worse. The media loves to run stories about how Millennials will never afford a home or be able to retire, and on how the Boomers are taking over the world with their burgeoning buy-to-let property and share portfolios.

Millennials are resigned to a life of financial strife. They have submitted themselves to never owning a property, never having substantial assets and possibly never being able to retire – and this message of doom and gloom is being propagated by the media every single day.

What's worse is that Millennials are starting to accept this as the status quo. They're hanging themselves out to dry and thinking, *why bother?*

Something has to give. Something has to change.

Having read all of this, you may have reached the conclusion I have a problem with the Boomer generation. In fact, this couldn't be further from the truth. I love the Boomers. They're the clients I work with every day and who I'm fortunate enough to help with their retirement and estate planning. They're the reason I have a business and the reason I'm well on the way to achieving my Freedom Figure by the age of 35!

The Boomers I work with all have a fascinating story to tell. They've often come from humble beginnings, they've suffered and strived to get where they are today and I believe they deserve the wealth they've accumulated. They also happen to be the people who pay my bills and I could not be more grateful to the clients who've chosen to work with me.

You might also be thinking I'm about to go on a socialist rant and demand the world's wealth be divided up fairly between the generations. *Let's tax the rich and give it to the poor!* Again, you would be very, very wrong.

I believe in capitalism and the free market. I believe that hard work, ingenuity, innovation and value creation are the reason people become wealthy in the majority of cases – so why shouldn't the people who've added the most value benefit from their life's work?

The Boomers have invested a significant amount of blood, sweat and tears to accumulate their wealth. They've often lived fairly simple, frugal lifestyles in order to scrimp and save during their working lives. They have foregone the fantastic experiences and travel adventures that some Millennials take for granted in order to build their nest egg, so why should they be deprived of their life's work?

Is this also the solution for us Millennials, then? Perhaps we need to stop enjoying the world, stop eating out, stop enjoying experiences and adventures, too? Perhaps we should all live at home until we're 30, eating baked beans so we can save a deposit, do the sensible thing and buy a house and live out our days scrimping and saving every penny so we can carve out a reasonable retirement. Doesn't appeal? Didn't think so!

The genie has been let out of the bottle on all of these things that Millennials love to do, and I'm sure it would be pretty hard to put it back in.

Once you are used to a certain type of lifestyle it's very hard to scale it back – and let's be frank, who would want to? Why would you want to stop travelling and enjoying the world? Who doesn't want to enjoy different experiences and take in different cultures? Why would you want to sit there with the lights off, shivering, just so you can save a house deposit? I would rather not, thank you very much!

There Is Another Way

I believe there's a third way. Somewhere between the extreme saving of the Boomers and the extreme spending of the Millennials. I believe there's a new world order. One where people can enjoy fantastic experiences on a regular basis, travel the world and see all it has to offer, eat out with friends over wine and laughter at the weekend yet STILL be able to buy a house, accumulate a nest egg and STILL enjoy more of the same during their retirement (if that word even has a meaning anymore).

You might now be kicking yourself you're not a celebrity or a YouTube star or some other special person. After all, what normal people achieve True Financial Freedom by the age of 40, while still enjoying fantastic experiences, travelling the world, taking extended sabbaticals and so much more? Surely this is just fairy-tale land?

The truth is there's a growing, underground movement of Millennials doing just this. These are not pop superstars or the latest Instagram sensation. They're normal people with normal jobs who've decided to do things differently.

They've decided they can have it all – the house, the lifestyle, the retirement – all while doing the work they love every day. They're using a simple tool (one we've all grown up with and is still under our noses) to create income streams they never thought possible while sitting on a beach sipping margaritas.

So, at this point you have a choice. Do you subscribe to the self-fulfilling prophecy of Millennial doom and gloom? Do you bury your head in the sand, spend every penny you earn and then live a retirement on fish finger sandwiches with the heating turned down (if you can even afford to have it on at all) in your rented apartment? Do you believe the media who tell you you'll never have a house or a retirement, because it makes you feel better about yourself?

OR, do you take matters into your own hands? Do you decide right here and right now to do something about it? To craft a life of True Financial Freedom, one where money works for you and not the other way round? A life where you can do the work you love every day because you want to, not because you have to? A life where money is your friend, not your enemy? A life where you are truly free?

If the latter appeals, join me as we start on this most amazing of Journeys.

Matthew Smith
London, February 2021

---

1 www.ons.gov.uk/peoplepopulationandcommunity/personalandhouseholdfinances/incomeandwealth/
2 www.gov.uk/government/collections/english-housing-survey
3 www.bbc.com/news/business-43788537
4 www.gov.uk/government/collections/english-housing-survey
5 www.forbes.com/sites/ashleystahl/2020/05/01/new-study-millennial-women-are-delaying-having-children-due-to-their-careers/?sh=127fbcf7276a

PART 1
THE
ESSENTIAL
LESSONS

What you must know and
understand in order to find
True Financial Freedom

1

Meet Our Protagonists (Spenders vs Savers)

As I've moved beyond the Big 3-0, I've found myself reflecting more and more on my childhood and the way my parents handled money. You see, I think my parents actually had things pretty much bolted down when it comes to the financial game of life.

We went on good holidays, had a nice home, good food, and hosted events for friends and family. It's easy for children to take all of this for granted. It becomes part of their day-to-day life. It's not until you're much, much older that you start to appreciate the financial cost of this wonderful lifestyle.

Before you start picturing me in a mansion with a silver spoon in my mouth, let me be clear: my parents were not rich. We were comfortably middle class, distinctly average, but certainly not rich.

My mum stayed at home to look after my brother and me for the majority of my childhood, before returning to her job as a school chef once we were a little older. My dad was a sales and marketing manager and used to travel to all sorts of exotic-sounding places for work. Perhaps that's how I caught the travel bug – I was always curious where Dad was going on his adventures.

We lived in what you might describe as the average 4-bed detached house in a village on the outskirts of town. Our old family home would probably be just above the UK average house price, but there were certainly no electric gates, sweeping driveways or Range Rovers on the drive!

For a significant part of my childhood, my dad drove a Toyota Picnic (perhaps one of the worst cars Toyota has ever made) and my mum had a clapped-out Ford Fiesta that had a choke to get it started (Millennials – Google it if you don't know what a choke is!). So you see, we were comfortable, but certainly not rich.

As a child, money seems to grow on trees, doesn't it? Children are always asking their parents for the latest gadget, the newest pair of trainers or the next must-have collectible toy or game, but they never pause to think about the pressure this puts on their parents. As kids, my brother and I were no different.

||||||||||||||||||||||||||||||||||||||||||||||||||||||||||||||||||||||||||||||||||||||||||||||||||||||

 A whopping 6 in 10 parents admitted to buying their children the latest gadgets or toys just so they could fit in, according to a report from the Skipton Building Society.[1]

||||||||||||||||||||||||||||||||||||||||||||||||||||||||||||||||||||||||||||||||||||||||||||||||||||||

What I didn't appreciate back then (and have only come to learn later) is that while all this fun was going on, behind the scenes, my father in particular was preparing a nest egg for the future.

He had a philosophy of Spend Half, Save Half when it came to any excess income and I guess in this respect he was rather unusual, both back then but over time as well. He found a balance many people never achieve. He was enjoying his money now while also making sure he had something put aside for the future.

Perhaps this is because he was in the generation between the Boomers and the Millennials: Generation X. Meanwhile, each week, my mum would keep tabs on our family budget using an A4 ledger book and she still does this to track her budget to this day. Some might call it a little old-fashioned (I prefer Microsoft Excel myself), but it is the principle that matters – those who track and monitor what they spend generally have a better handle on their finances.

As children, we received a small amount of pocket money each week, but if we wanted anything extra, we had to earn it. My parents would usually have a couple of little jobs to do around the house for me to earn an extra pound or two, but these jobs always ran dry before I was done earning (I guess my love of finance started at an early age). Dad would always tell me that if I wanted to earn more I had to go and find ways to make more – and that's exactly what I did.

Aged eight, I started my first business washing cars on our street. I would gather up a group of friends and go knocking on doors along the road asking if people wanted their car washed for £5. This worked great for a week or two, but then people got tired of being asked and the business dried up. That was my first experience of how the world of business and money really works.

Dad would often set us little challenges, though, and in doing so he instilled a work ethic that remains to this day. The pocket money we received was sort of like social security, a small weekly payment that you received regardless of your effort. The jobs Mum and Dad had available in the house were the low-hanging fruit, the easy money, but they were always limited. If you wanted to earn the big bucks, you had to go and innovate something that would generate cash.

I was incredibly lucky to have these money lessons so early in life, but the truth is that many people don't have any financial education at all.

Spender or Saver?

Most people fall very heavily into one of the main money archetypes: the Spender or the Saver. They happily assume one label or the other and think it defines them. They never see the other side, and this makes them rather dysfunctional with money as a result.

Spenders tend to live for today and throw caution to the wind. They don't care about saving for tomorrow. Savers tend to save for tomorrow but sacrifice their enjoyment today. Clearly, neither delivers the happy middle-ground that many of us seek.

Developing the habit of spending is very easy when it's not your money you're spending and you can just ask your parents for all the things you desire (not that you always get them, mind).

These habits became ingrained and as I entered my early teenage years, with the increased financial responsibility that came with it, I started to struggle. I was learning just how hard it was to accumulate money to buy the expensive things I craved. When you're earning £3.30 per hour working in the local pub, it takes a long time to save up for the latest iPhone (or Sony Walkman phone as it was back then).

It took so long in fact that I couldn't wait to get that shiny new phone in all its orange glory. No, I begged and begged my dad to get it for me until he couldn't take it anymore and agreed I could buy the phone, but with one big condition. He insisted I borrow one of his credit cards (I know, what was he thinking?!) on the basis I would pay the monthly payment and any interest incurred while paying it off.

Brilliant, I thought as I scurried down to the shop to get my phone. This was great as I could get the phone now and only have to pay back £16 per month – what could be better?

I remember that trip down to Dixons to buy the new phone. I felt so grown-up paying with my credit card (with Dad there to supervise of course).

I rushed home with the bright-white box and ripped it open with the excitement of a child on Christmas morning. I remember plugging in the headphones for the first time and playing my favourite album (yes – it was a big deal for phones to play music back then).

However, the joy of those initial moments with the phone soon wore off (as they always do with new purchases), and over time it just became normal. As the years passed, the phone started to become obsolete and eventually I replaced it with the latest model.

The problem with all of this, however, is that I was still paying off the credit card bill. The £16 per month was barely covering the interest, so even three years later the balance had barely changed.

It was only many, many months and years later as I entered my early 20s that I appreciated the gravity of what was happening to me. I had become a Spender. I was spending as much as or, in many cases, more than I was earning. I was reliant on credit cards to fund my lifestyle, merrily adding to my balance as time went on.

This was my first (and last) experience with consumer debt and fortunately the balance only grew to a few thousand pounds, but it could easily have been much more.

The initial joy of the new purchase soon wears off and you're left with an ever-increasing pile of debt to manage and worry about at night.

I Blame the Parents

Because my parents had never taught me all the lessons about money they were using in their own lives, I only got to see the spending part – and I became a Spender. I yearned for the lifestyle I'd enjoyed growing up and a little bit more. I'd subscribed to the children-should-have-a-slightly-better-life-than-their-parents motto and this had pulled me off track.

I'm grateful to my dad for letting me borrow his credit card at such a young age as it taught me so much about how easy it is to *spend* money and how difficult it can be to *pay it back later on*. I am not sure if he knew what he was doing when he let me have that shiny rectangle of plastic, but it has been one of the greatest financial lessons of my life and the catalyst for financial success I have enjoyed since.

It's the reason I've made the transition that most people never make, from Spender to Saver (NB – it's equally hard to go from Saver to Spender). But more than this, I've learned to find a happy medium, which is where we're heading on this Journey.

In order to appreciate how to find True Financial Freedom and true balance in your life, first you must understand where you're at right now. The vast majority of people fall firmly into the Spender or Saver category and it's important you are honest with yourself about where you are. Only then can you start to make progress towards where you want to be.

If you're a typical Millennial (there I go generalising again), then the media would have us believe you're a smashed-avocado-on-toast-eating, paid-up lifetime Spender, so let's start with figuring out exactly what characterises a Spender and see if you're the exception or the rule.

So, What Is a Spender?

A Spender is someone who generally spends as much as, or more than (often much more than) they earn. They will often enter the world with a sense of entitlement and when it comes to a big purchase they will think, *why shouldn't I have it? I deserve this.*

Hey, big Spender!

As our Spender grows up, their parents provide nice things and they have a good life. They go on holidays, have the latest trainers and always get a new iPhone when the time comes to upgrade.

After they graduate from school or university they get a job, and at the time the starting salary seems huge. After all, when you've lived for three years on a student budget, even minimum wage seems like a big pay rise!

They use this newfound income to enjoy things they couldn't before. Perhaps they go out to eat more? Perhaps they buy convenience food to enjoy at home? Soon, along comes an opportunity to take a holiday with friends. *Why not?* they think. *I've been working hard for this holiday, I deserve it!*

A few years later, they want to move out. The Spender is tired of living under Mum and Dad's feet and wants some more freedom and independence. They look at buying a house and gulp when they realise a huge deposit will be required. *Fat chance! That's never going to happen,* they think.

They decide to rent a flat because they don't want to wait for 10 years or more while they save up. They choose a nicer, new-build flat overlooking the river because 'it's only £200 a month more' than the tired, older flats around the corner. This might put a bit of a strain on the budget, *but what the heck?* The Spender's career is going well and they're bound to get a pay rise before long.

(It's important to mention that the flat our Spender will rent is probably owned by one of their Saver counterparts.)

To go with the new flat, the Spender wants some new furniture. After all, you wouldn't want a shiny new flat with tattered, hand-me-down furniture in it, would you? The deposit on the flat and the rent in advance have cleared out what little cash the Spender has available, so they put the furniture on a credit card. The monthly payment will only be about £45, so they'll easily be able to afford it with that big pay rise on the horizon.

A few months later, the old banger the Spender drives around breaks down. It isn't cost-effective to repair it so a new car is a must. The Spender looks at a few second-hand cars with low mileage and very reasonable prices, but the salesman tells the Spender they could have a brand-new car with all the bells and whistles for only a £2,000 deposit (less than they would've spent on the second-hand car) and £329 per month.

The Spender can't resist. *Why not have the new car? The deposit is less than I was planning to spend anyway and the monthly payment is affordable. I will definitely be in a better position in three years' time when the balloon payment is due.* (The balloon payment is the big, lump sum payment due at the end of most car finance deals.)

|||||||||||||||||||||||||||||||||||||||||||||||||||||||||||||||||||||||||||||||||||||||||||||

 86% of new cars in the UK are now purchased on credit – this has more than doubled since 2011.[2]

|||||||||||||||||||||||||||||||||||||||||||||||||||||||||||||||||||||||||||||||||||||||||||||

As the Spender enters their early 20s, love is in the air and a proposal is made. Wedding plans start to go into overdrive and of course the Spender wouldn't want to skimp on the most important day of their lives. *Only the best will do!*

The most extravagant venue, the best DJ and a free bar are all must-haves and the wedding dress and shoes need to match the occasion. The final bill: £32,000! The Spender takes a loan from the bank to pay for all this luxury. They quietly tell themselves it'll all be worth it for the best day of their lives but, deep down, there's a sense of discomfort about blowing so much money on just one day.

A few years later, child number one arrives. The Spender feels a little scared at this point because they're already spending more than they earn (if they're honest about the credit card bill creeping up over the past few months), but they tell themselves not to worry. 'We will manage' is what everyone else says, so they will too. Nevertheless, the Spender has a knot in their stomach that feels a little tighter every time a bill hits the doormat.

The Spender simply has to have the latest designer pushchair and clothes for the baby *(who cares if the baby will only wear them for five minutes?)* and all these luxuries go on the credit card. The knot tightens further.

As time goes on, the cost of having children hits home. As the months and years go by, more and more of the weekly shopping bill has to go on a credit card and the monthly budget simply won't stretch.

Whereas before the credit card was being used for non-essentials, now it's relied upon to cover the basics. The Spender knows this is not healthy financial behaviour, but what choice do they have? They start to become stressed and ratty, even when at rest, because the financial burden is taking its toll.

The sharks start to circle

As the credit cards and other debts build up, the bank makes a suggestion. Why not clear all of these credit cards with a lower interest consolidation loan? It will reduce your interest and your monthly payments! *Brilliant*, the

Spender thinks, *this is my saviour. I will get the loan, pay off all the credit cards and then cut them up. Once the loan is paid back in five years I will be debt-free and can start saving for a house.*

By some miracle, the loan is granted for the princely sum of £25,000. The credit cards and other debts only had a balance of £22,000, but the Spender takes the extra £3,000, just in case.

Sure enough, the Spender pays the credit cards off and gets a huge sense of relief as the bills come through the door with a zero balance. As they go to cut the cards up, the Spender hesitates. *Perhaps I should keep just one of these in case of an emergency?* The Spender puts the card with the highest credit limit in the drawer. *I won't use it unless I get really desperate,* they think.

Cue gallows laugh.

A few years later, baby number two comes along. The current car is simply too small, so the Spender must get a new one. They go back to the friendly salesman, who informs the Spender they can trade in their old car for a bigger one. They just need a £2,000 deposit contribution and their monthly payment will go up to £459 per month.

||||||||||||||||||||||||||||||||||||||||||||||||||||||||||||||||||||||||||||||||||||||||||||||||||

 Around 80% of car finance deals are never paid off. Most people just roll them over and take a new car on finance, keeping them forever burdened with monthly car loan payments.[3]

||||||||||||||||||||||||||||||||||||||||||||||||||||||||||||||||||||||||||||||||||||||||||||||||||

The Spender gulps. *Where will the £2,000 come from? We can't afford it!* Then the Spender has an idea: *that credit card in the drawer we saved for emergencies... This feels like an emergency!* Sure enough, the credit card comes out and the £2,000 deposit is paid. They now have the credit card bill to pay again, but at least they get the new car.

Around this time, the Spender gets an interesting offer from their employer. They are improving their pension scheme and if the Spender pays in an extra £50 per month, then the employer will match this with another £50 of free money. *What could be better?* the Spender thinks, but they then come to the realisation they simply can't afford the extra £50 per month. *Oh well, I can always sign up next year.*

Some weeks later, during the weekly shop, the total at the checkout comes to a bit more than expected. The Spender thinks for a second they are going to have to go through the embarrassment of putting some items back. But then, they have a thought. *That credit card is still in my wallet from when we bought the car. I will put the extra on that, it won't make much difference.*

Before long, the credit card is maxed out again. *How did that happen?*

‖‖‖

FACT
While these examples may seem extreme, a recent study by the Financial Conduct Authority in the UK reports that 52% of 18 to 25-year-olds are struggling with debt and that 35% of 18 to 25-year-olds are already over-indebted.[4]

‖‖‖

As time goes on, this cycle continues. The credit card balances continue to climb, the car gets a little nicer (and a little more expensive) each time and the cost of living continues to rise.

As the Spender gets into their 40s, they have the surprise arrival of another child. *Oh dear, we don't have room in the house,* they think. Of course, by now, the Spender had hoped to be able to buy a house, but the pay rises are never quite as big (or as fast) as expected, are they?

We will just have to rent somewhere bigger, thinks our Spender. This time the flat will cost an extra £700 per month. *We are so used to our shiny flat, the new one should really be nicer than the old one, right?* the Spender thinks.

(Of course, our Saver owns this bigger flat too! As property prices have been rising the Saver has been adding to their rental portfolio!).

As the children grow a bit older, the Spender treats them to a nice holiday to Disneyland. All of their friends are going, why should our kids be any different? There's no way they have the money for it so this too goes on the credit card, taking it back up to its maximum limit.

The children have a great time and come to expect this type of holiday regularly.

As the Spender reaches 50, they are feeling the strain of their financial mismanagement. The family finances are on a knife-edge, the bills are piling up and there doesn't seem to be an end in sight. The Spender can't sleep at night for worrying about the family finances.

As the Spender reaches retirement they breathe a sigh of relief. *Surely now things will get better?* Because their employer had a pension scheme, they do have a little bit of money saved up in a pension. They take the lump sum from their pension when they retire. For the first time in decades, the bank account is not at the bottom of the overdraft. Things are looking up. Or are they?

The Spender takes a look at their retirement finances and is disappointed by the meagre pension their employer scheme will provide. Only £2,500 per annum! *Why didn't I pay in those extra contributions?* they think.

In order to balance the books, the Spender has to use their pension lump sum to pay off the car loan and the credit card. *This is the only way we'll ever have enough to live on each month,* they think.

The Spender pays all the bills off, but now the bank account is back into the overdraft.

They only have the state pension and the employer's pension to live on in retirement – only just over £10,000 per year – less than £1,000 per month!

The Spender realises they'll have to move out of their fancy flat into something much smaller and nowhere near as nice. Even then, their meagre income will only just stretch. The credit card limits all get reduced because the Spender no longer has an income, so even borrowing to fund their lifestyle is no longer an option.

The Spender is resigned to their fate. Their retirement will be spent indoors watching TV, counting the pennies, eating food from the discount section. *Why didn't I buy a house? Why didn't I save for a pension? Why didn't I plan for the future?* The Spender realises it's too late to do anything about it.

When the Spender passes away, the family are surprised when they go through the Spender's affairs and find some unpaid bills and credit card statements – it seems the Spender had hidden some debts that no one knew about. Oh dear!

The debts wipe out what little money the Spender had in their bank account (which was only a few pounds in any case) and the rest is written off. Of course, there is nothing left for a funeral, so the Spender's children will have to pay the bill.

The children don't have any money either as they have followed in their parents' footsteps, so they put the funeral bill on a credit card and the vicious cycle starts all over again.

So, What Is a Saver?

A Saver is someone who generally spends less (sometimes a lot less) than they earn. They will often enter the world with an underlying fear of money (or rather not having enough of it). When it comes to making a big purchase, the Saver will think, *I can make do with what I have. I don't need that new shiny thing. I don't deserve it; I can't afford it.*

As they grow up, their parents watch every penny. They have second-hand furniture from the charity shop, their socks are always a little too thin and when they go to bed at night, the house is always a little chilly as their parents turn the heating off.

They never have the latest phone or those new trainers and get stick at school for never having the latest gadget.

||||||||||||||||||||||||||||||||||||||||||||||||||||||||||||||||||||||||||||||||||||||||||||||||||||||||||||

FACT
Over half of school-age children report peer pressure or bullying over having the latest branded consumer goods such as phones and trainers.[5]

||||||||||||||||||||||||||||||||||||||||||||||||||||||||||||||||||||||||||||||||||||||||||||||||||||||||||||

As they graduate from school or university, they get a job, and at the time the starting salary seems huge. After all, when you have lived for three years on a student budget, even minimum wage seems like a big pay rise!

They use this newfound income to start saving for a house, because it's the sensible thing to do. They continue to eat the discount-section food their parents eat, even though it never quite tastes as good as the food their friends seem to enjoy.

A year or so later, a group of friends suggest a holiday abroad. The Saver quivers with excitement at the thought of going away, but then thinks, *I'd better not, that £700 could go towards my house deposit.* The Saver says they can't afford the holiday and tells everyone else to have a great time.

The Saver sits at home the following week, watching the adventure unfold on Instagram (on their six-year-old, and now rather slow, smartphone).

A few years later, the Saver has amassed a deposit for a house. *Now my time has come,* they think. *All my friends have been off enjoying themselves, but now I can buy a home!*

They look at a few different houses and are rather taken with the gorgeous Victorian terrace a few roads from their ideal location, but the price sends a shiver down their spine. They continue looking and settle on a rather drab and run-down fixer-upper a mile out of town. *The walk will do me good,* they think, *and the price is £25,000 less. Imagine what I can do with that £25,000!*

As they move into their new home, the Saver starts to realise the place really is rough around the edges. They go through the house making a list of jobs and repairs to be done. They get some quotes to re-plaster the kitchen *(it really is in a bad way, and is that mould I see on the ceiling?)* but they decide to make do when they see the £900 quote for the work.

When they go furniture shopping for the new home, they look at the lovely oak bedside cabinets and matching headboard but settle on a second-hand divan from the charity shop.

Now they have a house, the Saver can start saving and investing money for retirement. They max out the contributions to their pension plan, start a regular Saver account with their bank and scour the high street for those current accounts that pay 3% on the first £1,000 of your balance. The Saver opens six current accounts and starts to shuttle money between all of them every month to meet the account criteria to earn the interest. *This is a bit of a hassle,* they think, *but I am earning an extra £6.60 a month in interest.*

A few months later, the old banger the Saver drives around breaks down. It isn't cost-effective to repair it so a new car is a must. The Saver thinks about getting a new car (after all, they could easily afford it with all those savings and investments they've been making) but they settle on a cheap and cheerful second-hand car with a small engine and slightly-faded interior. It'll be cheap to run and won't cost the earth to insure, so the Saver is happy.

When they drive the car, they always have a sense of dissatisfaction because it takes so long to accelerate and the air-conditioning doesn't really work. *But that doesn't matter,* the Saver thinks, *the car was really cheap!*

A few years later, baby number one arrives. The Saver doesn't need to worry about the finances because they've been saving for years for just this type of event. They scrimp and save on all of the baby gear, picking up a cheap pushchair with a dubious-looking stain on the fabric.

The Saver starts a university fund for their new bundle of joy immediately and starts building a nest egg for their future.

As the Saver's pot of assets grows, they decide to purchase a rental property. *This will generate some more income for us that we can re-invest for the future,* they think. They purchase a nice new-build flat (much nicer than their own home) because this one has the best rental income. The Spender visits a few days later and decides to rent the property from the Saver.

A few years later, baby number two comes along. The current car is really now too small, but the Saver decides to make do with the (now rather tired) car purchased a few years back. *No one has any room and long journeys in the summer are miserable without any air-conditioning but, what the heck, at least we are saving money!*

When the boiler breaks down, the Saver doesn't break a sweat – there's money saved up for this type of emergency. No problem.

As the Saver gets into their 40s, their nest egg is growing larger. The Saver has several hundred thousand pounds now saved in shares and bonds. This sounds great; however, because so much hard work has gone into the savings pot, they worry about losing the money or having an unexpected expense. *Now we have saved it we wouldn't want to lose it,* they fret.

A few years later, the Saver decides to buy another rental property. This time a much larger one. Despite the fact the other property is generating quite a lot of work (repairs, tenants coming and going, etc.), it's generating a good income, so they decide to push ahead with another one. The Spender visits a few days later with their expanding family and rents this property from the Saver.

As the children grow a bit older, the Saver wants to treat them to a nice holiday to Disneyland. All their friends are going, why should their kids be any different? Then the Saver looks at the price. *£4,000! You must be joking, there is no way we can afford that,* they think. The children will have to settle for a camping holiday in the rain instead.

As the Spender reaches fifty, their finances are becoming increasingly complex. They have accumulated all manner of stock accounts, bank accounts, term deposits, policies, plans and rental properties. The problem is that all these finances cause a huge amount of paperwork. The Saver spends all of Saturday morning each week just sorting and filing it all.

The Saver is also now spending a large part of their evenings and weekends reading about the investment and property markets. The Saver has worked so hard to build up their nest egg, they want to be in the loop on the latest investment news and grab every opportunity to buy or sell a stock. Their spouse is a bit concerned by this behaviour as the Saver becomes increasingly withdrawn. This money business is obviously playing on their mind.

As the Saver reaches retirement, they breathe a sigh of relief. They've saved so hard for this very moment; things should be rosy. They've amassed a huge pot of money for retirement so they should have no financial worries at all. So why the uneasy feeling?

Because the Saver has spent so long building their war chest of assets, the thought of spending it makes them feel sick. They've been building this pot for 40 years, so the psychological shift to move from saving the money to spending some of it is just too great.

The Saver lies awake at night worrying about all the disasters that could befall their huge pot of money. *What if the Stock Market crashes? What if I get defrauded? What if that stock I bought turns out to be a dud?* The Saver tosses and turns at 3am every morning just playing out these potential disasters in their mind. They have a tight feeling in their chest as they ponder all of this. They start to wonder, *what was the point in saving all this money to feel so uncomfortable about it?*

The Saver starts to spend more and more time managing their investments and researching the market. Before long, the Saver is spending over six hours a day just managing their money.

The Saver's spouse also starts to question what the point is if they can't go and enjoy the money.

The Saver is resigned to their fate. Their retirement will be spent indoors watching TV, counting the pennies, eating food from the discount section. All so they can keep saving and building up their huge pile of assets.

When the Spender passes away, the family are surprised going through the Spender's affairs to find out just how complicated the finances had become. There are thousands upon thousands of pages of statements and reports. The Saver's family wonder how they will ever sort through it all.

The Saver's family tidy up the estate. They complete the probate forms and are shocked to see how much of the money gets lost to estate and inheritance taxes. The Saver's children wonder why their father worked so hard to build up this impressive pot of assets if half of it is going to be lost to tax anyway.

The children take their inheritance (minus tax, of course) and start to wonder what to do with it. They think about buying a new car or taking a nice holiday. In the end, they decide to add all of the money to their pensions and pay off the mortgage. After all, that would be the sensible thing to do. The children now have a huge pot of money they're scared to spend and the vicious cycle starts all over again.

Spot the Difference

So now we've looked at the life of both the Spender and the Saver, we can start to see that – although at opposite ends of the money spectrum – both have significant problems with money. It could be argued that both have dysfunctional relationships with money, just in totally different ways.

It could also be argued the above examples are extreme – and in some ways they are, but they're also representative of the way the vast majority of people in Western cultures manage their finances. Even if you can't relate to all of these imaginary case studies, there will be elements you recognise in yourself or others.

In their early years, both the Spender and the Saver are forming habits of a lifetime. We could even call them addictions. These behaviour patterns are very difficult to break free from once they are established, and we've seen how much anguish is caused at both ends of the scale.

These behaviours become embedded and when the time comes to stop, they can't – that's the problem. This is often most-pronounced when people come to retirement. It's at this point where ideally you need to switch from one archetype to another. The Spender needs to become a Saver (or at least cut back on their spending) because they can't afford to sustain their lifestyle with their reduced retirement income. Similarly, the Saver needs to become the Spender and enjoy some of the fruits of their labour.

The problem is that in both cases there's no balance. They've gone all in on their method of dealing with money without ever really questioning whether it was the right way.

Did you notice how both the Spender and the Saver are kept up at night worrying about money? Did you see how they both did a disservice to their family and children when they passed away because of the financial mess they had left behind?

Ironically, the extremes of money seem to cause worry in equal measure: there is worry when you have no money at all and worry when you have too much.

||||||||||||||||||||||||||||||||||||||||||||||||||||||||||||||||||||||||||||||||||||||

FACT
A recent study in the US suggested that 63% of wealthy Baby Boomers were more scared of running out of money than death.[6]

||||||||||||||||||||||||||||||||||||||||||||||||||||||||||||||||||||||||||||||||||||||

Did you spot the fact that both Spender and Saver were dissatisfied with their purchases along the way too? The Spender always wants something a little bit more than they can afford and the Saver is always a little bit disappointed because they scrimped.

The Spender tends to view the world through the eyes of an optimist. They think things will always be better in the future. They tell themselves on a whim there'll be a pay rise or bonus that'll make all their money problems go away. We all know, though, that pay rises are sometimes not as generous as we'd like or that occasionally we don't meet the criteria to earn that big bonus at the end of the year. The Spender continues to believe that everything will be OK in the end, no matter how delusional that might be.

The Spender also tends to feel entitled to things – *I deserve that car or holiday*, is the thinking pattern that can cause so much trouble.

The Saver, on the other hand, views the world through the eyes of a pessimist. They worry that things will get worse in the future or there'll be some big disaster they must prepare for. They agonise about future events over which they have no control, and they can't stand to spend any of their money because they might need it in the future.

The Saver feels they're not entitled to anything. *I don't deserve this*, is their thought pattern.

Did you spot the irony over the holiday to Disneyland? The Spender convinces themself they can afford it and they should take the holiday, despite the fact it's clearly a bad idea and will only cause more financial misery in the future – long after the holiday is forgotten.

The Saver, on the other hand, tells themself they can't afford the holiday, even though they clearly could.

If you pay attention in the real world, 'I can't afford it' is something that people with money tend to say more than people without money, even though the opposite is clearly true. Why do you think that could be?

So, What Does This Have to Do With Me?

You might be wondering what any of this has to do with you. You might be reflecting on how the story of two imaginary characters could have any bearing on your own life.

The truth is, most of us fall very heavily into either Spender or Saver archetypes. You may not even see it yet (these characteristics can often remain hidden beneath the surface for many years) but chances are you had a Spender or a Saver personality factor installed in you by your parents. Your own situation will probably not be quite as extreme as the examples above, but most people I meet fall into one of the two camps to a greater or lesser extent.

One option is to let that character, that archetype, take over and run the show.

You can be the Spender, enjoying all of life's experiences and luxuries, but then wonder why your life is so miserable in retirement.

Or you can be the Saver, amassing wonderful pots of gold, but then look jealously at your Spender friends and wonder why you missed out on so much in life.

As we have seen, both of these paths lead to misery. They both involve sleepless nights and stress. They both mean we miss out on something. They both do a disservice to our family and loved ones.

But imagine if there was a third way. A best-of-both-worlds, Goldilocks scenario. A way that means you can have it all:

> Where you can experience all of life's rich tapestry without consigning yourself to a retirement of misery.
> Where saving for the future doesn't mean scrimping in the present.
> Where early retirement doesn't have to mean living in a yurt in Timbuktu on less than £1 a day (unless that's your idea of a dream retirement, in which case go right ahead – there's no right or wrong here).

If you think this sounds far-fetched or out of reach, then think again. This is happening right now to hundreds of thousands of people. They could be the person sitting next to you in Starbucks on a Tuesday morning or they could be that rather ordinary-looking chap who seems far too relaxed on the train into the city on Friday afternoon.

These people are not loud or flamboyant. You won't necessarily notice them (unless you know where to look), but they're there, living a life of True Financial Freedom right before our eyes.

These people are defining a new world order and it's a world you can be a part of too.

The Journey to True Financial Freedom won't be easy – there will be trials and challenges along the way, and there will be many times when you need to leave your comfort zone (you have been warned).

But, when you think about the alternative, can you afford not to take a leap of faith? After all, what do you have to lose?

So, join me, if you will, as we take the first steps along the road to True Financial Freedom.

Summing Up

We have learned in this chapter about the Spender and the Saver:

> The Spender views the world with optimism, thinking the future will be better than the past. The Spender tends to spend more (sometimes much more) than they earn.

> The Spender will generally not have any savings and will struggle to make ends meet.

> The Spender will spend money on experiences and enjoyment, making the most of life.

> The Saver views the world with pessimism, thinking the future will be worse than the present, and fears disasters and emergencies that need to be prepared for. The Saver tends to spend less (sometimes much less) than they earn.

> The Saver will generally have a lot of savings and be financially comfortable, but will still worry about money.

> The Saver will tend not to spend money on experiences and enjoyment, preferring to save it for a rainy day.

> Both groups of people worry about money. The Spender worries about not having enough; the Saver about losing what they have.

> It could be argued that both groups are dysfunctional with money, just in totally different ways.

What can you learn about yourself and your own money habits by looking at these two money archetypes?

1 www.dailymail.co.uk/femail/article-2188742/How-modern-parents-childrens-demands-buy-latest-toys-gadgets.html
2 www.theguardian.com/money/2017/sep/19/car-finance-debt-dealers-consumer-credit
3 www.theguardian.com/money/2017/sep/19/car-finance-debt-dealers-consumer-credit
4 www.fca.org.uk/publications/research/understanding-financial-lives-uk-adults
5 www.dailymail.co.uk/femail/article-2188742/How-modern-parents-childrens-demands-buy-latest-toys-gadgets.html
6 www.planadviser.com/americans-fear-exhausting-money-in-retirement-more-than-death/

Resources

The following tools and resources will help you learn more about the concepts in this chapter:

Books

Rich Dad, Poor Dad

Robert Kiyosaki, Warner, 1997

Arguably the original modern-day personal finance book, *Rich Dad, Poor Dad* has much to teach about the Spender and the Saver.

Using his own life story as an example, Robert Kiyosaki tells us about his Poor Dad (his actual dad, who was the Spender) and his Rich Dad (actually his friend's dad – the Saver) and what he learnt from each of them.

An essential read for anyone even remotely concerned about their financial future.

The New
World Order
(The Best of
Both Worlds)

I remember the moment I first looked over the Pacific Ocean from the Post Ranch Inn. It's a moment that changed me forever. We were on honeymoon in the summer of 2013 and life could not have been better.

The Post Ranch Inn is a super high-end luxury resort in the Big Sur region of California. It's little known, but if you read any of the luxury magazines it may seem familiar. The Post Ranch Inn appears on all sorts of top-10 lists. Top 10 Views, Top 10 Infinity Pools, Top 10 Restaurants, etc. I would have no hesitation in putting it as my number one place to be on earth.

The reason for this, however, has nothing to do with the luxurious accommodation, the mind-blowing food or the impeccable service. It's more to do with the place itself, the setting. The magic of the California coast does something to me. Being in this place gives me a sense of inner calm. I don't get this anywhere else and to me it's priceless. It's like fairy dust has been sprinkled all over the place.

I'm not sure I could describe the sheer beauty in words alone. Pictures don't do it justice. But as I stared in dumbfounded awe over the wonderfully calm, deep-blue ocean, I knew this was somewhere I wanted to visit again and again and again.

The only problem? The Post Ranch Inn costs over $2,000 per night!

On the day we left, I vowed I would return regularly in the years that followed. I just hadn't quite figured out how I would pay for it.

Now, at this point you might be thinking I was on a self-indulgent rampage and being sucked in by the pomp and poshness of it all. However, on that same honeymoon trip, we stayed in several places that were similar in terms of price and luxury, but none of them had the same effect on me as the Post Ranch Inn.

My visit here was a turning point in my life and is probably the moment I can pinpoint as being the start of my Journey to True Financial Freedom. I wanted to come back here again and again. I wanted to feel that feeling again and see that view again and I didn't want money to stop me.

Despite the almost life-changing effect this place had on me, the significance of those few nights would be profoundly overshadowed far sooner than I could have expected.

The Story Takes a Turn for the Worse

As we continued our trip down the Pacific Coast Highway (you must do this drive, by the way) I continued to be stunned by the scenery. We stopped for a night in LA, before completing the drive across the desert to Las Vegas. On arrival, we were upgraded to the Honeymoon Suite and had champagne delivered to our room – life was good.

At this point the story takes a nosedive. We walked across the street from the Vdara hotel via the Bellagio, stopping to gawp at the magnificent fountains, and went to a wonderful steak restaurant.

We ordered glasses of wine and waited to be seated. After we were guided to our table the waiter wheeled over a trolley covered in an impressive array of steaks for us to choose from. Porterhouse ordered, the waiting staff then proceeded to bring over a woven basket with a crazy selection of breads: rye wheels, olive ciabatta, sourdough – all my favourites were there. A few bites in, I felt my throat start to tighten and immediately knew that something was very wrong.

I'm allergic to nuts – and there must have been a nut in the bread.

I knew I was in trouble very quickly, but didn't mention anything to Katherine. *It will get better,* I lied to myself, knowing it wouldn't.

The allergic reaction worsened and I asked for the bill while Katherine raced off to vainly buy allergy tablets.

The waiters showed their concern, but I think they were just happy to get me out of there without a lawsuit. They even packed up our leftovers to take home!

Then the anaphylactic shock got me in its jaws. I remember trying to make it back to our room but collapsed in front of our hotel. Katherine acted fast and called 911.

She tried to pull me to my feet but I was too weak. The anaphylaxis had taken hold. Apparently, I was then violently sick in the doggy bag!

As the ambulance arrived, a paramedic asked me a question I will never forget:

"Are you sure you want to be treated?"

WHAT THE! I thought. *Of course I want to be treated, I'm dying!*

However, the question behind the question was, "Can you afford to be treated?"

I could see in Katherine's eyes she was both seething with rage and consumed with worry. Her expression turned to helplessness as the realisation hit her: the people we thought were there to save me wanted paying first.

In the US you pay for medical treatment as you go along. The cost of the ambulance ride alone was $1,200!

As we arrived at the Desert Springs Hospital, my condition seriously deteriorated. My ears started to drum and it felt like I was underwater and disconnected from the real world. I almost blacked out in the hospital corridor.

When I made it to the Emergency Room after what seemed like a lifetime, I breathed a sigh of relief. *At last they are finally coming to treat me,* I thought.

The next words out of that doctor's mouth will be etched in my mind forever:

"Can we please take a $6,000 deposit before we can take you up to the wards?"

Can you imagine Katherine's anguish, her eyes bleak and tired from the whole experience, as she started the lengthy process of logging into Internet banking to start moving money around as her husband lay there dying? Thank God we had some savings left over from the wedding. I wonder what happens if you can't afford to pay. Do they just let you die?

||||||||||||||||||||||||||||||||||||||||||||||||||||||||||||||||||||||||||||||||||||||||||||||||||||

 45,000 Americans are estimated to die each year because they have no health insurance and can't afford treatment.[1]

||||||||||||||||||||||||||||||||||||||||||||||||||||||||||||||||||||||||||||||||||||||||||||||||||||

I was finally admitted to the ward and medication began.

Usually this would be the end of the story. But, by a bizarre twist of fate, the medication they gave me caused deadly pancreatitis and plunged me into a three-week fight for survival.

When you have three weeks in a hospital bed doing nothing but contemplating your impending mortality, a lot goes through your mind. You start to question your purpose in life, what you have achieved and what it all means.

The view from the hospital window left a lot to be desired. The dramatic cliffs and turquoise sea of the West Coast had been replaced by a car park.

I'd been put on incredibly strong painkillers that pretty much put me to sleep each time they were administered. I'm told pancreatitis is one of the most painful conditions for a human to go through (yes, up there with childbirth apparently), and although the medication was heaven at the time, I quickly started to feel it was doing me no good.

Two weeks into my stay I made the brave decision to ask the medical staff to take me off the painkillers. They looked at me as if I was an alien, asking why I'd make such a ridiculous decision, but they finally submitted. Two days of withdrawal later and I finally started to feel (a little bit) better.

It was a desolate time during which I felt nothing but emptiness and regularly turned to contemplating my demise. I started asking myself some pretty big questions: *Will Katherine be OK? What legacy have I left behind? What things have I missed out on?*

In those vital weeks, although I perhaps didn't realise it explicitly at the time, I made some pretty big decisions. First of all, I promised Katherine we would re-do our honeymoon. Let's be honest, I'd made a bit of a hash of the first one! I know you vow 'in sickness and in health', but you don't generally test that theory a week into the marriage!

I also vowed from that moment onwards I would only do work that I loved. No more running on a treadmill to stand still, no more hamster wheel. Only deep, meaningful work that made me feel alive.

Finally, I promised myself I wanted to have a great life. I wanted to achieve True Financial Freedom as soon as possible, but not by ignoring all the wonderful things the world has to offer (and especially not by sacrificing a visit to the Post Ranch Inn again).

This experience was the worst of my life... except one...

Another Nosedive

About a year later, Katherine was expecting our first baby. Everything was going according to plan and life was good. We were delighted at the prospect of becoming parents and were looking forward to our life as a new family.

Around two months into the pregnancy she called me at the office.

"Don't go off on one, Matt, but I just want to let you know that I'm going into hospital because I just collapsed at work. I'm feeling OK, though. There's nothing to worry about. I'll call you in a few hours and let you know how things are going. No need to rush back," she blurted before I could get a word in edgeways.

A few hours later, the phone rang again and this time it was a more panicked Katherine.

"I've lost a lot of blood and I'm being rushed into theatre. You better come!" she gasped. She didn't have time to say much more than that.

I got straight up from my meeting, made my apologies and ran hell-for-leather out the door. That train ride home was the longest of my life, consumed with worry, thinking about what might be happening.

It turned out that Katherine had suffered an ectopic pregnancy, which had ruptured and around three litres of blood had gushed into her abdomen. She got dangerously close at times to not pulling through. Lady Luck was on our side once again it seemed; the surgeons got there just in time.

To have one pivotal moment in your 20s is a life-changer. To have two is just plain revelatory.

As we both reflected on our near-death experiences, in the 12 months that followed we made some pretty big decisions about our lives.

After a decade of working for other people, we both decided we were done, but for totally different reasons.

I actually quite liked my old job (in fact, I'd recommend my old employer to anyone). I had a certain degree of control over my time, I could work from home, I had a company car and a great salary. For many people this would be a dream job. Except that it never gave me a feeling of meaning or purpose. I never felt like I was making a difference.

Katherine, on the other hand, hated the over-work and over-stress in her role as an accountant. Twelve-hour days were not at all uncommon and working at weekends became the norm for her.

I decided to start a Financial Planning firm in London, which had been my dream ever since I began in Financial Planning almost a decade previously. What seemed impossibly scary only a year or two earlier, all of a sudden seemed very tame compared to nearly dying. What was I so scared of? What's the worst that could happen?

Katherine decided to quit her job and join me in the new business. Very quickly she started to feel happier. The only problem was that it had taken a decade (and nearly dying) to make the change. A decade of unhappiness at work. A decade of doing what we were supposed to do, because everyone else told us we were supposed to do it.

Just a few short years later and I was well on my way to True Financial Freedom. I had earned more than I ever thought possible in my corporate jobs and, best of all, I was loving it.

Like all good stories, I'm pleased to say this one has a happy ending (although I do hope it's not really the end, more a new beginning). A year later, Katherine fell pregnant again and gave birth nine months later to our beautiful daughter, Amy.

We have not yet returned to the Post Ranch Inn since the Honeymoon Part 2 (as we now call the trip we took a year after our actual honeymoon), but it's not money that's stopping us, just a young family. We have vowed to return very soon and the wonderful thing is, we don't have to worry about the cost anymore.

A New World Order

As I look back over those three transformative years I realise that, completely by accident, I've discovered a brand-new way of living.

Money is no longer a concern. It no longer gives me sleepless nights. I have taken control of money, rather than it controlling me.

So, what does this new world look like?

Well, for a start, I'm able to afford things I couldn't have dreamed of a few years ago. I'm saving and investing much more for our future. We've been able to buy a house in a nicer area, closer to where I now work in London. Even better, we're able to pay the mortgage off at a much faster rate than before.

My commute into London is dramatically reduced to 45 minutes, which I now secretly enjoy (don't tell anyone, but the train is one of the few places left on earth where you're unlikely to be disturbed – perfect for reading, or writing a book!). This leaves me with much more family time too.

We have the office in London I always dreamt of, in the best part of town, with views looking over to St Paul's Cathedral and the London Eye.

I work with the best team in the world, full of like-minded people and they love the work they do too.

But the best part of all is the *freedom* I feel. I'm my own boss. I can travel freely, both at home and abroad, and we feel a greater sense of ease with our financial affairs.

Another fascinating bonus of getting your finances under control is the possibility of making *more* money. As you begin to save and invest, not only does the money itself create more money, but you also stumble across far more opportunities. Since starting my business, I've written books, spoken on national radio, been featured in several national newspapers and invited to speak at national conferences. All things I would've thought impossible a few years earlier.

You can also capitalise on other opportunities. At the time of writing, a friend of mine is about to raise finance for his business in the artificial intelligence space. Although far from certain, this is an investment with the potential to make a 100x or 1,000x return. There's no way I would've been in a position to participate three years ago, but since making the Journey to True Financial Freedom, I have the available cash to invest in ventures like this.

Finally, as I've immersed myself in the True Financial Freedom world, I've stumbled across so many other Millennials who have created the same freedom in their lives too.

But How Is This Possible?

At this point in the story, you're probably thinking: *well that won't happen for me, those other people are special somehow* (or some variation on that theme).

The truth is I used to feel just the same way. I never thought it was possible to achieve the level of True Financial Freedom I now have in such a short space of time. I thought that only happened to special people too, not to average 30-something guys like me. How wrong I was.

Although a lot is said about Millennials' money problems (rising property prices, static incomes, high rents, the list goes on), I believe they're the generation with the easiest path in history to achieve True Financial Freedom.

The Boomers' path to True Financial Freedom sometimes involved 40+ years of soul-destroying work for a big corporation, trapped in a booth somewhere doing work for a machine that didn't really move the needle. So why do this?

Well, for starters, that's how it was. Boomers' parents had nothing like the lifestyle their children were now enjoying. The corporations offered generous pensions, pay packages, bonuses and other perks. What became clear through the 80s and 90s, however, was that it didn't really make anyone happy. In fact, it was making everyone miserable. Rates of suicide and depression skyrocketed during those decades.

||||||||||||||||||||||||||||||||||||||||||||||||||||||||||||||||||||||||||||||||||||||||||||

FACT
UK suicide rates in the 1980s were the highest they had been since the Great Depression in the 1930s.[2]

||||||||||||||||||||||||||||||||||||||||||||||||||||||||||||||||||||||||||||||||||||||||||||

Millennials, on the other hand, have an easier much more fulfilling route to True Financial Freedom. To say *easy* would be wrong (there's no such thing as a get-rich-quick scheme – believe me I've tried) but definitely *easier.*

Millennials have tools and capabilities enjoyed by no previous generation. The funny thing is the key to your True Financial Freedom – the most game-changing tool that will transform your financial life forever – has been right under your nose for a decade or more. You just haven't noticed its transformative power yet. This magical tool is called... the Internet!

Don't worry if all this seems daunting (it did for me when I started this journey) because I'm going to walk you through the whole process step by step. In *PART 2* of this book, I'm going to give you the full 6-Step Process to Financial Freedom:

> In *Step 1* I'll show you how to evaluate your current situation so you've a clear idea of where you're starting from.
> In *Step 2* you'll visualise your new life and I'll show you how to calculate how much money you need to make your dreams a reality.
> In *Step 3* I'll show you how to protect yourself from all the potential pitfalls and dangers along the road to True Financial Freedom. This is not a well-charted route and there will be people who put obstacles in the way of your success.
> In *Step 4* I'll explain how you can escape the misery of debt and use debt only where it serves your interests and not anyone else's.
> In *Step 5* you'll learn how to build Financial Resilience, so the next time the boiler breaks down (or you have a medical emergency), you're well prepared.
> Finally, in *Step 6* I'll show you the financial advantages sitting right in front of you for the taking – when you know how!

In *PART 3* of the book, things get really interesting. In *PART 3*, we'll explore the Hallowed Ground of the financial freedom world: Passive Income!

But Let's Not Get Too Carried Away With Ourselves!

Before we examine how the Internet and the 6-Step Process can solve all your financial worries and create the financial freedom you never dreamt possible, we need to explore the principles that govern the economy of the New Rich. The economic world is changing fast and most people simply haven't noticed. If you can learn to understand and harness the power of this new economy, the Journey to True Financial Freedom will be a lot easier, faster and more enjoyable. So join me as we begin to explore the 6 Essential Truths of the New Rich in *Chapter 3*.

Summing Up

We have learned in this chapter how, after my near-death experience, I took a long hard look at what I wanted from life.

> I made some big decisions, some of which changed my life forever.

> You don't have to have a near-death experience to wake up. You can choose to wake up right now if you want to.

> I made some promises or vows to myself.

> I vowed that I would return to the Post Ranch Inn – arguably my favourite place on earth – and I didn't want money to hold me back.

> I vowed to only do work that I loved.

> The rules of the finance game are changing. Millennials have a different set of challenges and a different world in which to face them.

> But Millennials also have the best opportunity to make more of their life.

Would you like to have the best of both worlds? Imagine that you had a near-death experience... how would you react? What would you change in your life if you had the chance?

---

1 https://news.harvard.edu/gazette/story/2009/09/new-study-finds-45000-deaths-annually-linked-to-lack-of-health-coverage/
2 https://academic.oup.com/ije/article/39/6/1464/736597

Resources

The following tools and resources will help you learn more about the concepts in this chapter:

Books

The 4-Hour Work Week (Expanded and Updated)
Tim Ferris, Harmony, 2009

This is the book that coined the phrase 'The New Rich'. Need I say more? A must-read for anyone interested in leveraging the Internet to help you achieve True Financial Freedom.

The 6 Essential Truths Of The New Rich (How The New Rich Play By Different Rules)

If you're to make a success of your Journey to True Financial Freedom, you must first understand, appreciate and internalise some essential truths and lessons. The following pages contain the secrets that have led so many to True Financial Freedom.

These rules and principles may seem illogical, even cruel, but they are all universally true. If you harness the power contained in the following pages, your own Journey to True Financial Freedom will be a lot smoother.

Without further ado, let's begin with the first Essential Truth.

Essential Truth #1
Not All Effort Is Rewarded Equally

If you think about it logically, we know that all efforts are not rewarded equally. On a practical level we appreciate that someone working at a bar in a pub or in a factory might earn £10 per hour, whereas a doctor or a lawyer might earn £400 per hour. These different rates are created by the market and are based on the demand for the skills of each person, as well as the value they create in the world.

Regardless of the hourly rate, however, these roles revolve around an old economic model of trading time for money. An extra hour of work equals an extra hour of pay, and so forth.

This model has two fundamental flaws:

Flaw #1

There are only so many hours in the day/week/year. As such, your earnings will always be limited by the number of hours you're able to work. There's an intrinsic cap on the amount you can ever earn in the Time for Money Economy.

Working more hours does not create freedom. It does the opposite. As such, working more hours to earn more is very rarely the long-term solution to achieving True Financial Freedom (although it can be useful for short periods of time as we will see later).

Flaw #2

Trading time for money doesn't work exponentially. The problem here is you can't scale up when you're simply trading your time for money. Let's say you're already working 60-hour weeks and then extra at the weekend and you still need to earn more money. In the Time for Money Economy, you can't. This won't work if we want to achieve True Financial Freedom – we need another way. Which brings us nicely to...

Essential Truth #2
The Power of the Value Economy

In order to find True Financial Freedom, you need to leave the Time for Money Economy behind and move across into the Value Economy.

In the Value Economy, what you get paid is dependent on the value you add to the people you work with. In my business, I'm sometimes able to make more than £30,000 per day. This is not because I'm worth more than anyone else. Nor is it because I'm special in any way. It's simply that I'm able to add enough value to enough other people in a day that they want to pay me £30,000 in return for that value.

||||||||||||||||||||||||||||||||||||||||||||||||||||||||||||||||||||||||||||||||||||||||||||||||||||

 Amy Porterfield, who creates online courses to help people build online businesses, recently earned over $5,000,000 in a 14-day period as she launched her latest programme. This is the Value Economy at its best![1]

||||||||||||||||||||||||||||||||||||||||||||||||||||||||||||||||||||||||||||||||||||||||||||||||||||

As you make the transition into the Value Economy, you need to leave all the old rules behind. It can be very difficult to snap out of the Time for Money Economy mindset – it will take time to adjust.

From now on, however, it is important that you think about your activities in the context of the value they add to other people and to the world, rather than in terms of how much your time is worth per hour.

Do you see the shift in thinking here? The Time for Money Economy is all **internal**. How much do I feel I'm worth?

I used to suffer terribly with so-called imposter syndrome and to a certain extent I still do. When I joined my first business coaching group, I recall one of the more senior members telling a story about how they'd charged a client £25,000 for a single day's coaching session.

I will never be worth that, I thought to myself. *How can I be? How could little old me EVER be worth £25,000 to someone?*

It was only later in the session that I learned that the client paid £25,000 because they had an idea that generated them over £3 million in revenue. Would you pay £25,000 to make £3 million? I think so!

This is the power of the Value Economy. In this case, the £25,000 for a day's coaching probably seemed like a bargain because it generated £3 million in value.

Essential Truth #3
The Importance of Self-Belief and Self-Talk

From experience, the main thing that holds people back from earning more is a lack of self-belief. They max out at a certain level of hourly earnings because they don't feel they're worth any more. Their internal self-talk tells them they're unworthy or they don't deserve it.

This could be at different levels for different people. Some will think they're worth £50 an hour, others £1,000, but in most cases each person has a cap on what they feel they deserve.

This is imposter syndrome in action. It happens when people simply don't feel worthy of moving to a higher level of success – they don't feel that they are special enough to justify it.

I can tell you now that you're special and you have unique skills and abilities that could be the key to your financial freedom.

The Value Economy is all **external**. How much value can I add to the people I work with and to the world? With this new way of thinking, your hourly rate becomes totally irrelevant. Everything you do can be judged and rewarded based on the value you add. If you add £100,000 of value to people in a day, why shouldn't you be paid £100,000?

It's in this Value Economy where almost all people who achieve True Financial Freedom and early retirement live. They break free from the time vs money equation and start to play by different rules. In fact, they start to play a different game entirely.

Essential Truth #4
The Power of the Internet

Video Game Visionary

The name Felix Arvid Ulf Kjellberg won't mean much to you, but you may have heard of his online persona, PewDiePie.

Felix set up a YouTube channel after dropping out of university to do what made him happy. By 2012, his was the most subscribed to YouTube channel, with over 5 million followers. At the time of writing, PewDiePie has over 63 million subscribers!

What's more impressive, though, is that at the age of 28 PewDiePie is estimated to be worth a cool $20 million.

So how did he achieve such huge success? Had he created an online video course about how to make gold out of coal? Had he stumbled upon the fountain of eternal youth and was showing people how to find it?

No. Not even close. The thing that made PewDiePie over $20 million was... playing video games.

That's right. He simply records himself playing video games and comments on what he's doing and people love it. He's created a community of people who love to follow along and he's become one of the world's richest people as a result.

This is one of the best examples of the Value Economy in action. If you asked most people what the hourly rate should be for someone to play video games for them, most people would say zero. In fact, why would you want to hire someone to play video games for you at all? This is a role that would have no place at all in the Time for Money Economy.

In the **Value Economy**, however, PewDiePie is worth a fortune. So how does this work? PewDiePie simply creates videos that his community of 63 million followers enjoy. They watch them for entertainment. Nothing more, nothing less.

This audience is a big draw for advertisers who can communicate with a very specific demographic of people via the videos. If you run an ad on TV, you don't really know who will be watching. On YouTube, however, it's far easier to target ads based on the types of videos people are watching.

If you watch a video on YouTube about video games, you probably won't find many ads running about rowing boats. What you will find is lots of ads about video games, video games' accessories and other things that people who like video games are also likely to be interested in. This is an advertiser's dream.

The result of all this is that advertisers pay YouTube to run ads before and after videos. Some of the revenue from those ads is then shared with the content creator, in this case PewDiePie.

So, in the Value Economy, it's possible to become a multi-millionaire without even charging your customers (viewers) a penny. Pretty cool, huh?

||||||||||||||||||||||||||||||||||||||||||||||||||||||||||||||||||||||||||||||||||||||||||||||||

FACT The Forbes Rich List 2019 contained a record 71 billionaires under the age of 40. Many of them leveraged the power of the Internet to make their fortunes.[2]

||||||||||||||||||||||||||||||||||||||||||||||||||||||||||||||||||||||||||||||||||||||||||||||||

OK. So that example is a bit extreme. Let's look at some other case studies that are a bit more down to earth.

Made up by Doing Make-up

Tiffany Bymaster sells online courses on make-up and beauty. A professional make-up artist by trade, she decided to take her passion and turn this into an online business teaching others her skills. Her online business now turns over more than six figures and she's able to work wherever and whenever she wants.

Going Potty for Potatoes

There are people using the Internet to make money from just about anything.

One of the biggest influences on my online business journey has been Russell Brunson, author of *DotCom Secrets* and *Expert Secrets*, who had his first success online selling how-to DVDs on making potato guns. It seems you really can make money selling anything online.

You might be thinking at this point that you need a superstar idea to make this work for you, but you really don't. People will pay for the knowledge you already have. Perhaps you know how to play the guitar, or make cushions, or basic first aid or all the timesaving hacks for Microsoft Word. Your knowledge and experience is valuable to other people, no matter what it is you know. Don't worry if all of this seems a little daunting at the moment, we're going to cover everything in much more detail in *PART 2*. For now, what follows is just a taster to whet your appetite.

Let's Look at the Numbers

All of these people, and thousands more besides, operate in the Value Economy. They're paid based on the value they create multiplied by the number of people they help. There's no concept of an hourly rate or an annual salary in this world. Simply the value you add multiplied by the number of people you serve.

Let's look at some examples at different ends of the spectrum. PewDiePie has 63 million YouTube subscribers. If he added just $1 of value to each of them, that would be $63 million.

By now you are probably thinking: *how on earth am I going to get 63 million followers or have a six-figure business?*

The good news is that you don't need anything like 63 million followers. In the Value Economy, you can achieve True Financial Freedom with as few as 30. Let's look at some more examples.

Upsell to the same market

Perhaps you could reach a thousand people and sell them something you made yourself, such as a doormat that explains how to remove the smell of cat pee (yes, someone did just this!), for £10. That gets you a pretty cool £10,000. Let's say that once you've added £10 of value for someone, they want more. Perhaps this time you can add £100 of value. You now have your six-figure business serving just 1,000 people.

Subscriptions

In other cases, people use memberships or recurring subscriptions to generate their financial freedom. This is where the numbers get even smaller. Perhaps you could charge 100 people £50 per month for membership to a course or online community – that's £5,000 per month.

How big is your bucket?

Now, you might still be wondering how on earth you could reach 100 people, let alone 1,000. The good news is that the task looks a lot less daunting if you look at the size of your potential audience on the Internet.

The population of the US is 325 million people; the UK has 65 million. Add in Canada, Australia and New Zealand – which have populations of 36 million, 24 million and 5 million respectively – and we already have a potential audience of 455 million English-speaking people who live in developed economies.

Given the vast majority of Europeans have taken the time to learn English as a second language, you can add in another 680 million or so potential customers for your online business, selling to them too.

In total we have over a billion (yes, a billion) potential clients, subscribers, customers or whatever else you would like to call them. All of a sudden, finding 100 people doesn't seem so daunting, does it? To put it another way, that's just 0.00001% of our potential audience.

Heck, even PewDiePie's 63 million followers only represent 6.3% of the potential population.

If you add in the growing middle classes in Asia and other emerging markets (most of whom also speak very good English), you could well argue your potential audience is 2 or even 3 billion people.

The Internet gives you a tool to monetise your passion. This is brilliant on so many levels. It allows you to do what you love and probably make more money than you ever dreamt possible. I have businesses based in both the online and offline space, but the Internet is the single most important tool in the success of all of them.

In my Financial Planning business in London, we use the Internet and the power of our e-mail list (an e-mail list alone can buy you True Financial Freedom – much more on this later) to generate interest in our services and invite prospective clients to our seminars. From there, they are so impressed by the value we add (for free) they often then want to become a paying client.

The Internet allows me to get the messages on my blog out to a potential audience of millions of people, who then go on to subscribe to online courses or membership services.

The power of the Internet and the Value Economy allows you to have the best of both worlds. You can do work you love that helps loads of people along the way, you can do everything you want to do today (travel, buy a home, etc.) AND you can still save for your future.

Now, this does not happen overnight, but it can happen sooner than you think. If I told you that three-to-five years from now you could be enjoying complete True Financial Freedom, would you sign up? Thought so!

Right now this might seem like the stuff of fairy tales, but as we continue on this Journey I'm going to show you how to make this happen in *your* life as well. While I won't go as far as to say any of this is easy, it's probably not as tough as you think, either. But... you do have to give it time.

Essential Truth #5
The Power of Patience

The reason most people fail at most things is simply a lack of time, patience and resilience. In this world of always on, 24-hour, instant gratification, we often want to experience immediate results.

Much is said about the fabled get-rich-quick scheme, but frankly, it's all lies. There's no such thing as *get rich quick* and no such thing as *get rich easy* – unless of course you win the lottery, and the odds on that stand at around 1 in 45 million, so do you fancy your chances?

When we start something new, most people give up after they don't see results in a short space of time.

We can see the impact of this when we make New Year's Resolutions. It is assumed that everyone actually wants what they resolve, whether it be to lose weight, get fit or get out of debt. If we make a New Year's Resolution, surely this is something we want to achieve?

Why is it, then, that so many of us give up on our resolutions so quickly? It's thought that only something like 8% of people actually fulfil their resolutions for 12 months and more than half of people have given up within two weeks![3]

Worthwhile change always takes time and commitment. When I started my business it was so hard for the first 18 months or so. The hours were long, the pay was rubbish compared to what I'd earned in the corporate world and I was feeling under a serious amount of pressure to pay a mortgage.

Under those circumstances a lot of people just give up. It's sometimes easier to go back to the old way of doing things. I could have closed down my business and gone back to a normal job, but I knew the rewards would justify the effort – in the end.

When we start a new website or host a new offer, we are often disappointed we don't get thousands of hits on day one. But, like everything else, it's consistency and time that generate results.

In our first year in business, we only got around 300 names on our e-mail list. In year two this grew to 3,000 and then to 12,000 within four years. We could easily have become despondent after that first year because of the lack of quick results, and given up.

Change takes time.

You need to commit to this process for the long term. Most Millennials who have achieved financial freedom tell me it took three-to-five years from when they started their Journey to feel they were getting somewhere. It has been the same for me.

Sometimes when you commit to change it can be really exciting and romantic to do it immediately. We have all read the stories of people who decided to change their life overnight, and this is great.

But these types of overnight change are not always possible or practical. Sometimes there's a mortgage to pay that means you can't just walk out on the job you hate.

Sometimes there's a health issue holding us back and we need to give ourselves permission to take our time in these situations.

The important thing is to commit to making the change and start the Journey to get there. This could mean that the change doesn't happen for three months, a year or perhaps even five years. The key is making the commitment and taking the first steps.

So at this point you have a choice: do you want to work hard at something you love to earn your financial freedom for the next three-to-five years? Or do you want to spend the rest of your life doing something you don't love and potentially have no freedom at all?

The decision seems simple to me!

Essential Truth #6
Compounding Compounding

There's one final Essential Truth that you need to understand before we set off on our Journey: the miracle of compounding.

Did you know that compound interest is often described as the 8th Wonder of the World? That's how powerful it is!

So what is compounding?

Compounding is simply the process where interest earned on a sum of money goes on to earn more interest, which in turn earns more interest, and so on. Let's look at a simple example.

If you invested £100 at 5% interest a year for one year, you would earn £5 interest and have £105 at the end of the year.

If you now re-invest that £105 for a further year, you get £5.25 in interest – 25p more than last year – so we now have a total of £110.25.

At this stage you're probably thinking that extra 25p in year two is not very exciting. You would be right, but bear with me.

In the third year, we earn around £5.50 on our investment so we now have a total of £115.75.

If we extrapolate this for 10 years, we end up with £162.89 – an almost 63% return on our initial £100 investment.

This assumes that interest compounds annually (i.e. interest is only added at the end of each year). Most investments compound daily, so the actual return would be slightly more.

But the more time you give it, the more powerful compounding becomes. Bear in mind we earned £62.89 in our first 10 years. If we leave the investment for a total of 20 years, we get £265.33, meaning we've earned more than £100 in the second 10 years, which is more than we invested originally.

||||||||||||||||||||||||||||||||||||||||||||||||||||||||||||||||||||||||||||||||||

FACT Albert Einstein described compound
interest as the 8th Wonder of the World.[4]

||||||||||||||||||||||||||||||||||||||||||||||||||||||||||||||||||||||||||||||||||

So what do we mean by *compounding compounding?*

Well, this is where we take the above principle of compounding and apply it not only to the returns we are making on an investment, but also to the contributions we are making.

We've all seen the scary reports on the news that say if Millennials want to have a comfortable retirement, they need to be saving gazillions of pounds a month from their 20s to make it happen. The problem with this is it's simply not affordable.

So let's look at things slightly differently. Let's say we want to begin saving £100 per month and we're still earning 5% per year in interest. If we stick with a £100 per month payment for 10 years, earning 5% each year, we will have £15,592 at the end of 10 years.

If, however, we added 5% to our monthly payment each year (i.e. we paid in £105 per month in year 2, £110.25 per month in year three, and so on) then at the end of 10 years we have a massive £19,223 – over 25% more.

If we extend the results to 20 years we get around £41,000 with the level payment of £100 per month, but a huge £62,000 if we add 5% to the payment each year.

Using this double-compounding effect is the best way to make your savings goals achievable. Next time you think about how much you need to save, think about how much you can afford and how much you need to add to that payment in each future year to achieve your goals.

Let's say you want to save £100,000 in 10 years' time. In order to do this with a flat monthly payment, you would need to pay in £650 per month, assuming you are earning 5% per year. Seems quite tough, right?

On the other hand, you could commit to saving £400 per month, but adding 10% each year to your payment – still a lot of money, but sounds a bit easier, doesn't it?

What I'm saying here is that you very rarely go from zero to your savings goal all in one go. You can start small and then add to your savings contributions over time. Something is always better than nothing. Even if you can only afford to save £5 per month now, start there and build on it. Don't get caught in the trap of thinking what you can afford to save is too little to bother. This is one of the biggest mistakes I see people make in their financial lives.

When people ask me in their 20s and 30s, "How much should I be saving?" or, "How much should I be putting into my pension?" my answer is nearly always the same: as much as you can afford right now. This figure is usually less than the ideal savings amount, but any more than that is clearly unaffordable.

Start small, start somewhere, but whatever you do, just start! You can build on things from there.

Now that we have a good understanding of these basic truths, we're ready to begin the Journey to True Financial Freedom. So why is it, then, that so many people either never start or give up too soon?

The Near-Death Experience

The sad thing is that most people don't begin this journey of their own accord. Most people who make the Journey to True Financial Freedom do so because something causes them to wake up and see how much better their life could become.

For me, when I nearly died, it made me re-evaluate every single part of my life. I considered how I wanted my life to unfold from that moment onwards. I felt like I had been given a second chance and I wasn't going to waste it.

In hindsight, nearly dying was one of the best things that's ever happened to me. If it were not for that experience, I'd probably still be working that corporate job, doing long hours, earning okayish money, but never really feeling truly fulfilled. I'd still be bored, and for me the boredom was the worst of all. In my corporate jobs, I never felt challenged. I would sit and stare at the wall all day waiting for the next client to walk into my office, but the boredom of doing so almost killed me.

Today, every day when I wake up I feel alive. My work gives me purpose and meaning and I simply love it. I have a sense of freedom that I've never had before.

Dan's Four Freedoms

Dan Sullivan of the company Strategic Coach defines four freedoms that motivate us:

> Freedom of time (doing what you want with your time).
> Freedom of money (having the freedom to spend what you want to spend).
> Freedom of relationship (only working and being with people you love to be with).
> Freedom of purpose (having the freedom to do only the things that give you meaning and purpose).

I feel like I am well on the way to achieving all four.

Perhaps the biggest benefit of all, however, is that since the turning point in my life where I said 'what the heck, what's the worst that could happen?' and started my business, I have never, not once, not for one single moment, been bored. My days (both business and pleasure) are filled with excitement and joy – and that, my friends, is simply priceless.

My hope for all of you is that it doesn't take a near-death experience to wake you up and jolt you into action. If you're unhappy with your job, your financial situation, your debt or your freedom, you can change all of it, quickly and relatively easily. All you have to do is take the first step. What seems almost impossibly scary at first, quickly becomes second nature. Every single person I know who's been brave enough to take the first step down this road has said the same thing: "Why didn't I do this sooner?"

So... you have to ask yourself... *what am I waiting for?*

Don't worry if this all feels a little bit intimidating right now. The whole of *PART 1* was just to help you believe that this is possible.

In *PART 2*, I'm going to walk with you every Step of the way on your path to True Financial Freedom. I am going to show you, in detail, what you need to do and give you all the tools and resources you need.

Ready? Let's go!

Summing Up

We have learned about the 6 Essential Truths of the New Rich and that...

If you are to make a success of your Journey to True Financial Freedom, you must first understand, appreciate and internalise the 6 Essential Truths.

Essential Truth #1 – Not All Effort is Rewarded Equally

> Some people earn £10 an hour; others earn £1,000. Some even earn £10,000. Not all effort is rewarded equally. You must focus your efforts on high-value, high-reward activities.

Essential Truth #2 – The Power of the Value Economy

> Some people are paid based on the number of hours they work.
> Others are paid based on the value they add multiplied by the number of people they can add value to.
> The Value Economy is exponentially more powerful than the Time for Money Economy and contains almost unlimited potential.

Essential Truth #3 – The Importance of Self-Belief and Self-Talk

> Only those who believe they are worthy and have what it takes will succeed in this new world.
> Many people have done it before. None of them were special. They were just normal people who had a dream and the belief and desire to pull it off.

Essential Truth #4 – The Power of the Internet

> The Internet is the most powerful wealth-building tool of all time, not just for online businesses, but for traditional bricks-and-mortar businesses as well.
> If you leverage the Internet to reach more people for a product or service, you can achieve True Financial Freedom faster than you can imagine.

Essential Truth #5 – The Power of Patience

Change takes time.

> The Internet and the Value Economy can help you to achieve True Financial Freedom in record time, but it won't happen overnight.
> You have to give it time.
> Most successful entrepreneurs say it took three-to-five years to gain huge traction in their businesses.

Essential Truth #6 – Compounding Compounding

> Compound interest is one of the most amazing tools we have in our quest for True Financial Freedom.
> But it's deceptively slow at first.
> Compound interest takes time to work its magic.
> The interest earned on interest will seem almost insignificant at first but, over time, the snowball will grow until it becomes unstoppable.
> You can take the concept of compounding one step further by compounding not only the returns on investments, but also the contributions to those investments.
> You must understand and internalise the 6 Essential Truths if you are to succeed. Ignore them at your peril.

How do you feel about the 6 Essential Truths? Can you see how internalising these beliefs could help you on your quest for True Financial Freedom?

---

1   www.amyporterfield.com
2   www.forbes.com/sites/kathleenchaykowski/2019/03/05/the-worlds-youngest-billionaires-in-2019-meet-the-71-under-age-40/?sh=3ca436e7411e
3   www.inc.com/jeff-haden/a-study-of-800-million-activities-predicts-most-new-years-resolutions-will-be-abandoned-on-january-19-how-you-cancreate-new-habits-that-actually-stick.html
4   www.theglobeandmail.com/investing/investment-ideas/article-compound-interest-may-not-be-einsteins-eighth-wonder-but-it-is-a/

Resources

The following tools and resources will help you learn more about the concepts in this chapter:

Books

DotCom Secrets: The Underground Playbook for Growing Your Company Online

Russell Brunson, Morgan James, 2015

An essential read for anyone who wants an introduction to the world of online business and just how powerful it can be.

Expert Secrets: The Underground Playbook for Creating a Mass Movement of People Who Will Pay for Your Advice

Russell Brunson, Morgan James, 2017

A variation on the above theme, but this time for 'experts'. If you feel that you have expertise in any field, this book will explain how to package and sell that knowledge online.

The 4-Hour Work Week (Expanded and Updated)

Tim Ferriss, Harmony, 2009

Yes, I have already spoken about this book, but it is that important it deserves a second mention. If you want to learn more about the Value Economy and how it can work for you, you have to read this book.

Feel the Fear and Do It Anyway

Susan Jeffers, Ballantine, 2006

If you struggle with self-belief and self-confidence when trying new things and going outside of your comfort zone, this book is for you.

Websites

Compound Interest Calculator

www.thecalculatorsite.com/finance/calculators/
compoundinterestcalculator.php

Use this compound interest calculator to experiment with the power of compound interest. Play around with contribution rates, interest rates and timescales. See how powerful time and the rate of monthly contribution can be in building wealth.

Strategic Coach

www.strategiccoach.com

PART 2
THE 6-STEP PROCESS TO PREPARE YOU TO ACHIEVE TRUE FINANCIAL FREEDOM

Putting the 6-Step Process into action in your life

Step 1
Tell The Truth
(Where Are
You Now?)

So, you've decided this financial freedom thing is for you. That's great. But how exactly do you get there?

The good news is there's a proven, tried and tested method you can apply in your own life that will take you there. You'll have to work at it; there will be effort involved. But if you follow the 6-Step Process to True Financial Freedom outlined in the following pages, I promise that you'll find True Financial Freedom sooner than you can imagine.

Before we go anywhere, though, before any journey begins, we need to know where we're starting from.

Much like you need to know your current location before you plot your route on a map (OK, so I know no one uses maps anymore, but stick with me here), you must have a clear understanding of your current financial position before you can embark on the Journey to True Financial Freedom.

You have to tell the truth (and be brutal with it). This could well be uncomfortable. You may have to admit to yourself that you've made financial mistakes in the past. Perhaps you even need to admit that you've just been plain stupid with money.

It could be you have a spending problem – perhaps you're addicted to debt or have a gambling issue that's the cause of your financial problems.

Whatever your current situation, you have to be honest with yourself about it before any progress can happen.

Whenever an addict goes to a help programme, step one is always to say something along the lines of:

"Hello, my name is Matt and I'm a (insert problem here)."

This has been the first step in almost all addiction recovery programmes for nearly 100 years and this is because it works.

If you want to change, you have to admit to yourself where you are now, why you want things to change and what the benefit will be when change is complete.

So, What Does This Have to Do With Financial Freedom?

Although not being Financially Free isn't an addiction as such, chances are you've not been managing your money how you wanted to in the past, right?

Before you can start on your way to True Financial Freedom, you've got to be really honest about where you are *now*.

This can be really hard, especially if you're in a bad situation. It can be difficult to face up and admit that you've made poor money decisions in the past.

If you're in debt or spending more than you earn, the temptation is to simply bury your head in the sand and not think about it too hard – this will get better in the end, right?

WRONG!

Unless you tell yourself the truth about where you are now, there's no hope of moving forward.

Fortunately, I'm going to make this really easy for you.

Before you start on your Journey to True Financial Freedom, we need to do a full audit of where you are now. Not only will this create the foundation for everything that is to come, it's really awesome to have something to look back on when you've made it.

Although I wouldn't say I've achieved my ultimate goal just yet, when I look back at the progress I've made since I started my quest for financial freedom five years ago, the results are outstanding.

When I started this process, I had £25,000 of consumer debt and was consistently spending as much as (or sometimes more than) I earned. I wasn't investing anything worth writing home about and I wasn't planning for my future. Truth be told, I was a passenger in my own life.

Now, at the age of 32, I've repaid all of that debt, started a business that is worth over £2 million and saved over £425,000. Yes, in five years!

When I first started this Journey, I completed a very crude, prototype version of what I'm about to show you.

I had to admit to myself that I'd been stupid with money before. I had to look at some of the silly purchases I'd made and how I'd let money rule me (not the other way round).

This realisation has been one of my best motivators. As time passes I can always look back at the answer to my early *Tell the Truth* exercise (see *Step 1*) and see how far I've come. There is nothing more motivating than to witness progress being made – just like those before-and-after diet photographs that abound.

Hopefully someday soon you can look back and see how far you've come.

Build a Budget

The first part of telling the truth about your money is to establish where you're spending it. From experience, most people (rich and poor) have no clue where their money goes.

As we discussed in *PART 1*, most people are simply hard-wired as Spenders or Savers and they just spend their money in the way that seems natural to them. This is all instinctive – there's no purpose tied up in how most people spend their money, they just spend on autopilot.

The only thing that separates the rich and poor, most of the time, is simply the coding that was installed when they came out of the factory. Were they given a Spender or a Saver mindset?

Having a solid budget in place changes all of this. It allows you to see where you're spending your money in the first place. Then, and only then, can you start doing something about it.

It's a common misconception that only people who are bad with money, or who have debt, need a budget. I think everyone should have a budget. If you have problems with money already, a budget can be the first step in getting everything under control.

Even if you think you're currently pretty good with money, a budget can help you to spend and invest your money on purpose, rather than just being a passenger in your own financial life.

The first step in any good budget is to think about your expenses.

Expenses

How you spend your money probably has the biggest influence on your financial success. More so than how much you earn, more even than how your investments perform. When I look at my clients, most of them have become rich by having their spending under control.

Before we get too carried away, please note that I'm NOT saying all spending is bad. I hate the idea that to be Financially Free you have to live on £1 a day and live in a tent somewhere. No thank you!

Spending money is great: it can give us fantastic experiences, it can allow us to travel the globe, start a business or change the world.

BUT, when we spend money, we need to do so *consciously*.

||||||||||||||||||||||||||||||||||||||||||||||||||||||||||||||||||||||||||||||||||||||||||||

 Around 70% of Americans fail to correctly answer a basic financial test that contains simple questions about spending and interest rates.[1]

||||||||||||||||||||||||||||||||||||||||||||||||||||||||||||||||||||||||||||||||||||||||||||

We also need to be aware of when we're spending too much. If you're spending more than you earn (meaning you're taking on debt), this is going to end badly. You have to put a stop to this now.

In *Step 6*, I will show you how to dramatically increase your income so you can spend money on whatever you want, but before we get to that, we need to get our expenses under control.

OK – let's get started.

Keep a tally

First off, if possible, you need to add up all your expenses for the past year. Yes – the past year.

Although this will take a bit of hard work (you can use some great apps, such as Yolt or You Need A Budget to make this easier) it's absolutely worth it.

Adding up expenses for just one month will not tell the full story. What about the car service you had three months ago or the new bed you bought last year? What about Christmas presents and the slightly over-the-top office party you attended and all the other one-off things you spent money on throughout the year?

If we add up expenses on a monthly basis, we miss a lot of this stuff and it doesn't give the true picture. Remember: we need to tell ourselves the truth, even if it hurts.

If you really can't bring yourself to add up the past year's expenses, just add in the last month for now and then continue adding to it in detail on a monthly basis moving forward. This will still be *way* better than nothing – but I do recommend you try and go back a full year if you can.

The best way to do this is to simply log in to your Internet banking and download your statements. It's better to pull the data out as a Spreadsheet rather than a PDF document because this means you can use Excel to add things up and make other calculations.

The good news is you can go to www.millennialmutiny.com/budget and download my ultimate budgeting Spreadsheet to help you with this.

Once you have a record of all your expenses for the year from your bank statement, you can create categories so it's easy to see what you have spent on what.

There's no right or wrong number of categories, but I suggest creating around 20–30. Not so many that you get overwhelmed, but enough so the data is useful.

There will always be the basics – food, housing, etc. – but perhaps you have an expensive hobby or love getting dinner out or a takeaway after work. I would suggest you give these things their own category so you can see exactly how much they're costing.

I will give some examples of each category as we go through the next section.

Once you have the expenses all totalled up, I put them all under four master headings as follows:

1) Bedrock Expenses

These are expenses which you effectively have no control over. These are the costs that you can't really reduce, whatever you do. I can't think of many expenses that actually fall into this category.

Perhaps you might include a very basic allowance for food and some utilities, but other than that, most expenses are negotiable.

The reason we classify some expenses as Bedrock Expenses is so we know that they're non-negotiable. There's no point trying to reduce them because they're totally fixed and immovable.

Some examples of Bedrock Expenses:

> Council or property taxes (although even this can be reduced by moving to a cheaper home, I guess).
> Water rates (set by your water company – you have no choice about switching provider).
> Food (just a basic allowance to cover a sustenance level of groceries).

2) Foundation Expenses

This is where most of your day-to-day living expenses will be. In here you have mortgage or rent payments, most utilities, the majority of your food bill and any other basic costs of living.

You might think that your rent or mortgage payment should be under the Bedrock Expenses heading, but this isn't quite true. If you're renting a house, you could always rent somewhere smaller or move out of town to reduce your rent. If you have a mortgage, you might be able to get a better deal. If you're paying money for your gas and electricity, perhaps a different supplier might offer a better rate.

Costs in the Foundation Expenses category are generally considered to be *essential* (although I think we all know that most of them are not a matter of life and death). Although we acknowledge we have to pay them, it's possible that we can save money by getting a better deal or being smarter with our shopping.

Some examples of Foundation Expenses:

> Utilities
> Mortgage or rent payment
> Food
> Home repairs
> Motor insurance
> Home insurance

3) Lifestyle Expenses

These are any costs you incur to make life nicer. While Bedrock and Foundation Expenses are pretty much necessities (even though you can possibly get a better deal), Lifestyle Expenses are things that you definitely, categorically, do not *need* (although you might really want them).

Lifestyle Expenses can be anything from that coffee you grab on the way to work to your probably-slightly-over-the-top cable TV subscription.

Other things to include here will be eating out, takeaway food, cinema visits and other leisure activity.

It could be said that Lifestyle Expenses are what make day-to-day life fun and I think there's some truth to that. If we had no Lifestyle Expenses (meaning we are just living on the basics), life would probably not be that exciting.

Lifestyle Expenses are, however, possibly the biggest threat to your True Financial Freedom, so take care here.

Unlike Luxury Expenses (described below), which are generally planned in advance, considered and looked forward to, Lifestyle Expenses can be incurred almost without thinking about it if you're not careful.

My coffee expenditure is a great example of this. I had definitely fallen into the Lifestyle Expenses trap. What was just one coffee on a Friday as a treat for a week's hard work, became one coffee every morning – before I knew it, there was one sometimes sneaked in at lunchtime too.

The same can be true for eating out, takeaway food or even eating convenience food at home. What starts out as an occasional treat can quickly develop into a habit, and at this point it starts costing you hundreds or even thousands of pounds a month.

Lifestyle Expenses are most likely to be the cause of that *HOW MUCH?!* moment, when you realise how much you're spending on something.

Don't despair, though – I'm not going to say you *can't* have that coffee at work or you *shouldn't* eat out. It's just that you need to spend money on purpose, on things that matter to you and on things that you value.

In *Step 6*, you'll also learn how to increase your income before you increase your expenditure, so even if you do want regular treats, they don't have to be at the expense of your True Financial Freedom.

Some examples of Lifestyle Expenses:

> Eating out
> Cinema trips
> Takeaway food
> Lunch or coffee
> Shopping on Amazon
> Clothes shopping
> Day trips
> Entertainment

4) Luxury Expenses

These are the real life-making luxuries. Holidays overseas, private club memberships, spa weekends, high-end meals out and West End shows. All of these fantastic experiences go here.

As mentioned above, believe it or not, Luxury Expenses are potentially less dangerous than Lifestyle Expenses.

There are a number of reasons for this:

1) Generally, Luxury Expenses are pre-planned (but that's not to say the odd spontaneous splurge can't be fun).

2) Luxury Expenses tend to be researched and considered. When we're planning a holiday, we tend to take hours, days or weeks deciding where to go, checking every hotel on a review site and then using price comparison sites to get the best deal.

3) Luxury Expenses tend to be larger one-off items and thus we are more conscious of these expenses when we incur them. This is rather unlike the £3 coffee each day, which is small in isolation, but which can become a big expenses line if it gets out of control.

||||||||||||||||||||||||||||||||||||||||||||||||||||||||||||||||||||||||||||||||||||||||||

 Research in the US has indicated that most people spend more time planning a two-week vacation than they do planning their whole retirement![2]

||||||||||||||||||||||||||||||||||||||||||||||||||||||||||||||||||||||||||||||||||||||||||

Some examples of Luxury Expenses:

> Holidays
> Weekends away
> New car
> Expensive hobby (flying, horse riding, etc.)

So, Back to Your Spreadsheet

As you'll see in my Spreadsheet, I recommend tracking spending on a monthly basis and then also adding up a yearly total.

This exercise will probably take you a few hours the first time, but it's totally worth it!

Once you have added everything up – what do you see?

Are there things that shock you? Have you had any *how much?!* moments?

Perhaps you're spending less than you thought in some areas?

True Financial Freedom is not about frugality, as such. I believe you can achieve financial freedom AND have a great lifestyle.

Sometimes, though, we just waste money on stuff that doesn't make us happier, that serves no purpose or that's just bad value.

When I first did this exercise, the one thing that stood out to me was the amount I was spending on coffee – almost £1,000 per year!

Armed with this information I decided to buy the office a Nespresso machine (God bless Nespresso) and a nice cup of coffee now costs me 35p rather than £2.35!

I actually like Nespresso better than Starbucks – sometimes you can save money AND improve your life!

I also decided to cancel a load of subscriptions I wasn't using – £8 per month for a magazine doesn't sound much on its own, but everything soon adds up over the year.

Now that you have your monthly and yearly totals, you need to look at each of them in turn and really think.

Do I need this? Does this make me happier? Do I get value from this?

If the answer on all three counts is no, then this is a perfect place where we can look to reduce our expenses, but more on this later.

Income

Once you have your expenditure all figured out, we can then move on to consider your income.

This is probably going to be a whole lot easier for most people.

Add up your **net income** (this is the income you receive in your bank account after tax and other deductibles). Net income is the only type of income that's useful to us.

If you have a job, this is pretty simple: just add up all your pay cheques.

If you have a Side-Hustle already, you're self-employed or have other types of income, this could take a little longer.

You will also need to add in any income you receive from bank interest (probably not much in this low interest rate environment!), investments or rental property if you have any.

Compare

Now that we've looked at income and expenses for the past 12 months (or the past month at the very least), what does this tell you?

If your income is more than your expenses, congratulations – you have a great foundation to build on.

This could be totally intentional; you've been aiming to save for some time now or you've been focusing on reducing your expenditure. This could also have happened completely by accident; you were just born a Saver. Either way, congratulations. You made a great start.

The alternative result, of course, may be that your expenses turn out to be greater than your income. This means you're either spending your savings, if you have any, or you're accumulating some debt.

If this is the case, please don't worry. I'm going to show you how to reduce your expenses AND increase your income later on.

For the moment, the important thing is you acknowledge where you are financially and you commit yourself to True Financial Freedom.

That wasn't so hard, was it? You've just completed the first and potentially hardest part of the whole Journey.

Now that we've completed the income vs expenses analysis, we need to look at assets and liabilities.

Assets

Most people define assets as anything they own. This could be a house, a car, a watch, cash in the bank or investments, basically anything that you could call *mine.*

The problem with this definition of assets, however, is it's not very helpful for True Financial Freedom purposes. I've never seen a car contribute to someone's financial freedom; nor have I seen a watch be the reason someone could retire early. I apologise for the bluntness.

Many of the things people call 'assets' actually cost them money. Think about it for a second. If you have a car, this costs you money in maintenance, road taxes, fuel and tolls – not to mention the monthly payments if you bought the car on finance or lease (more on this in *Step 4*).

Even your own home, if you have one – everyone has been telling you it's your main asset for the last 20 years, but it costs you money.

You have the heating, repairs, improvements, insurance and, of course, a mortgage payment (unless you're lucky enough to be mortgage free).

All of these things actually take you further away from True Financial Freedom because they're increasing your expenses.

Don't get me wrong. I'm not saying any of these things are bad by nature. It can be great to own your own home and, in many cases, it's actually cheaper than renting.

I'm not saying that cars are bad. I *love* cars. They're one of my things and I will happily spend money on them.

All I'm saying is we must not get caught in the trap of thinking these things are assets when we think about them in the financial freedom sense.

Robert Kiyosaki was the first to make this distinction in his personal finance classic, *Rich Dad, Poor Dad*.

So how do we define assets, then?

When we're thinking about financial freedom, an asset is something that pays you. These are things that generate an income for you each month. Let's look at some examples.

If you own your own home, it's not really an asset in this sense, because it costs you money. If you have a rental property, however, this *is* an asset because it provides you with rental income each month. You need to be careful, though, because even rental properties can become a liability if they need huge repairs or if you don't have a paying tenant in place.

If you own a car, that's not really an asset – it's costing you money. If you rent your car out through a car-sharing club at the weekend and it generates an income, however, then perhaps your car is an asset.

Luckily, some things are more clear-cut. If you have savings in the bank and they're earning interest, they're an asset (not much of one at the moment, but an asset nonetheless).

If you have stocks or bonds that are paying you dividends or interest, these too are assets.

You need to add up all your assets and put them into categories. You can use my Spreadsheet for this too (find it at www.millennialmutiny.com/budget). I would suggest that you split things up into the following categories:

> Property
> Cash savings
> Investments
> Bonds
> Pensions
> Other assets (cars, watches, etc.)

For the moment, make a note of your own home and cars, but just make a mental note they're not assets as such.

OK, so now you have an idea of your total assets. Let's move on.

Liabilities

The final part of this exercise is to add up all of your liabilities. This is any money you owe to anyone of any kind.

That student loan you don't really think about because you're not paying it back yet – that should go on the list. That money you borrowed from a friend who you think has forgotten about it, that needs to go on the list too.

When you record all of your liabilities, you also need to note down the interest rate you're paying, the minimum monthly payment on the debt, the monthly payment you're actually making at the moment, the total amount outstanding and the term of the debt (its duration based on the current pay back rate). Once you're done, your table will look something like this:

Type	Current Payment	Minimum Payment	Interest Rate	O/S Balance	Term
Credit Card	£410	£300	15.9%	£4,560	14 Months
Overdraft	Nil	Nil	19.9%	£1,500	Forever!

You'll need all of this information later on when we banish debt in *Step 4*.

Compare

Now take your total assets and deduct from them your total liabilities. This is known as your **net worth**.

What we're looking at here is what you'd have left if you sold everything you own, including your house and car and then paid off all of your debt.

Assets (That Don't Pay You)	Value
Your Home	£250,000
Your Car	£20,000

Assets (That Pay You)	
Rental Property 1	£230,000
Investments	£14,000
Savings	£12,000
401k / Pensions	£17,000

Total Assets (Standard)	**£543,000**

Total Assets (Rich Dad Definition)	**£273,000**

Putting it another way, if you wanted to leave the country and start a new life, you might sell everything you own and pay off your debts so you have a clean slate. Your net worth is the cash you'd have left to take on the plane with you.

For most people, their net worth will be a positive amount. If not, don't worry, help is at hand later on.

In most cases the banks will not let you borrow more than you own, but it can happen.

The other calculation we're going to do here is look at your real net worth. Assuming you want to have a house to live in and a car to drive, you can't really use these assets to help you achieve True Financial Freedom.

What you need to do here is take your net worth figure from above and deduct any assets that are not actually assets (as per our new definition). If the asset is not paying you, it's not an asset. Most people will deduct their house if they have one and their car here.

Liabilities	Balance Owed	Interest Rate	Minimum Payment	Current Payment	Term
Mortgage – Home	£123,000	1.69%	£543	£543	15 years
Mortgage – Rental property	£174,300	3.29%	£359	£359	17 years
Credit Card	£2,000	16.9%	£40	£65	Open-ended
Total Liabilities	£299,300	Totals	£942	£967	
Net Worth (Standard)	£243,700				
Net Worth (Rich Dad Definition)	£(26,300)				

What do you see now? Do you have a negative number? Most people will at this point, so don't worry.

The reason for this is that if you own a house, there will generally be a mortgage attached. We have just deducted the house from the calculation, without removing the debt.

The other reason could be student debt. Student debt is unusual in that there's no asset attached to it (unlike when you buy a house or a car, where the debt is attached to a tangible item).

The Truth Hurts

I will never forget the first time I went through this exercise with Sanjay and Jill – the look of sheer unadulterated shock on their faces when I revealed how much they were spending on eating out and convenience food each month.

A few weeks earlier, we'd had our first meeting and I had introduced my budget planner to them. I initially asked them to guess how much they were spending in various categories (bills, eating out, holidays, etc.), but they really, genuinely, didn't have a clue!

"Just give me an estimate," I said. "Something really high-level." Still puzzled looks.

Wondering how a couple could have such little grasp of their outgoings, I asked them to pull together all their bank statements and credit cards so we could look through their spending – line by painstaking line.

It's fair to say their finances were disorganised, and they had accounts scattered to the four winds. By the time they had finished putting the pile of paperwork together the meeting was running to 90 minutes long, and we had yet to tally anything up.

We agreed that I should take the paperwork back to the office and pull everything together ahead of our next meeting, which we booked for a few weeks hence.

It took my team almost 15 hours – poring over countless bank statements and credit card slips, categorising and summarising – to arrive at a completed budget planner that demonstrated the extent of the spending problem.

Sanjay admitted he had always wondered where the money went. He and Jill worked hard, he as a graphic designer and she as a teaching assistant, and they had a good household income – not spectacular, but well above the national average.

Yet, they still had little left (if anything) at the end of the month. They did have debts on credit cards and overdrafts – nothing too dramatic, but the situation was far from ideal.

As soon as I revealed the figure to them, everything became clear. The reason why they were struggling to make it to the end of the month in the black; the reason why they were unable to save for their future; the reason they were stressed and tense talking about money.

The reason for all of this financial pain and heartache was cripplingly simple: the couple were spending upwards of £1,450 per month on eating out and convenience food. £17,400 a year!

All of their other spending was in line with my expectations for a couple with their level of income (not that there is a *correct* level to spend on anything – more on this in *Step 2* when we design your

Perfect Life). They were not going on hugely extravagant holidays or indulging in designer handbags and jeans. They were not addicted to fine wine or jewellery.

Nope. The single line on their Spreadsheet that contained the answer to all of their problems was staring them in the face: eating out and convenience food. That was the reason they couldn't save anything. That was the reason they were sometimes taking on a little debt at the end of each month.

When we broke it down, it worked out they were eating out around three times a week and then purchasing ready meals and meal boxes most other nights. They were working hard and felt they 'deserved' to treat themselves 'occasionally'. Only 'occasionally' had become 'all of the time'.

Before our budgeting exercise, they were totally, utterly unaware of the amount they were spending in this one area. They were genuinely puzzled as to why they had no money at the end of the month. You see, they never consciously sat down and decided they were going to eat out three times a week. It just kind of happened over time. Once became twice, twice became thrice – you get the idea. These things can just kind of creep up on us.

In one breath, we had dispelled the mystery as to where all of their money was going – and the best part is, they took action, immediately!

You have to tell the truth to make progress and, in this case, the truth hurt! It hurt so much they knew they had to do something about it right there and then.

From the very next week, they committed to cooking at home four nights a week. Notice how they didn't cut this expenditure item out completely and go cold turkey. They really enjoyed eating out, so they didn't want to stop entirely, and that's OK!

The beauty of this budgeting system is that it's flexible; it's designed to allow you to have some fun, to have a life.

They also committed to spending less on delivered meal boxes and instead purchase better value (but still ready to eat) food from the supermarket.

The net result was over £875 per month of budget freed up. They were still spending £575 per month on eating out and other convenience food and they were OK with that – they were doing it consciously and enjoying it more as a result.

Eating out had returned to being a slightly less frequent treat and not just the day-to-day norm.

With that remaining £875 per month that had been saved, we set them up with a comfortable Emergency Fund and then looked to begin building an investment portfolio for their future – but that's a story for another time.

Pulling it all Together

Now that we have completed the summary of income vs expenditure and assets vs liabilities, we can start to learn from this information.

If you're spending more than you're earning and you're knee-deep in debt, the good news is there's light at the end of the tunnel (*Steps 4, 5* and *6* will be particularly interesting). But you need to be really honest with yourself... right now.

How has this happened? Are you a compulsive Spender? Do you buy things you don't need? Do you use debt to purchase things on impulse? Do you feel compelled to keep up with friends and family and this means you over-stretch?

There are plenty of examples of people out there who run very effective budgets on minimum wage jobs. It can be done. If you're not in a good financial position right now, it's normally (not all of the time, but most of the time) due to decisions you've made in the past. You may have made these decisions unconsciously, but you made them nonetheless.

Whatever the reason for your current situation, you need to be honest about it, admit to yourself there's been a problem and commit to making progress towards financial freedom.

If you realise your money problems are due to a deeper issue (alcohol, gambling or drug addiction, for example), then you need to stop reading right now and go and seek professional help with that issue before you go any further.

On the other hand, if your income is greater than your expenses, you're not in debt or you have a positive real net worth, then congratulations – we have a good foundation upon which to make progress.

Even if you're in a good situation, you don't get off easily. You still need to understand the reasons why you find yourself in this good financial position. It can help to ask yourself some of the following questions:

> Why is your situation currently pretty good?
> Did it happen on purpose?
> Did you actually plan to save and pay off debt?
> Or did it just kind of happen by accident?

Whatever the reasons, good or bad, write them down.

It's only by making a note of where you started from that you can measure your progress.

Trust me – someday soon you'll look back at this exercise and realise just how far you have come.

That's it for *Step 1*. Well done! You've just completed one of the most tedious parts of any journey, which is proper preparation.

Now the fun part starts – now we can begin to design your dream life!

Summing Up

We have learned in this chapter about the importance of telling the truth and how to create a budget:

> You must be honest with yourself about your current situation if you want to make progress.
> You must admit to and take responsibility for any past money mistakes.
> Once you've been true to yourself, you can begin moving forward.
> You must create a detailed budget if you want to be successful on your quest for True Financial Freedom.
> When you create a budget, you will reveal the true state of your finances.
> Whatever the outcome of this exercise, the following chapters are going to help you exponentially improve your current situation.

What did you learn as you created your own budget? How can you use this information in the future? Will you change your spending behaviour on the basis of this exercise? What little victories can you celebrate at this point in the Journey?

1 www.cnbc.com/2017/08/11/most-americans-cant-answer-these-basic-money-questions.html
2 www.cnbc.com/2019/08/02/1-in-5-people-spend-more-time-planning-vacations-than-finances-survey.html

Resources

The following tools and resources will help you learn more about the concepts in this chapter:

Apps & Software

Microsoft Excel

www.microsoft.com/en/microsoft-365/excel

Despite the rise of apps, smartphones and artificial intelligence, Excel is still by far my favourite financial planning software outside of the professional tools we use in the Financial Planning business. Using Excel you can create any sort of financial analysis you want. I use Excel for my monthly budgeting Spreadsheet, to track my net worth and to plan my financial future. You can download my master budget planner to use yourself at: www.millennialmutiny.com/budget

Yolt

www.yolt.com

Yolt is a free app from the people at ING Bank which allows you to connect your bank accounts and credit cards and then it will pull in all of your spending, categorise your transactions and give you a summary of where you are spending your money. Although the level of detail will never be as high as you will get with a custom Excel budget sheet (which is my recommended solution), something is always better than nothing. If you really can't muster the time or energy to do the full budget Spreadsheet (but please do – you will thank me for it later), then Yolt comes a close second.

You Need a Budget
www.youneedabudget.com

Goodbudget
www.goodbudget.com

This is another great budgeting app. This is a new term and is one for a bit further down the road. If you feel ready for some more advanced budgeting strategies, I suggest you head over to www.millennialmutiny.com/budget to learn more.

Step 2
See The Future
(Where Do You
Want To Be?)

Now that you've been honest about where you're at, you can start the fun process of designing the life you want to achieve.

For some, their priorities might not signify a major change in their day-to-day lives. Perhaps they just want to get out of debt, pay off a student loan or start planning for an early retirement.

For others, however, this exercise will see them imagining a life that's worlds apart from their current one. Some will have visions of exotic travel, quitting their job or writing a book.

Whatever's going through your mind right now, that's OK. This is your life and the great thing is you get to design it how you want.

When we start to think about the future, it can be a little daunting at first. We have to imagine things that don't feel possible or that seem overwhelming; it can seem a little scary.

The good news is, just like in the last chapter, I have a structured exercise you can complete to help you here. This one's called Your Perfect Life and it comes in three parts.

But before we do that, we need to consider a simple question...

The Question That Changed My Life

In the months that followed the creation of our Financial Planning business, things were pretty good. When you first set up a business, there's always a kind of halo effect that sees things off to a good start.

During those first few months, not only is everyone full of excitement and anticipation, but it's also when you tend to win the easy business.

In our case, the easy business came in the form of supportive friends, family members and an old client or two. These initial projects kept us going nicely for the first few months.

It was only as we approached the end of year one that things started to get dicey. The friends and family had already been taken care of and the contact list was looking a little thin on the ground. We were in trouble.

At about this time, I attended a free seminar hosted by a business coach in the Financial Planning sector. I'm not sure why I decided to attend, but there was something about the little advert that made it appealing to me.

I walked in the door (five minutes late), sat down and very quickly found myself transfixed. David was speaking about my problems as if he actually knew me.

"Are you working 60 hours a week and feeling burned out? Are you struggling to find new business? Are your clients not paying you what you are worth?"

I was realising that despite my intentions to find financial freedom after my near-death experiences, despite the commitments I'd made to myself, I'd got pulled off track.

I was working too hard, not feeling particularly satisfied and was certainly not feeling Financially Free.

There was an instant connection and I knew I had to work with this coach.

There was just one small problem...

Because the launch into business had been hard, our newly accumulated savings were starting to dwindle. We were down to our final £19,000.

The cost to work with this coach was £18,000 per year – GULP!

Can you imagine the conversation I had with Katherine to convince her that spending our only money on a business coach was a good idea?

But... to my surprise, she agreed and off we went.

The first thing we did was to arrange a two-hour discovery call with David.

We spoke on the phone for the first hour or so and then, ever so casually, David asked, "Do you mind if I ask you a question?"

Well of course not, I thought, *that's what coaches are meant to do, isn't it?*

"This is quite a big question, Matthew. Are you sure you're ready?"

"Yes!" I think I pleaded.

Little did I know just how profound this question would be.

This big question, the one that had such a massive impact on me, was so simple yet so life-changing:

Are you ready? Are you sure?

What do you really, really... *really* **want?**

David asked me just that five years ago and the answer I gave is what changed my life.

Now it's your turn.

Your Perfect Life Part #1 – What Do You Really, Really... Really Want?

I would like you to pause for a moment and think about this. It's not a question you can answer in 30 seconds.

In fact, take a sheet of paper and write the question at the top. You have to write it just like this (or personalise it if you like with coloured pens, perhaps):

What do I really, really... really want?

Now stare at it for a few minutes before you begin to write the answer.

This activity requires deep thought. Make sure you have a good hour or so free of distractions so you can really consider what you want in your future.

If you are on your second read-through of this book, I suggest you take a pause from reading now and complete the exercise before going any further.

When I first did this, I think I wrote for almost an hour. I won't replicate the three or four sides of paper I jotted down here, but some of my main points were:

> To live a happy and rewarding family life.
> To travel widely – America, Australia, New Zealand and more.
> To spend more time with friends and family.
> To work in a rewarding business.
> To have a business that could run itself effectively in my absence.
> To help other people achieve freedom in their business.
> To reach a level of financial freedom where I never had to worry about money ever again.
> To be in a position to semi-retire earlier than is usual.
> To give something back.
> To coach and train less-advantaged children.
> To get a PhD.
> To play a gig in a punk rock band (even though I'm a horrible singer and currently play no instruments).

The beautiful thing about this exercise is the answers you come up with are yours and yours alone. No one can tell you how you should plan your future.

When you think about what you really, really, really want, you tend to come up with high-level items. These are often things you want to become (*I would like to become a great teacher*) and sometimes they'll be things you want to do (*I would like to do a skydive*) or see (*I would like to see The Great Barrier Reef*).

At this point, it helps to begin thinking about what day-to-day life looks like in your ideal world. To get ready for the next exercise, go to www.millennialmutiny.com/budget and download my Perfect Life Worksheet. This is the second part of the exercise.

Your Perfect Life Part #2 – Your Perfect Day

Your Perfect Day

I'd like you to think about your Perfect Day. Imagine the best day in the whole world ever:

> Where are you?
> Who are you with?
> What do you do?
> Where do you travel?
> What do you eat and drink?
> Where do you sleep?

Write all of this down. Longhand. Yes, that's right, with a pen and paper – not a keyboard. It's been proven that moving your hand across a page like this allows you to access your subconscious more effectively than using a computer. When using a computer you can block the flow of thought by reading and editing as you go.

For most people, The Perfect Day is just that: a day. You wouldn't want to do the same thing every day for the rest of your life. Superficially you may think you want to, but if you're really honest, would you want to live this same day over and over for weeks on end? Which brings us to...

Your Perfect Week

Following on from The Perfect Day comes The Perfect Week.

This is slightly more of a bird's-eye view, but a week is still a sufficiently short period that you can really give it some serious thought.

The same questions as above apply here but think about each day in turn. If you could have your Perfect Week, how would it look?

> Where are you?
> Who are you with?
> What do you do?
> Where do you travel?
> What do you eat and drink?
> Where do you sleep?

No cheating. I need you to consider every single question again, in the context of a week rather than a day. Write it down with your pen, longhand as before.

While a week gives us more variety and a bit more time, it's still a reasonably short period of time. To get a true idea about your ideal life, we need to zoom out to look at a year.

You know what's coming next...

Your Perfect Year

This is where it gets a little harder. It can be easy to imagine a day or even a week and what you might do during that time. Thinking about a year, on the other hand, is a different matter.

Rather than getting bogged down planning each of the 365 days (it could take a year just thinking about it!) I recommend you think about the year as four periods of three months each – four quarters:

> January – March
> April – June
> July – September
> October – December

Within each quarter, think about the big-picture things you want to do and see.

Unlike The Perfect Day and The Perfect Week, you're not looking for granular detail here; you don't need to think about every activity.

Rather, let's think of some of the main things you'd like to do in each quarter.

Again, write it down on your paper.

When I completed this exercise for the first time, I included a significant winter sun trip in Q1 and time working on our home environment in Q2. I included a lot of summer travel while the weather was nice, followed by some skiing in the winter and Christmas at home with the family in Q4.

There might also be other things that you add into your Perfect Year.

Perhaps each year you want to learn a new skill (play the guitar, learn to speak Spanish, maybe). Perhaps there are other things you would like to accomplish (start a blog, run a marathon, etc.).

All of these things can go into your Perfect Year.

Your Perfect Life Part #3
– Adding it all up

Now, you might be thinking this all sounds wonderful (and believe me it is) but how much is it going to cost?

This is where the final part of this exercise comes in.

You now need to figure out the cost of your Perfect Life.

To complete this step, you need to go back to your expenditure summary that we completed in *Step 1*.

Current annual budget

After completing *Step 1*, you should have a very good idea about what you are spending on your lifestyle *now*. We are going to use this as a benchmark to help you work out the cost of the lifestyle you have just described.

We need to look at annual, rather than monthly, expenses here (if you cheated earlier and just added up a month's worth of costs, you will need to multiply this by 12 and then add in extra for things that might not happen every month, i.e. holidays, etc.).

Future Desired Lifestyle

Alongside your current annual expenses, we now need to add a new column to our sheets (if you downloaded my template from www.millennialmutiny.com/budget, it's already there for you).

This new column will be called Future Desired Lifestyle.

You need to take each item in turn and think what it would cost to incorporate into your Future Desired Lifestyle.

Some items might go up (perhaps by a lot), some might go down (again, possibly significantly) and others will stay the same.

Let's look at some examples.

Your property taxes are generally something that will remain the same – unless your desired lifestyle involves a much bigger house than at present or a holiday home, in which case you'll need to budget a lot more.

Other items that might remain the same are things like utility bills (again, unless you're planning bigger or second homes, as above) and insurances.

You might have decided that in your Perfect Life, you would like to travel a lot more often and even fly first class. If so, add up the cost of your desired trips over the year and add them to the Spreadsheet.

I suggest you put effort into this. Don't just do a finger-in-the-air estimate. Actually, log on to some travel sites and research the real-life cost of your desired trips. Don't forget to build in a budget for spending money and other travel costs while you're away as well.

If you currently drive or take public transport to work, your commuting cost could be something that reduces in your Perfect Life. This could be because you wish to quit your job completely, or work from home, perhaps.

Other things will actually be interlinked. A great example is your budget for grocery shopping and eating out.

Some people love to eat out, but they don't do it that often because they don't have the money.

Other people love to cook at home, but they eat out a lot because they don't have the time.

Let's say you are in the former camp. In your Perfect Life, you might budget more for eating out and less for your grocery shop.

You can use your current expenditure as the benchmark for all of this. In the above example, perhaps you currently eat out once a week and spend £200 a month. In your Perfect Life you want to eat out four times a week so you budget for £800 (unless you want to eat in more upmarket restaurants, in which case it'll need to be more).

At the same time, you might work out you spend £7 on the average meal you cook at home. You can now knock £21 off your weekly grocery bill as you'll not be cooking at home so much.

Once you've gone through the whole sheet, you should have an idea of the total annual cost of your dream life.

One-offs

The final thing we need to add in is one-off lump sum costs. This could be for the second home, the dream car or some other one-off purchase.

What do you see?

Is the number higher than expected? Is it a bit scary?

Perhaps it's actually less than you expected?

When I first did this exercise, I certainly had a sharp intake of breath.

My total was £96,000 per annum, plus £400,000 for one-off expenses – GULP!

Don't worry about the number right now. *Step 6* will show you how you can make almost any lifestyle a reality.

So, What Does This all Mean?

"So, what does this all mean?" I hear you ask. Now that you've figured out how much you need to live your Perfect Life on an annual basis, plus any extra one-off costs, you can begin to calculate your Freedom Figure.

Your Freedom Figure

Your Freedom Figure is the amount of money you need to live your Perfect Life, without the fear of ever running out of money.

Sounds good, doesn't it?

There are two ways that you can think about your Freedom Figure and they both have their pros and cons.

First, you can think of your Freedom Figure as a monthly income amount that you need to achieve.

Let's say you've decided your Perfect Life will cost £60,000 per year. In that case, you need a monthly net income, after taxes and other deductibles, of £5,000.

All you have to do is build a business or other income stream that will generate £5,000 per month, while allowing you the right level of time freedom to actually do what you want to do.

Simple, right? OK, it may not sound that simple, but it's actually not as hard as you think. Don't worry about the *how* right now – we'll cover that in detail in *Step 6*. For now, you just need to know the number, the Freedom Figure.

The second way to think about your Freedom Figure is to think about the lump sum of capital you'll need to generate enough income to give you your monthly £5,000.

In order to do this we can use some very simple maths that's known in the financial freedom community as the '4% rule'.

Basically, the theory says you can draw 4% out of an investment portfolio each year and it will still probably last forever.

Some studies have suggested the rate could be slightly higher or lower than 4% but, as a rule of thumb, it works fairly well.

To figure out the capital you need, you simply take your annual income target (in this example, £60,000) and divide it by 4%.

If you divide £60,000 by 4%, you get a figure of £1,500,000.

If you build up an investment portfolio of £1,500,000, you can draw off 4% every year to provide £60,000, and it should last forever.

So, Which Is Best?

As with many things in life, the answer is not black and white – it depends. When thinking about your Freedom Figure, consider the following pros and cons.

Monthly income amount
(the monthly cost of your Perfect Life)

Pros

+ Can be faster and easier to achieve than a big lump sum.
+ Can allow you to increase your income amount over time.
+ Can allow you to start living your Perfect Life sooner.

Cons

- Will generally involve *some* form of work, although this could be minimal.
- There's always a slight vulnerability that something in your business could change, which stops or reduces your monthly income.

Lump sum of capital (the lump sum you need to fund your Perfect Life, based on the 4% rule)

Pros

+ Generally requires no work to maintain.
+ Is a fairly safe and stable way to generate income.
+ You'll need to learn about the world of finance and investments (which is definitely a good thing and not that complicated).

Cons

- Will normally take longer to build up than a monthly income.

You don't need to decide right now. Just bear in mind your target monthly income and your lump sum amounts – note them down in your Spreadsheet and we will re-visit these in later steps.

That's Just Dreamy

It's fair to say it was almost impossible. Not quite impossible (nothing is *really* impossible, is it?) but very close.

Paul had just completed his Perfect Life exercise and he'd got a little carried away. There is nothing wrong with that, mind you. That's kind of the whole point of the process: to get people to articulate their Perfect Life, their money-no-object, do-anything-you-want Perfect Life. Paul had certainly remained true to the brief!

As we reviewed Paul's list there were certainly some big numbers on there:

> First class flights – £20,000 a year
> Overseas holidays – £35,000 a year
> Yacht maintenance – £15,000 a year

OK, now you are just being silly, I thought to myself. You see, at the time we first completed this exercise, Paul's income was only around £35,000 per year – gross, before tax. He wanted to spend more on holidays each year than his current annual net income!

The list continued:

> Weekends away – £6,000 a year
> Eating out – £6,000 a year

I went to interrupt Paul and tell him that his dreams were probably a little out of reach (*This really is getting out of hand*, I thought), but then I stopped myself. I was about to break my own rule. My promise to myself to always believe in what's possible when you put your mind to something.

Yes, Paul's income was fairly modest. Yes, his Perfect Life had a big price tag attached – a very big one. But, this was Paul's Perfect Life. This was *his* goal, *his* dream, *his* ambition and who was I to get in the way?

You see, Paul believed he could get there and that is what mattered. What I hadn't asked at this point was how. Had I been a bit more patient, I would have learned that Paul had a unique business idea that really did have the potential to make a lot of money. Although he was working in a fairly average job, he was already plotting his escape to freedom. He was already planning on how to make these dreams a reality.

You see, I was about to do what many people do when we hear others talk of their dreams and ambitions: they scoff, they laugh, they tell us it's all just a dream and it can never become a reality. But didn't every dream start off sounding a bit crazy?

When Elon Musk declared that he would put a Tesla into space, his family must have thought he was bonkers. When Obama said he was going to run for president, his friends probably thought he was in cloud cuckoo land. When Martin Luther King said "I have a dream", there were many who thought it was just that.

Having big dreams means you need to be prepared to fight for what you want, for what you believe is possible.

So I encourage you, very much like Paul, to let yourself go as you do this exercise – don't hold back. If you really want something, put it down.

From experience, a compromised dream is nowhere near as powerful a motivator as the fully-fledged, no holds barred version you really want to put down on the paper in front of you.

So, just go for it.

After all, as Paul so eloquently put it, "I would rather have a massive, ridiculous goal and get 80% of the way there, than have a tiny one and achieve 120% of it." I couldn't have put it better myself.

So there you have it.

Let's remind ourselves how far you've come on the road to True Financial Freedom, just in this chapter alone...

You should now have a clear idea of what you really want in your life. This is generally what you want to become.

You have imagined what The Perfect Day, Week, Year and Life might look like in your ideal world. This is generally what you want to see and do.

Finally, we've considered the cost of all of this and generated our Freedom Figure and expressed this in terms of a target monthly income or a lump sum necessary to consistently generate that income.

Before we get too carried away, though, we need to make sure we avoid some of the common traps people fall into while on their Journey to True Financial Freedom.

Summing Up

We have learned in this chapter how to create a vision of your Perfect Life – your destination on this Journey – the top of your mountain.

> You have considered what you really, really... really want in life.
> You have figured out what your Perfect Day looks like.
> Followed by your Perfect Week and Year.
> You have also then worked out how much money you need to make that dream lifestyle a reality – your Freedom Figure.
> Finally, you have started to think about if you want to aim to generate your Freedom Figure through a regular monthly income or a lump sum of capital.

How do you feel about your Perfect Life? Does it feel a little bit scary? Perhaps you are wondering how you will ever achieve all of this?

Resources

The following tools and resources will help you learn more about the concepts in this chapter:

Books

The Number: What Do You Need for the Rest of Your Life and What Will It Cost?

Lee Eisenberg, Free Press, 2006

What I call your Freedom Figure, Lee Eisenberg calls your number – basically, how much money you need for the rest of your life. This book delves deeper into Financial Independence and how to achieve it using a lump sum of capital.

Beyond The 4% Rule: The science of retirement portfolios that last a lifetime

Abraham Okusanya, 2018

The 4% rule is good, but it's not perfect. If you want to deeply understand the 4% rule and its potential pitfalls, you need to read this book by actuarial expert Abraham Okusanya. You will come away with a far greater understanding of this oh-so-important number!

Step 3
Avoid And Prevent Pitfalls (So You Don't Stumble Along The Way)

Shortly after I started my first job, I remember being all excited when the first pay cheque came through the post. I tore open the envelope with glee to look at my first proper monthly wage.

I was working at Dixons (a now-defunct electrical retailer that has morphed into Currys PC World).

My first pay cheque was for the grand sum of £982! At the time, I was on a basic salary of about £8,000 per year, plus a bit of commission on top.

That £982 doesn't sound like much now, but at the time I felt like a king. When you've been living on a part-time pot-washer's wage for two years, £982 seems like a fortune!

I quickly scurried to the shops to spend my hard-earned fortune. I bought some new shoes, a new mobile phone and some computer games and then

– everything was gone.

I was amazed how it'd only taken me a matter of hours to spend a whole month's worth of work.

I should've learnt the lesson there and then, but did I? Don't be silly.

As the months passed, I kept receiving my pay cheque, spending it within the first week and then waiting the agonising three weeks until the end of the month to top up my bank account again. I had inadvertently slipped into some poor money management habits.

What's more, at this point I really didn't have that many financial responsibilities. I was still living at home and I didn't have any bills to speak of, so I had no excuse for being broke.

As I developed in my role, I started to earn a little more and within a couple of years I was probably earning around £16,000 per year. Still not a lot, but it was a 100% increase on what I'd been earning before.

At this point, I moved out and rented a flat, which came with lots of new bills and expenses to keep up with.

Despite my income doubling, I'd taken on a load of new expenses that more than absorbed all my extra income. I was probably worse off than I was before. How could this be?

When I left the shop and got my first job in banking, my earnings increased again. Very quickly, I was earning over £30,000 per year – double again.

You'd think by now I'd have loads of money floating around to save and invest. But no!

Katherine and I moved out of the flat and bought a house, and I upgraded my car. We started to go on some holidays and spend more on food. Despite the fact my income was so much higher, I was still struggling to make any meaningful savings or investments.

By the time I left the bank only three years later, my earnings had increased to around £90,000 per year. A massive three times more than I'd been earning before, and a whopping 11 times my original £8,000 salary only five years earlier.

But, I still wasn't saving. I had little income left at the end of the month and I still prayed for the next pay cheque to come. What was going on?

Enter Lifestyle Inflation

I was suffering from a condition called *Lifestyle Inflation*. This is where the cost of your lifestyle increases at the same pace as, or even faster than, your earnings.

My little flat had been upgraded to a nice three-bedroom detached house. My old banger had been replaced by a shiny new car with all the latest gadgets.

Whereas we used to shop in the discount aisle for reduced items and short sell-by-date meat, we were now digging in the premium section and selecting all sorts of yummy treats to go with the weekly shop.

Our budget holidays had been replaced by 5-star luxury resorts.

And all of this had happened without us really noticing.

Generally when we get an increase in earnings, it doesn't happen overnight. I didn't go from £8,000 to £16,000 in a day – it took over two years. It was a gradual process.

As my earnings increased gradually, so did my spending, almost without my knowing it.

This might sound extreme. *How could he not notice?* you might be thinking. But this is how most people live. They get a small pay rise, their spending increases by a similar or even greater amount, and then they're back at square one, trying to make ends meet.

Lifestyle Inflation is perhaps the biggest danger on your Journey to True Financial Freedom.

In *Step 6*, I'm going to show you loads of ways to increase your earnings beyond your wildest dreams. But if your spending keeps up, then you'll be no better off and you certainly won't find True Financial Freedom.

The reason I mention Lifestyle Inflation *now* is because you have to get this under control before you start earning lots more money, otherwise your lifestyle will just increase at the same pace.

To be clear, I'm NOT suggesting you do all of this work and don't enjoy the fruits of your labour. That's not what True Financial Freedom is all about.

The Journey to True Financial Freedom should be almost as enjoyable as the destination, so you should be free to spend and enjoy *some* of your additional income as your earnings increase – but only *some*.

If you spend all of your additional income on additional lifestyle, then this will actually lead to more stress and anxiety around money.

||||||||||||||||||||||||||||||||||||||||||||||||||||||||||||||||||||||||||||||||||||||||||

FACT On average, it takes Brits just six weeks for a pay rise to lose its novelty factor and for people to absorb it into their lifestyle.[1]

||||||||||||||||||||||||||||||||||||||||||||||||||||||||||||||||||||||||||||||||||||||||||

When I was earning £8,000 per year, I didn't really worry about money that much. Although I wasn't earning a lot, I wasn't spending a lot either – a lot of that spending was discretionary, if I'm honest.

By the time I was earning £90,000, I had a family, a big mortgage, car payments to make, household bills and expenses and all of the other responsibilities that come with running a house. I now *had* to earn a certain amount or I'd get into a lot of trouble.

The Magic of the Savings Rate

The key to enjoying your life *and* finding True Financial Freedom is what I call your Savings Rate. Keeping an eye on your Savings Rate is also the very best way to avoid the trap of Lifestyle Inflation.

So what is your Savings Rate exactly? Put simply, your Savings Rate is the percentage of your income that you save or invest each month.

Let's say you have a monthly income of £1,000 and you manage to save £100 per month of that – you have a Savings Rate of 10%.

For a lot of people, their Savings Rate when they start this Journey will be zero – yes, a big fat zero. If that's you, don't worry, you're in good company.

Some people will even start off with a negative Savings Rate. If you earn £1,000 per month and spend £1,100, you have a negative Savings Rate of -10% (this means you're taking on debt and/or spending any savings you currently have).

Whatever your Savings Rate is now, the key is to always increase it from this day forwards.

Even if you currently have a 1% Savings Rate, aim to make it 2% next month.

If you're starting with a 10% Savings Rate, aim for 11%, etc.

When you begin this Journey, you will probably make incremental progress and that's OK.

Remember the power of Compounding Compounding from *The 6 Essential Truths of the New Rich?*

Even if you add just 1% to your Savings Rate each month, that's fine. The impact of this 1% monthly increase will compound beyond your wildest dreams and before you know it, you'll be well on your way to True Financial Freedom.

So How Does This Help Me Have a Great Life?

So long as you continually increase your Savings Rate, you're making more and more progress towards True Financial Freedom. This is not to say you have to divert *all* of your spare income into savings and investments.

How to Save More and Spend More

Let's take a look at a simple example.

Assume you're earning £1,000 per month. You have expenses of £900 and are currently saving £100 – this means you have a Savings Rate of 10%.

If you get a pay rise (or use a Side-Hustle to earn extra income – more on this later) and you're now earning £1,100 per month, you could choose to put all of this additional money into savings. Now you're saving £200 per month.

This would give you a Savings Rate of just over 18% (remember we now have to take the £200 savings as a percentage of £1,100, not £1,000).

The only problem is that it does nothing to help you today. You have no more spending power to spend on travel or experiences that could bring you joy right now. Some might call me short-sighted, but in the wake of my near-death experience I became more focused not just on having a great life in the future, but also in the here and now! Most importantly, I decided it made no sense to me that one had to come at the expense of the other – surely there was a way to make both things a reality?

Split it

The alternative is to take your £100 of additional income and split it. Let's assume we split it 50/50 for now, so you add £50 per month to your savings and you add £50 per month to your discretionary spending.

You're now saving £150 per month, which gives you a Savings Rate of around 13.5%. This might not sound like a lot, but a 3.5% increase in your Savings Rate is impressive – just wait until you see what happens next. Upping your overall Savings Rate by 3.5% actually means you are saving 50% more than you were before in pound note terms (£150 vs £100 before).

You also have £50 extra in your pocket every month to spend on anything you like. The best part is that you can spend that £50 guilt-free because you know you have your savings under control.

When my dad was making his money decisions back in the 80s, the term Savings Rate probably hadn't even been invented. But with his Spend Half, Save Half rule when it came to excess money he was, in his own way, increasing his Savings Rate. He probably won't even remember the conversation, but those four words – *Spend Half, Save Half* – have probably had a larger impact on my own financial freedom than any other advice.

There are many ways of keeping Lifestyle Inflation under control (we will talk about another one in a moment), but I believe that focusing on your Savings Rate is the best.

Not only does it keep your expenditure under control (while still allowing some flexibility to enjoy increased earnings right away), but it also gets you closer to True Financial Freedom as you go along – a double whammy! The best part about it is you get to keep your focus on something that's very easy to view through a positive lens (making additional savings) rather than viewing things through what can be a negative lens (your spending habits).

What if my Savings Rate is negative?

Don't worry. A lot of people start from this point on their Journey to True Financial Freedom.

In fact, it's the misery and stress of debt that gives a lot of people the wake-up call they need to begin this Journey in the first place.

If you currently have a negative Savings Rate, this means you're currently overspending and are not managing your money very well. I'm not attacking you here but remember *Step 1 – Tell the Truth?* We have to do this first.

A negative Savings Rate means you're using your accumulated savings to meet day-to-day living costs – if you have any, that is. If you don't have savings, it means you're taking on debt – most likely expensive consumer debt on overdrafts and credit cards.

Although I want you to have a great life, if you currently have a negative Savings Rate, it has to stop – right now!

A negative Savings Rate is not sustainable for any period of time and will only lead to debt and misery.

We can focus on improving your lifestyle later on, but first you must get on top of your overspending.

There are two ways to get this situation under control: reduce your spending or increase your earnings. We will deal with increasing earnings in *Step 6*, but for now let's focus on getting those expenses down!

Take Back Control – How to Reduce Expenses

If you have a negative Savings Rate, reducing your spending is a must. Even if you have a positive Savings Rate, it's always a good idea to see if you can reduce your spending. Even £20 or £30 a month of savings has the potential to add 1 or 2% to your Savings Rate.

When it comes to reducing expenses, it might help to review the definitions we covered on pages 71 to 75 before you go any further.

Take out your monthly spending summary that we completed in *Step 1*. You'll need it for this next bit.

Back to your Bedrock Expenses

By definition, your Bedrock Expenses are pretty fixed. These could be things like property taxes or other fixed expenses that can't be controlled or negotiated. (Other than by taking ultra-extreme action like moving house, which often costs money in any case. That's not to say that this is a bad idea – sometimes drastic circumstances call for drastic measures – but of course, this kind of decision is not to be taken lightly.)

As such, Bedrock Expenses don't really give us much scope for reducing costs. Let's move on.

Back to your Foundation Expenses

Your Foundation Expenses are potentially a richer vein. There are often some savings to be found here as follows:

1) Are there any insurances that can be re-negotiated? If you have car or home insurance, there's often a better deal to be had, especially if you've let the policy roll over from one year to the next.

   The deals offered to new customers are often better than for those that renew, so you should be checking your insurances on a yearly basis.

   If you've not done this recently, do so now – you could generate hundreds of pounds a year in savings.

   Be careful to check the level of cover, though – there's no point having crappy insurance that doesn't pay out when you need it to (I should know, my fortunately-very-good travel insurance picked up a tab of £210,000 from my American hospital visit!).

   With that said, it's often possible to get exactly the same cover you have now, with the same provider you use now, at a lower price just by picking up the phone and negotiating with them. Threaten to cancel the policy if you need to (you don't actually have to go through with it).

   Please read *Step 5* before you go ahead and cancel any insurances that are not needed – there could well be some further cost savings to be found here as well.

2) Could you get a better deal on your utilities? If you can, this really is a no-brainer. Gas and electricity are gas and electricity; there's no difference in the product you receive between different suppliers.

Most people don't even look for better deals on their utilities and they could be missing out on hundreds of pounds a year in missed savings.

3) Can you get a better deal on your mortgage if you have one? Lots of people don't renew their mortgage when it comes to the end of the fixed-rate term.

This leaves them paying the lender's standard rate, which can be double or even triple the rates available with the best deals. You could save hundreds every month with a new mortgage deal.

4) Could you reduce your grocery bill? Many of us spend more than we need to on groceries. Shopping in a different chain or using coupons could be a great way to reduce your expenses.

Back to your Lifestyle and Luxury Expenses

What you should do with these categories depends in part on your current Savings Rate.

If you currently have a negative Savings Rate, you should put a stop to as many of these expenses as you need to in order to reach a break-even point.

By definition, Lifestyle and Luxury Expenses are discretionary (you don't need them) and you should not be consistently taking on debt to fund these things. Sorry to be harsh – but it's true.

Don't worry, this nasty period won't be for long (we're going to increase your income later in *Step 6*) but for now these things need to go!

If you currently have a positive Savings Rate, you may not need to cut so deep here. In fact, I'd rather you look for ways to increase your income so you can maintain your current lifestyle – but let's save that for *Step 6*.

For now, it'd be a good idea to check through your Lifestyle and Luxury Expenses to see if you have anything there that's, well, a bit stupid.

Like when I realised I was spending £1,000 per year on coffee. It's just crazy. If you have anything like that in there, then you could consider cutting it to improve your Savings Rate.

On the other hand, perhaps you *really* love that morning coffee and don't want to let go. If you're doing this consciously and you really enjoy it, that's fine, go right ahead. If you currently have a positive Savings Rate – you've earned it!

What Is a Good Savings Rate?

Frankly, I think that any positive Savings Rate is good.

The vast majority of the population in Western economies have no savings or Emergency Fund and they consistently live from pay cheque to pay cheque.

If you have a consistently positive Savings Rate (even 1%), this is a great start and you should be proud of yourself.

|||||||||||||||||||||||||||||||||||||||||||||||||||||||||||||||||||||||||||||||||||||||||||||||||||||||

 40% of Americans could not cope with an unexpected expense of $400 or more.[2]

|||||||||||||||||||||||||||||||||||||||||||||||||||||||||||||||||||||||||||||||||||||||||||||||||||||||

So, What Savings Rate Should I Aim for?

If you want to achieve first Financial Independence and then True Financial Freedom quickly, you need to be aiming for a Savings Rate of more than, wait for it... 50%.

*WHAT THE ****?!?*

Yes, you read that right, you need to be aiming for a Savings Rate of over 50%, which means you'll be saving over half of your income.

At this point you probably think I'm totally mad and could be tempted to throw this book out the window, but bear with me.

You could be thinking that you're lucky to save 1% of what you earn, let alone 10%, 20% or even 50%!

A 50% Savings Rate will sound bananas to start with – it certainly did to me – but as you make progress, it will start to seem more obtainable.

As with all things, progress at the start is slow. Perhaps you can grow your Savings Rate by 1% or 2% in the first few months and that's a great start.

From small acorns big oak trees grow and by the time you've completed *Step 6*, you could be well on the way to a 50% Savings Rate as well.

When I started this Journey, my Savings Rate was probably zero or 1% at best and perhaps even slightly negative on occasion. Now, I routinely save over 30% of my income and in many months I'm able to achieve the fabled 50% Savings Rate.

Why is 50% so important?

So, why is 50% the magic number, then?

The truth is there's not much significance in the 50% number itself, other than meaning you can reach financial freedom super fast and be totally in control of your finances.

Let's look at the maths.

For this example, assume you're earning £50,000 per year to keep it simple.

Using the 4% rule, you need a portfolio of £1,250,000 to maintain that type of income (£50,000 / 4% = £1,250,000 and £1,250,000 x 4% a year = £50,000).

The two ways to save 50%

From this point, there are two (or maybe three) ways to achieve a 50% Savings Rate.

1) **Reduce your expenses to £25,000 per year, leaving you with £25,000 to save**

Although it might not seem immediately obvious, because you've chosen to reduce your expenses you now only need a portfolio of £625,000 to maintain your new level of expenses at the rate of £25,000 per year.

This might not give you your Perfect Life, but by the time you have £625,000 saved up, work becomes a choice. You could quit your job and carry on living your current lifestyle just from your portfolio income.

This is the key difference between financial freedom and True Financial Freedom. If you can build up your portfolio to a level where it could support your current lifestyle, then work (at least the work you currently do) becomes optional. If you wake up one morning and decide you don't like it, you can just hand your notice in and move on to something else with very little risk – because you can continue living the life you had before.

Your Freedom Figure could well be a lot higher than this, however, because £25,000 may not be enough to pay for your Perfect Life. When you have enough in your portfolio to fund your Perfect Life, *then* you can say you have reached True Financial Freedom

– living your Perfect Life without having to worry about money again in the future.

Now, if you're currently taking home pay of £50,000 a year and you're spending most of that money, you might be thinking you can't possibly reduce your expenses by 50%, but let's get real for a second (tough love alert). You *can* live comfortably on £25,000 a year. In fact, millions of people in the UK and across the world live on much less than this and would bite your right arm off to have an income of £25,000, let alone £50,000 a year!

Chances are *you* lived on much less than that when you started your first job, or when you were a student.

The fact you're spending more than £25,000 is a choice. You have chosen your house, your car and your current lifestyle. Your current rate of spending is a by-product of those choices.

Don't get me wrong. I'm the first one to admit how much I love spending money on lifestyle. There's nothing wrong with that, but just be aware that it's a choice.

It's not that you *can't* reduce expenses below £25,000 (pretty much anyone can if they need to), simply that you *don't want* to. That's fine, but please be aware that you're choosing not to reduce your expenses, which will mean it could take longer to reach True Financial Freedom.

2) **Increase your income to £100,000 per year, leaving you with £50,000 to save**
With option 1, the assumption is you can reduce your expenses drastically, which *might* not be the case, or you may simply not want to. Option 2 is to increase your income.

Now, finding an extra £50,000 per year of income is no mean feat, but all will become clear in *Step 6*.

3) **The third way – do both!**
The truth is there's actually a third way where you can do both of these things.

If you look to reduce your expenses *and* increase your income, this can have a compounding effect and you can see your Savings Rate really rocket.

Using the same example above, if you could increase your income to £67,500 *and* reduce your expenses to £33,750, you now have the magic 50% Savings Rate. I'm not saying any of this is easy, but it's possible. It will take hard work, commitment, dedication and grit, but it *is* possible. I am living proof of that. If I can do it anyone can.

Easy for You to Say

I'm often attacked online when I talk about my Savings Rate and the amount of money I'm able to save. People will say things like, *easy when you have a six-figure income, I could save 50% too if I took home that much each month.*

But while I do now enjoy a healthy income and a high Savings Rate, both of those things are a *result* of this Journey. They weren't there at the start.

I first committed to finding True Financial Freedom and *then* the income and the Savings Rate followed. I attribute my success to my commitment to this Journey. I am not special. I'm just a normal guy that decided to make a change and stick to it. When you're really focused on something, opportunities begin to present themselves to help you achieve your objective. Things become apparent that weren't before. But this only happens when you really, truly, set your mind to something.

It took time, it took blood, sweat and tears – there have been countless failures and frustrations along the way. But, I'm almost sure I would not find myself where I am today if I hadn't made those promises to myself five years ago.

Anything Else?

So, once you have Lifestyle Inflation under control, is there anything else you need to be worrying about?

Well, yes and no.

The only other thing holding back your potential is you. As we discussed in *PART 1*, you need to get your own mindset under control and believe this is possible.

You also have to be disciplined, and this is where good budgeting comes in. Once you have committed to increasing your Savings Rate, there is no use doing it for two months and then going back to your old ways. You have to keep your promises to yourself and stick to your new budgets.

Unfortunately, human beings are not very good at being disciplined; we have a habit of sticking to old habits. The good news is we're very good at inventing systems to save us from ourselves – enter the Envelope!

Enter the Envelope

Budgeting is hard; there are no two ways about it. Especially if you've been spending willy-nilly in the past, having a restricted budget might feel impossible, but it's really the only way to make this Journey work.

There are lots of different budgeting strategies and solutions out there. There are hundreds of expensive software packages and apps that promise to revolutionise your budget. The good news is you only need one system, and you can run it using Microsoft Excel or even Google Sheets: enter Envelope Budgeting.

Yes – Envelope Budgeting is by far my favourite budgeting system for lots of reasons. For starters: it works. Plain and simple. If you stick to your Envelope budget, it will work. Envelope Budgeting is also far more flexible than most other budgeting systems, so you have no excuse not to.

Envelope Budgeting is easy to understand. In fact, I'd argue it's the simplest way to keep track of your money.

The best part is you've already done a lot of the hard work. Ready to get financially organised forever?

Here goes...

A history lesson

First, a history lesson. Envelope Budgeting has been around for a long time. Probably for as long as money or cash-like money has been around. It probably wasn't called Envelope Budgeting (I doubt we had envelopes when people first started doing it). People probably didn't even know they were doing Envelope Budgeting because it's so instinctive, so natural – but the fact remains it's been around for hundreds if not thousands of years.

The reason it has existed so long is that Envelope Budgeting is a system designed to work with us: human beings. It's designed to save us from ourselves while giving us confidence and freedom in the spending decisions we make.

Here's how it (doesn't) work...

When they get paid at the end of the month, most people put all of their money into one bank account. They then have all their expenses come out of that bank account, including bills, utilities, mortgage, eating out, holidays and any other random expenditure that might come along.

They intend to save whatever is left at the end of the month, but the problem is there's never anything left over, is there?

You see, we human beings have an uncanny ability to live with what we have, to cut our cloth according to our means. But we really do tend to take this to extremes. If you earn £1,000 a month and this all goes into your one bank account, chances are you'll spend about £1,000.

I'm not having a go at you here; it's just human nature.

In his great business book, *Profit First*, Mike Michalowicz likens a single bank account to a single large plate of food. His contention (that I certainly agree with) is if you serve up a large plate of food, you tend to eat it all. After all, your mother told you that you couldn't have any ice cream until you finished your dinner!

Many weight-loss programmes have been successful by making one seemingly ridiculously simple change: use smaller plates. If you have a smaller plate, you can't fit as much food on it. If you can't fit as much food on the plate, you won't eat as much – simple. I bet you didn't think you'd be getting weight-loss tips in the book too!

The problem with having all of your money in one bank account is that you spend (eat) it all, just because it's always sitting there in front of you just waiting to be spent (eaten).

The solution to this problem is Envelope Budgeting.

When you're new to the concept, it helps to think about it in an old-fashioned sense. Some of this might be hard to believe, but it wasn't really that long ago.

In the so-called olden days, when you got paid, you tended to get a pay cheque. You would take that cheque down to the bank or the post office and they would give you cash (I know – what a pain, right!). Most people would take all of that cash – let's assume £100 – and shove it in their pocket in one nice big wedge.

They would pay their olden-day mortgage and settle their olden-day utility bills (by taking another trip to the bank I might add – how did these people cope?). They would then go to the grocery store and buy food for the week and whatever was left would be available for discretionary spending. After all that was done, there would rarely be anything left.

So, our smarter-than-average ancestors invented a system to solve this problem: Envelope Budgeting.

Here's how Envelope Budgeting works

Instead of putting all of their money into their pocket when they got paid, our smart ancestor would take their pay cheque to the bank, collect their £100 and then IMMEDIATELY when they got home divide it up into several envelopes.

How many envelopes would depend on the person and the situation, but it might have looked something like this.

Our smart ancestor knew their mortgage was £30 a month (I know – things were crazy back then!), their utilities were £10 per month and their home insurance and other bills were £5 a month. As such, they would put £45 into an envelope with the word *Bills* written on the front. When one of these bills became due, the money to pay it would be taken from the Bills

Envelope – nowhere else.

Our smart ancestor knew their weekly grocery shop tended to be around £5, so they put £25 into an envelope called *Groceries*. They put £25 in and not £20 because there are slightly more than four weeks in a month and, of course, occasionally the grocery bill is a little more than expected.

When our smart ancestor went to the grocery store, they only took the Groceries Envelope to the store. That way, there was no temptation to spend any money that wasn't intended for groceries. When the money in the envelope was gone, it was gone – simple as that – no more groceries. But (and here's the magic of Envelope Budgeting) if there was money left in the Envelope at the end of the month, it could stay there and roll over to the following month.

Because our smart ancestor was smart, they knew on average they spent around £22 a month on groceries, but they put £25 a month into the envelope – leaving roughly £3 per month behind. That meant that when Christmas rolled around, there was a nice excess fund of all those £3 savings to pay for the turkey – but it was all still coming out of the Groceries Envelope.

So, to recap. Smart ancestor started with £100. They put £45 into the Bills Envelope and £25 into the Groceries Envelope. A total of £70 – meaning they had £30 left. What did they do with that?

Well, if our smart ancestor was not-so-smart, they probably would've put that final £30 all into a final Envelope called *Discretionary* and then spent it all on eating out at Nando's (they did have Nando's back then – right?).

But if our smart ancestor was smart, they did something slightly different. They had another Envelope. This Envelope was extra special. So special in fact they put £10 into this Envelope before they put money into any of the others.

This envelope was called your *Freedom Fund* (otherwise known as *savings and investments*). Before our smart ancestor put money anywhere, they paid £10 into the Freedom Fund Envelope. Next came £45 into Bills and £25 into Groceries. This means they only had £20 left in their Discretionary Envelope.

The Freedom Fund Envelope was locked safely away so it couldn't be accessed, apart from in an extreme emergency (and no – Nando's does not qualify as an emergency, I'm afraid).

When our smart ancestor went out to the pub or went to a restaurant or went on holiday, they only took the Discretionary Envelope. This removed any temptation to spend more than they could afford. What it also meant was their savings and investments were already taken care of.

They weren't waiting until the end of the month to see if there was anything left to save, because they already made their savings payment right at the start of the month – this is a concept known as Pay Yourself First and is one of the most important lessons you must learn on your Journey to True Financial Freedom. Let's just take a moment to understand this vital tool.

Pay Yourself First

Paying yourself first was first popularised in Robert Kiyosaki's excellent book, *Rich Dad, Poor Dad*.

Basically, the concept of Pay Yourself First means you make payments to your savings and investment accounts before you pay any of your other bills and expenses.

The one exception to this is if you have debt, but as we will learn in the next chapter, you should focus on eliminating debt (apart from, perhaps, good debt) before you start saving and investing.

The theory is that a lot of people tell themselves they'll save and invest whatever is left over at the end of the month. Only there's never anything left over, is there?

If you Pay Yourself First, the debit for your investments and savings comes out before you have a chance to spend the money.

Human beings are not very good at being disciplined with money. If we pay ourselves first, on the day we get paid, we remove all temptation to spend, therefore guaranteeing the money will be added to our savings and investments.

But how will I afford to save anything, you might ask, *when I'm just about making ends meet as it is?*

I'm glad you asked. The key is to start small and build from there. If you've cleared all your debt and you're now just about getting by on your income, I would suggest starting with a Savings Rate of 1% or 2%.

If you can live on 100% of your income, you can sure as heck live on 99% or 98%. From there, try and increase your Savings Rate by 1% each month. So if you started at 2%, you move to 3%, and so on.

I promise that you'll barely feel it and you'll soon reach the point where you don't even notice the money leaving your account.

We humans have an uncanny ability to adapt and make do with what we have. If you take the money off the table first (before you have the chance to spend it), you will just spend less – trust me, it works!

Some people might think it's irresponsible to pay your investment or savings account before, say, your mortgage or your water bill –

but again, it's not true. Though it sounds totally mad to pay your investments before these vital household bills, this is what you must do.

Human beings are very bad indeed at being disciplined and very good indeed at surviving on what we have. If you take the money off the table at the start of the month (rather than promising to save what is left at the end of the month), then you'll save more money. Fact!

Spot the difference

So let's look at the differences here and summarise.

Our not-so-smart ancestor's monthly cashflow looked a little like this:

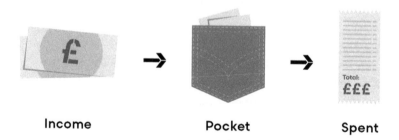

| Income | Pocket | Spent |

Our smart ancestor, on the other hand, was using Envelope Budgeting and so their monthly cashflow was a little more like this:

Income – £100

Freedom Fund Envelope – £10 → Don't spend
Bills Envelope – £45 → Spend on bills
Groceries Envelope – £25 → Spend on groceries
Discretionary Envelope – £20 → Spend on discretionary items

Of course, our ancestors were using cheques and cash, but Envelope Budgeting is just as relevant today.

Assuming you use a bank account of some kind to manage your money, there are two options available to you to implement Envelope Budgeting, depending on whether you're a beginner or an advanced Envelope Budgeter. The good news is these options stack on top of each other. If you're new to all of this, I suggest you begin with Option 1 below to get you started and then come back to Option 2 when/if you feel ready to do so.

How to use Envelope Budgeting today

Option 1 – Bank accounts for beginners

If you're living in the modern world, you simply need to replace Envelopes with Accounts.

You might think that having multiple bank accounts makes things more complicated but, in fact, it will make your financial life much simpler – here's why...

When you get paid, you will now get paid into your Income Account. This bank account is only used to receive your income. Any kind of income can go in here – salary, rental, Side-Hustle, etc. Put all your income in here.

You now need to open a new bank account for each of your Envelopes. To get started, I recommend you categorise your expenditure and just open a few accounts. *Bills, Groceries* and *Discretionary* are my favourite ones.

You'll also need to open a new savings or investment account, which we're going to call your Freedom Fund (if your bank has a facility to change the account's name, I'd suggest you actually call it Freedom Fund – it makes it far more fun when you pay money into it!). Don't worry too much about investing for now, just open a savings account.

All the different bank accounts should be with the same bank, if possible, apart from perhaps the Freedom Fund bank account. We're not looking to make your financial life much more complicated by having accounts with a ton of different banks.

When you get paid into your Income Account, you immediately transfer money into your other accounts, based on your Envelope budget. Don't worry – we're going to decide how much to pay into each account in just a moment.

At the end of this process, your Income Account will be back down to zero and you'll have your funds spread across your other accounts.

For your Bills Account, I suggest you set everything up on direct debit, which means you don't really need a debit card for this account.

For your Groceries and Discretionary Accounts, you should have a debit card.

When you want to eat out that evening and you're wondering if you can afford it, you just look at the Discretionary Account. If there's money there – happy days – Nando's here we come! If there's no money there – bad luck – no dinner out for you.

Using this system, you can always see at a glance how much money you have available for different things. If you're at the supermarket and you're wondering if you can afford that nice bottle of wine on top of the weekly shop – just check the Groceries Account.

The other great part is that you put the money in your Freedom Fund account first – so this is all taken care of. When you spend money on eating out, you can do so knowing that you budgeted this money for just that purpose – having fun – which removes a lot of the guilt we often feel when we spend money on ourselves.

OK – so we have a couple of other things to get right here:

Bank accounts

All of your Accounts should be with the same bank, except one – the Freedom Fund.

You should open your Income, Bills, Groceries and Discretionary Accounts with a single bank. The idea here is that you want to be able to see at a glance how much you have available in each category.

Your Freedom Fund, however, you want to have at a different bank – one that is hard to get to.

The whole idea is you don't want to be looking at your Freedom Fund all the time. If you see it, there's the temptation to spend it. We want it out of sight and out of mind – so use a different bank.

You can add other accounts if you have some other category of expenses you want to keep track of. Perhaps you ride horses as a hobby and this is a major part of your spending. In this case you might want to create a whole separate Horse Riding Account and have a separate allocation to that account each month.

How much in each account?

I'm glad you asked. How much should you allocate to each account each month?

Well, you remember your budgeting Spreadsheet we completed earlier? You'll need that to hand here.

Your starting point will be your current lifestyle figures from the past 12 months (you did do the work and add them all up, didn't you?).

Of course, we want to begin saving into your Freedom Fund. If you found yourself with any excess income each month, then this is a good place to start.

Looking at your Spreadsheet, let's say that you earn £1,000 a month and you've determined that you're spending £450 on rent, £300 on bills and groceries and £250 on leisure and entertainment. Thus, you are spending the full £1,000.

Having gone through the expense-reduction activity, you identified that you were spending £50 a month on coffee (I feel you) and you've decided to reduce this to £25 (notice how we've reduced it and not necessarily stopped it completely – you're allowed to have some fun you know). This means you've freed up £25.

In addition, you managed to negotiate on your car insurance, saving £25 a month and you have also committed to having one less takeaway a month, saving a further £25.

What this means is we have £75 per month of excess income. This now becomes the allocation to your Freedom Fund, giving you a starting Savings Rate of 7.5% – not bad!

If you have significant excess income at the moment, then this should also be allocated to the Freedom Fund. The idea is to save as much as possible in the Freedom Fund to start with and then ratchet the payments up from there.

So now, when you get paid £1,000 into your Income Account you'll allocate:

> £75 to Freedom Fund (always done first).
> £700 to Bills Account (£450 rent + £300 bills – £50 of savings made above).
> £225 to Discretionary Account (£250 minus the £25 saving on coffee).

This is how Envelope Budgeting works. As we discussed above when talking about Lifestyle Inflation, now when you get any sort of extra income or a pay rise, you can allocate some to your Freedom Fund and some to the other Accounts (Envelopes). The aim of the game is to increase your Savings Rate while also increasing the amount you can spend on leisure and lifestyle.

So what happens if you don't have excess income?

Two points here. If you're currently spending more than you earn, even after cutting out everything you can, then you have a problem. You should try to reduce expenses further or increase your income as fast as possible. If you're really struggling with debt, I suggest you finish this chapter quickly and move on to *Step 4*, which is all about ridding yourself of the scourge of debt.

Alternatively, you could be in the position that most people are, which is you're pretty much spending all you earn and you don't want to cut back too much.

This is OK (it's your life and your money) but you have to appreciate it will take a little longer to reach True Financial Freedom if this is where you're starting from. You're starting with a Savings Rate of zero, instead of 7.5% like in the previous example.

What I would like you to do is begin by allocating 1% of your pay to your Freedom Fund the next time you get paid. You should still set up the other accounts as detailed above, but just allocate 1% to your Freedom Fund. The rest of your money you can continue to allocate as you've been doing before, but the beauty of Envelope Budgeting is it makes you a lot more conscious and intentional in how you spend your money.

Option 2 – Apps for advanced budgeters

For many people, using bank accounts as in Option 1 will suit them just fine forever and they won't even need to move on to Option 2. Option 2 is for people who have mastered using bank accounts for their budgeting and want more control or detail on where they're spending their money.

If you're feeling ready for the next step – this is where we start to use one of the excellent budgeting apps out there to introduce some further *imaginary* Envelopes.

Here's how this works. For starters, you'll still have your bank accounts as in the previous example. Let's assume you have your Income, Bills, Groceries and Discretionary Accounts with one bank and the all-important Freedom Fund somewhere else.

Using an app lets you sub-divide some Envelopes into extra categories or save up for some longer-term purchases. You could always open an extra account or two to do the same thing, but for most people there are only so many bank accounts that they can keep track of, so an app is a good solution.

Sub-dividing accounts is most common in the Discretionary camp, so let's use that as an example.

Going back to our previous example, we were allocating £225 per month to the Discretionary Account, having made some savings so we could add to our Freedom Fund. The problem is that Discretionary is a large category. Some of the money in here might be for short-term things like eating out or cinema visits, whereas some of the money going in here might be used to pay for an annual holiday. In this case, if you spent all the money in the Discretionary Account every month, there would be nothing left over to pay for that summer holiday. This is where the app comes in.

Using your app, you could sub-divide your Discretionary Account into two sub-accounts. Let's call them *Day-to-day* and *Holiday* for now. Each month, you would use your app to set aside let's say £100 into the Holiday Account, leaving the remaining £125 to spend how you please.

At the end of the month, assuming you spent all of the £125 allocated to the Day-to-day Account, your bank account would show you had £100; your app would show you had £100 in the Holiday Account and nothing in the Day-to-day Account.

At the beginning of the following month, you get paid and you add another £225 to the Discretionary Account. If you didn't have the app, you would now be looking at a balance of £325 and thinking you could go on a spending spree.

However, you consult your app and see that you have £100 of that balance set aside for holidays. You add another £100 to your Holiday fund as it's the start of a new month, meaning you now have just £125 to spend on day-to-day things as expected.

The other great thing about using an app like this is the flexibility it provides.

Let's say that at the end of the month you haven't spent all of your Day-to-day money (I know – shock horror) and you have £25 left over. Using your app, you might decide to shuffle that money over into your Holiday Account to pay for an extra round of margaritas – sounds good to me.

Our Flexible Friend

When credit cards first came out they were called 'your flexible friend' on the ad campaigns, but really they were anything but – debt traps, more like. Envelope Budgeting is the real friend here.

The beauty of Envelope Budgeting lies in its flexibility – and we have one final thing to consider before we wrap up here, which we touched on in the previous few paragraphs. What happens if you have some money left over in one of your Envelopes (Accounts) at the end of the month? This is where Envelope Budgeting really comes into its own. You have four options, as follows.

Let's imagine you get to the end of the month and you have £20 left over in one of your accounts. With Envelope Budgeting, you can choose what to do with that £20:

1) Keep the £20 in the current Envelope and roll it over to next month. This can be very useful for bills that are variable and unpredictable. Food shopping is a great example. You might have some cheaper months during the year, but then need to dig into the accumulated funds (those extra £20s a month) to pay for a more expensive time like Christmas.

2) You can move the £20 (or part of it) to another Envelope. Perhaps your entertainment fund could do with a boost or you need some more money to cover an unexpected car repair. Please be careful not to do this too quickly, though. Sometimes you want an Envelope to build up a little balance over the year – like in the above example where we want to save some money in the Groceries Envelope for Christmas shopping. Envelopes are designed to have an excess balance at times to cover leaner months – like a squirrel putting away acorns for the winter.

3) You can use an excess in one Envelope to repay a deficit in another. Perhaps in the final week of the month you have already spent your £225 discretionary budget, but you just have to go and see the latest *Star Wars* film. If you have a £20 excess in your grocery budget, you can use this to spend a bit more in another area. Again though – this comes with a health warning – sometimes you'll need that extra £20 in the original Envelope a bit later on, so be careful with this one.

4) Finally, best of all, you could choose to save and invest the extra £20 at the end of the month and add it to your Freedom Fund. Some people would call this 'sweeping' because you sweep any remaining funds at the end of the month into a savings or investment account.

For beginners, I would suggest you just stick with the first of these options, which is to let the funds roll over into the following month – you might need them sooner than you think. You can always come back in a year or so and sweep up any excess balances. The other flexibilities should be used by more advanced budgeters only.

Envelope Overload

"Matt, Matt, I think I've messed it all up." The line went silent for a half-second as Sandra paused for breath. "My Envelopes, I've messed them all up. There must be something I've done wrong."

Around six months earlier, I had introduced the concept of Envelope Budgeting to Sandra and she had taken to it like a duck to water. Sandra was always reasonably good with money; she didn't have any major debts and she always just about seemed to be able to make ends meet. But she was never really able to save a great deal and she wanted to get started with building a Freedom Fund for her future.

As soon as we finished our conversation, Sandra logged in to her Internet banking and opened the requisite accounts for her Envelope Budgeting to begin. You could see she was excited to finally have some clarity around where her money was going. Bills, Food Shopping, Leisure & Entertainment and Holidays were the four accounts she decided to open. Holidays were super important to her and she wanted to make sure she was putting something away each month.

Finally, she opened her Freedom Fund savings account with a different bank – out of sight is out of mind. She even chose a bank that allowed account nicknames so she could actually call the account 'Freedom Fund'.

We went through the income and expenditure analysis and identified that Sandra did seem to be spending the majority of her £1,450 per month take-home income. There were a few months where there was a little left over, but nothing to write home about.

Sandra really wanted to begin saving for emergencies and her future freedom – she was prepared to cut back on a few discretionary items.

We managed to make around £40 per month of savings on existing bills and expenses. Things like her home insurance and utilities. The beauty of these savings is that they didn't cost Sandra anything in terms of her lifestyle. She was just leaving money on the table by using uncompetitive deals.

Sandra also committed to spending a bit less than she had been on lunches at work. She would make sandwiches at home, saving £50 per month. Finally, she shaved just £10 per month off her holiday budget to make a total of £100 per month in savings.

This was to be her first regular payment into a savings account – £100 per month – a starting Savings Rate of around 7% (£100 / £1,450 = 6.9%). Not too bad for a day's work. Of course, we made sure that Sandra paid herself first and set this up as a standing order into her savings account on payday.

The reason Sandra called me in a fluster six months later was that she had made the switch to app-based Envelope Budgeting the previous month. She wanted to have more control and greater visibility over where she was spending her money. She was in a panic because, for the first time since she started the Envelope Budgeting system, all of her Envelopes were in the green at the end of the month.

"I must have done something wrong," she repeated. "Perhaps I screwed it up when I set up my app."

We paused for a second and then set about checking that the Envelope system was working correctly. We looked through Sandra's bank accounts, compared them to the entries on her app and sure enough, everything was hunky dory. She had made it to the end of the month and had a little left over in every single Envelope.

Now, of course, some Envelopes are *supposed* to have money left over in them. If you are saving for a holiday, the whole idea is to carry a balance from one month to the next. But Sandra had excess cash in her food shopping Envelope and the bills one, too.

Although Sandra was finding all of this very hard to understand, her experience is actually fairly common. You see, when people become more conscious of their spending – when they have a system in place so they can see how each item of expenditure fits into their bigger picture – they often just naturally spend less.

Now, don't get me wrong, the balances Sandra had left over in her Envelopes were not spectacular. Maybe £10 here, £20 there, but they were significant.

My advice to Sandra was simple: wait until next month. If the same thing happens again, then you might want to reduce your allocations to some of the Envelopes and then you can increase your payment to your Freedom Fund.

I think Sandra took this as a challenge because the following month, not only did she have excess in each Envelope again, but in most cases, there was even more left over.

Sandra was able to increase her savings contribution by another £80 per month, to £180. Now, her Savings Rate was up to just over 12%. That's a 5% improvement, in just a few months!

As I keep banging on about, it's from small acorns that big oak trees grow. Sometimes when you take the first step and commit to the process, you will be amazed at how much you can achieve.

The Two Tools

So there we have it. You now have the two tools that you will need to begin propelling yourself towards True Financial Freedom – Your Savings Rate and Envelope Budgeting.

Using one of these tools is a game-changer in terms of your financial success. If you use both of them together, you'll be amazed at the progress you can make.

Now that you're armed with these awesome tools, there's really nothing to stop you other than yourself. You also have to commit to change. Remember one of The 6 Essential Truths of the New Rich? The Power of Patience?

All this takes time. If I'd given up on our business when it got hard, I wouldn't be where I am now (actually, I think the reason most businesses fail is that the owner gives up too soon, rather than the business itself being unviable).

When we're making changes to our finances, it can be really hard. It will be tempting to turn back and revert to our old ways.

You have to commit to financial freedom for the long term and stick at it when it gets tough!

Like any big journey, the key is to bear in mind that each step brings you a little closer. When you're at base camp staring up at Everest, taking one step may feel rather insignificant. But the fact remains, you're closer to the top than when you started – remember that!

OK, so now you have your spending and Lifestyle Inflation under control, we need to deal with the menace of debt!

Summing Up

We have learned in this chapter how to prevent setbacks on your Journey to True Financial Freedom:

> Lifestyle Inflation is one of the biggest threats to your future financial success.
> Lifestyle Inflation occurs when your expenses keep up with (or outpace) any pay increases you might get.
> The key to getting Lifestyle Inflation under control is keeping an eye on your Savings Rate – this is the percentage of your income you save each month.
> In order to improve your Savings Rate you can reduce your expenses, increase your income or both.
> There are many ways to reduce your expenses, but you should look to your Foundation and Lifestyle Expenses for the easy wins.
> We have learnt about Envelope Budgeting, another tool to prevent you getting pulled off track.
> Envelope Budgeting means that you Pay Yourself First – putting money into your savings and investments (your Freedom Fund) before you pay any other bills.
> Envelope Budgeting allows you to be much more intentional and conscious with your spending.

Have you ever suffered from Lifestyle Inflation? How might you prevent it from catching you out in the future? How do you think Envelope Budgeting could help you achieve True Financial Freedom?

---

1 www.directlinegroup.co.uk/en/news/brand-news/2019/living-it-up--the-novelty-of-a-pay-rise-only-lasts-43-days.html
2 www.federalreserve.gov/publications/2019-economic-well-being-of-us-households-in-2018-dealing-with-unexpected-expenses.htm

Resources

The following tools and resources will help you learn more about the concepts in this chapter:

Books

Profit First: Transform Your Business from a Cash-Eating Monster to a Money-Making Machine

Mike Michalowicz, Portfolio, 2017

This book is designed for business owners and is essentially 'Envelope Budgeting for business'. But, it might be worth a read for anyone interested in the Envelope Budgeting concept as this book really does a fantastic job of breaking it down in an easy to read and entertaining way. In any case, the lessons will be invaluable if you ever decide to start a business of some kind in the future or if you have one now.

Rich Dad, Poor Dad

Robert Kiyosaki, Warner, 1997

Websites

Compare the Market, Money Supermarket, etc.

www.comparethemarket.com, www.moneysupermarket.com, etc.

Despite the annoying ads featuring larger-than-life characters, price comparison sites do take a lot of the hassle out of getting a better deal. If you are looking to negotiate a better rate on your insurances, utilities or mortgage, a price comparison site is a good place to begin your search. Don't be fooled by the marketing – most of them have access to a similar range of deals. Just pick the one that feels right and get comparing!

Apps

Good Budget

https://goodbudget.com

Good Budget is my favourite app for Envelope Budgeting. It is all manually controlled (i.e. it doesn't integrate with your bank, which in this instance is a good thing). The best part is you can create up to 10 'envelopes' without needing to pay a penny – meaning your budget stays intact. Envelope Budgeting is supported fully and it even has some useful reporting tools so you can see where your money went at the end of the month.

Step 4
Banish Debt
(Mostly)

Now that you have your budget, a clear idea of your future and measures in place to stop yourself tripping along the way, the biggest thing holding most people back is debt.

Debt has been described as a 'menace', as a 'virus', as a 'destructive force of evil' and indeed it can be all of these things – IF YOU LET IT.

Debt can also be used in certain ways to your advantage; however, these methods are only for the most disciplined.

You have to be honest with yourself here. If you're likely to misuse debt if it's available to you, then you're better off paying off all your debt and having none available at all.

Before we start to look at some of the ways that debt can be used to our advantage, let's deal with the issue of paying off debt first.

Dealing With Debt

Remember back in the *Tell the Truth* chapter I asked you to make a list of all your debts or liabilities? Take that out again now; you'll need it for this part.

On your list, you should have:

> A total for how much you owe on each debt.
> The interest rate you are currently paying.
> The end date of the interest rate if you are on a special or limited time interest rate. This is common for mortgages and credit cards.
> The minimum payment you *have* to pay each month.
> The monthly payment you are currently making.
> The term of the debt, if it has one. Mortgages, for example, usually have a total term (25 years) whereas some debts, like credit cards, are open ended.

If you are missing any of the above information, take some time to add it into your table now – it will be vital for this section.

When it comes to clearing down and repaying debts, there are two things you can do. Which of them suits you will depend mainly on your personality type, but we're going to consider both in detail in just a moment.

Before we look at debt repayment, though, there's some vital groundwork you *must* do before you continue...

Debt Re-negotiation

Many people have debts on credit cards and overdrafts, which carry very high rates of interest.

It's often possible to re-negotiate the debt in order to secure a better interest rate, either for a fixed period of time, or for the whole time it takes you to pay off the balance.

For example, many people carry debts on credit cards with interest rates between 15% and 30%.

There's usually a whole load of so-called balance transfer deals available from other credit card providers.

Let's say you have a credit card balance of £5,000 with provider A and it has an interest rate of 19.9%.

A balance transfer means that you transfer the balance on your credit card with provider A to a new credit card with provider B.

Provider B is keen to win your business, so may offer all kinds of deals to attract you – like interest-free balance transfers for 15 months or a low interest rate of, say, 3.9% for as long as it takes to repay the balance.

This is clearly better than paying 19.9%.

The same can be said for loans and overdrafts.

You should always check to see if you can secure a lower interest rate with either your current provider or a new provider.

So many people have debts on deals that are simply not competitive – it's always worth seeing if you can do better.

|||||||||||||||||||||||||||||||||||||||||||||||||||||||||||||||||||||||||||||||||||||||||||||||||

 The UK population owes £72.5bn on credit cards, most of which is at uncompetitive interest rates.[1]

|||||||||||||||||||||||||||||||||||||||||||||||||||||||||||||||||||||||||||||||||||||||||||||||||

Once this is done you *must* close down the old account with provider A. There's no use doing a balance transfer deal to a new credit card, but then keeping the old one and building up a balance on that card as well.

Once you have looked into re-negotiating debts, you can also consider...

Debt Consolidation

The other way to really reduce the interest rates on your debts is to think about consolidation.

Imagine you have a balance on a credit card, an overdraft and a finance agreement for a new car you bought – all with fairly high rates of interest.

If you have a good relationship with your bank, a personal loan may be possible to repay all of your debts at a much lower interest rate.

Personal loans are available from around a 3% interest rate nowadays, which is much cheaper than most overdrafts and credit cards.

This option comes with one massive caveat: you must, must, *must* close down the credit card or overdraft accounts you have consolidated. Failure to take this step just leaves too much temptation on the table and before you know it you've maxed out that credit card again AND you have a loan to pay back on top.

I saw this story all too often when I worked at the bank. We would offer consolidation loans (often at very low interest rates) but a couple of years later that same person was back to do the same again, having maxed out their credit cards.

I will say it one more time for dramatic effect – if you take a consolidation loan or balance transfer deal, you MUST close down and shut off the accounts you have consolidated or transferred once they are repaid.

OK, Back to Our Repayment Plan

Now that you've re-negotiated or consolidated your debts if possible, we can start to think about how to clear those pesky debts once and for all.

If you managed to do any balance transfers or consolidation, make sure you update the new debts in your table and take any old ones out.

From this point onwards, there's an assumption you have some spare income each month to use for debt repayment.

If you've been through the previous chapter about your Savings Rate and have still not got to a point where you have at least some spare income, you need to get this under control right away.

If you're regularly adding to your debts on a monthly basis and you don't feel like you can get this under control – or even worse you're using one debt to make payments on another – then you may need to seek some professional debt help.

There are loads of organisations that can help you if you're in serious debt trouble. (I will summarise them at the end of the chapter.)

Assuming you have at least some spare income each month (even if this means cutting back for a little while) then read on.

Two Strategies for Debt Repayment

There are two main ways to repay debt. Let's look at them in turn:

Strategy #1 – the Debt Snowball

With the Debt Snowball, you put all of your debts on a list, starting with the smallest debt first, followed by the next smallest, and so on.

Let's use an example to make this clearer:

Debt Type	Balance Owed	Interest Rate	Minimum Payment	Current Payment	Term
Credit Card 1	£1,000	15.9%	£50	£50	Open-ended
Overdraft	£2,500	19.9%	N/A	£150	Open-ended
Car Loan	£9,500	6.9%	£300	£300	3 years
Credit Card 2	£12,000	22.4%	£150	£300	Open-ended

Please note: the assumption here is we've already gone through the previous steps of re-negotiating and consolidating where possible and this list now contains the best possible debt deals on the market for this hypothetical person.

You can see here that Credit Card 1 has the smallest outstanding balance, so that goes at the top of the list, followed by the Overdraft and so on.

Credit Card 2 is last on the list as it has the biggest balance.

The theory behind the Debt Snowball is that you focus all available monthly budget on paying off the smallest balance first.

This even means we divert money *away* from other debts in order to focus on the smallest.

Of course, you'll still need to pay the minimum payments on all of your other debts, but that should be all.

Looking at the list in turn, you can see that on Credit Card 1 the minimum payment is £50 and you're currently paying £50. As such, there's no spare budget here.

On the Overdraft, however, there is no minimum payment, but a payment of £150 per month is being made. With the Debt Snowball, we would stop making this payment completely (because we can) and divert the whole £150 per month to pay off the smallest balance, which is Credit Card 1.

The Car Loan has a required payment of £300 per month and that's what is being paid, so we can move on.

Finally, Credit Card 2 has a minimum payment of £150, but £300 is actually being paid. Again, we would divert the £150 per month extra payment here and use it to pay off Credit Card 1.

This means we have the original £50 (that we were paying on Credit Card 1 anyway) with an extra £150 taken from the Overdraft and £150 from Credit Card 2, giving a total monthly payment to Credit Card 1 of £350.

Your table would now look like this:

Debt Type	Balance Owed	Interest Rate	Minimum Payment	Current Payment	Term
Credit Card 1	£1,000	15.9%	£50	£350	Open-ended
Overdraft	£2,500	19.9%	N/A	£0	Open-ended
Car Loan	£9,500	6.9%	£300	£300	3 years
Credit Card 2	£12,000	22.4%	£150	£150	Open-ended

Now we have a nice healthy payment of £350 being chipped off Credit Card 1 each month, which means the total balance would be repaid in just over three months – pretty good progress.

At this stage, we would divert our attention to the next smallest debt, being the Overdraft. There's no minimum payment on the Overdraft, so we'd take the full £350 per month we were paying off from Credit Card 1 and pay this off the Overdraft.

The table would now look like this:

Debt Type	Balance Owed	Interest Rate	Minimum Payment	Current Payment	Term
Overdraft	£2,500	19.9%	N/A	£350	Open-ended
Car Loan	£9,500	6.9%	£300	£300	3 years
Credit Card 2	£12,000	22.4%	£150	£150	Open-ended

At the rate of £350 per month, the Overdraft should take a little over seven months to repay. This means after 10 short months, the two smallest debts have been totally repaid.

Once the Overdraft is gone, we divert all of the £350 to the Car Loan. The payment on the car is already £300 per month, so we add the £350 to this and make a total payment of £650. This comes with the important caveat to check there are no penalties or charges for making overpayments – some debts penalise you for paying them off, cruel I know!

Your table is now:

Debt Type	Balance Owed	Interest Rate	Minimum Payment	Current Payment	Term
Car Loan	£9,500	6.9%	£300	£650	3 years
Credit Card 2	£12,000	22.4%	£150	£150	Open-ended

At the rate of £650 per month, you can clear that Car Loan in as little as 15 months – less than half the three-year term!

Finally, once the Car Loan is gone, we divert all remaining budget to Credit Card 2 as follows:

Debt Type	Balance Owed	Interest Rate	Minimum Payment	Current Payment	Term
Credit Card 2	£12,000	22.4%	£150	£800	Open-ended

At £800 per month, Credit Card 2 will be gone in around 16 months.

So there we have it, the Debt Snowball in full effect.

The other option we have available is...

Strategy #2 – the Debt Avalanche

The Debt Avalanche is similar to the Debt Snowball, with one vital difference. With the Debt Avalanche we focus our attention on the interest rate being paid on the debt, rather than on the size of the balance.

With the Debt Avalanche, you would put all of your debts in order based on the interest rate you are paying.

Using the previous examples, your debt table would now look like this:

Debt Type	Balance Owed	Interest Rate	Minimum Payment	Current Payment	Term
Credit Card 2	£12,000	22.4%	£150	£300	Open-ended
Overdraft	£2,500	19.9%	N/A	£150	Open-ended
Credit Card 1	£1,000	15.9%	£50	£50	Open-ended
Car Loan	£9,500	6.9%	£300	£300	3 years

Notice how Credit Card 2 goes at the top of the list, as it has the highest interest rate, followed by the Overdraft with the next-highest and so on.

The strategy here is similar to the Debt Snowball, but instead of focusing our entire available budget on the smallest debt, we focus on the one with the highest interest rate.

So in this example, we'd continue to pay the £300 per month already being paid on Credit Card 2. We would also stop making the Overdraft payment for now and divert that £150 to Credit Card 2, making a total payment of £450 per month.

Your table now looks like this:

Debt Type	Balance Owed	Interest Rate	Minimum Payment	Current Payment	Term
Credit Card 2	£12,000	22.4%	£150	£450	Open-ended
Overdraft	£2,500	19.9%	N/A	£0	Open-ended
Credit Card 1	£1,000	15.9%	£50	£50	Open-ended
Car Loan	£9,500	6.9%	£300	£300	3 years

At this rate, Credit Card 2 is likely to take around 27 months to pay off. Notice how with the Debt Avalanche, we potentially have to wait quite a lot longer to see real progress (with the Debt Snowball, we paid off the first balance in just three months).

With Credit Card 2 now gone, we would focus on the debt with the next highest interest rate:

Debt Type	Balance Owed	Interest Rate	Minimum Payment	Current Payment	Term
Overdraft	£2,500	19.9%	N/A	£450	Open-ended
Credit Card 1	£1,000	15.9%	£50	£50	Open-ended
Car Loan	£9,500	6.9%	£300	£300	3 years

Then we move on to Credit Card 1:

Debt Type	Balance Owed	Interest Rate	Minimum Payment	Current Payment	Term
Credit Card 1	£1,000	15.9%	£50	£500	Open-ended
Car Loan	£9,500	6.9%	£300	£300	3 years

And finally, the Car Loan:

Debt Type	Balance Owed	Interest Rate	Minimum Payment	Current Payment	Term
Car Loan	£9,500	6.9%	£300	£800	3 years

So there you have the Debt Avalanche. But you might be asking yourself the question...

So, which is better?

When asking if the Debt Snowball or the Debt Avalanche is better the answer is, as with many things in life: it depends.

In the strictest possible sense, the Debt Avalanche is the most logical option. If you're looking only at the pounds and pence of matters, the Debt Avalanche will come out on top.

The reason for this is you're paying off the high-interest debts first, meaning you pay slightly less in interest overall as you go through your debt repayment journey.

The Debt Snowball, on the other hand, delivers the quickest win on the basis that you pay the smallest balance off first.

The repayment of that first small debt gives a psychological boost (it feels great to be making progress) which then spurs people on to pay off the next debt, and so on.

With the Debt Avalanche, although you're technically being slightly more sensible, you often have a long and hard wait to get that first victory.

My advice is as follows.

Unless you really are super disciplined (let's be honest, if you're in this debt in this first place, can you honestly say you're that disciplined? Sorry to be harsh, but we have to tell the truth), I would suggest that you go with the Debt Snowball.

My experience is that people actually have far more success with the Debt Snowball because of that early psychological victory.

When you look at the psychology of motivation and goal setting, it's almost universally agreed we should break big goals down into the smallest possible steps and look to celebrate small wins along the way to boost our motivation.

Yes, you may pay a little more interest paying debts off this way (we're often only talking a few pounds) but the goal here is to get rid of that nasty debt, not just to optimise every penny we spend.

The best of both worlds?

Having just looked at the difference between the Debt Snowball and the Debt Avalanche, could it actually be that you can have the best of both worlds?

Well, in many cases the answer is yes, or very nearly yes. Let me explain:

You see, smaller debts *tend* to have the largest interest rates. If you think about it, this does sort of make sense. We tend to carry smaller balances on things like overdrafts and credit cards, which often have high interest rates. We also tend to carry larger balances on things like car loans and mortgages, which have lower interest rates.

As such, a real-world debt repayment table might actually look like this:

Debt Type	Balance Owed	Interest Rate	Minimum Payment	Current Payment	Term
Overdraft	£1,000	19.9%	N/A	£100	Open-ended
Credit Card	£2,500	15.9%	£50	£150	Open-ended
Car Loan	£9,500	6.9%	£300	£300	3 years

In this case, you can have the Debt Snowball rolled (sorry – I had to) into the Debt Avalanche as the balances and interest rates happen to fall into place. The smallest balance has the highest interest rate, and so on.

Based on the fact that smaller debts tend to have bigger interest rates, it's very likely that you can reach this best-of-both-worlds situation with your own debt repayment strategy or, if not, you can probably get pretty close. Let me show you with one final example:

Debt Type	Balance Owed	Interest Rate	Minimum Payment	Current Payment	Term
Overdraft	£1,000	19.9%	N/A	£150	Open-ended
Credit Card	£2,500	21.9%	£50	£150	Open-ended
Car Loan	£9,500	6.9%	£300	£300	3 years

In this case, the Credit Card has a higher balance than the Overdraft, but also has a slightly higher interest rate.

I would set things out as in the table above in terms of repayment.

Although the Overdraft has a lower interest rate, the cost of paying this off first instead of the Credit Card (19.9% vs 21.9%) is so minimal I'd rather have the motivation boost of getting that Overdraft cleared.

So, does this mean you should clear all of your debts and have no debts at all?

As with most things, it depends – not *all* debt is bad you see.

There are some forms of debt that are neutral and even some types of debt that are really good.

The Good Side of Debt – The Good Debt 5

There are some forms of debt that, used wisely, are actually really good for your financial health.

Despite them being good, all these debts come with a significant health warning.

Unless you are super disciplined and you know you will not spend more money when you have debt available, you should skip this section and move on.

Although these good debts can be great, they can also be dangerous. If you're likely to submit to temptation, best not to have any debt available at all.

So, how then can debts be good? Well, there are actually a number of beneficial types of debt. Some of them are better than others, but I'm going to outline below five types of good debt.

This list is in order of preference. That is, if you can choose between one or more of the options below for your purchase, always pick the one closer to the top of the list.

Good debt #1 – debt that pays you

Believe it or not, there's actually some debt that pays you. Yes, you did read correctly – some debts could earn you money.

The best example of debt that pays you is a cashback or rewards credit card.

These credit cards let you earn cashback or rewards points, usually on everything you spend.

I use a cashback credit card that gives me 1.25% back on everything I spend throughout the year. I now put as much of my spending on the credit card as I can and I earn around £400 per year in cashback – just for spending money I was going to spend anyway.

Alternatively, you can get rewards credit cards from almost anywhere nowadays. With a rewards card, you will generally earn points that can be converted into vouchers to spend with the retailer issuing the card. You can get rewards cards that give you air miles and other bonuses too, if you travel a lot.

The good debt ground rules

There are some ground rules that you MUST follow if you are going to take advantage of debt that pays you:

> ALWAYS pay your credit card off in full at the end of the month. Most cashback and rewards cards have higher-than-average interest rates. If you're going to be carrying a balance on a credit card for any period of time, a cashback card will probably not be very efficient.

> NEVER spend money on the card just to earn the rewards. At the very most the cashback or rewards will be worth around 5% of what you spend so this is a zero-sum game.

> NEVER spend more than you were going to, just because you have the credit card. When you have a line of credit, there's the temptation to spend a little bit more than you might have otherwise. If you will be tempted, don't have the credit card in the first place.

Good debt #2 – debt that's free

If you can't obtain a credit card that pays you, the next best thing is to use debt that's free.

There are lots of interest-free credit deals out there, most often from retailers looking to incentivise people to buy their products. Interest-free finance is available on anything from a new dining table to a new car.

If you're planning on making a purchase and you have the money in the bank to pay for it, but you then realise there's an interest-free finance deal available, I would always buy the product on the interest-free deal if possible.

This is advantageous in several ways. First of all, you're borrowing money for free. Assuming the rate of inflation is positive, the value of the debt you owe is actually falling in real terms over time.

The other big benefit is you can keep the money in your bank account or investments earning interest and then only pay off the debt when it is due.

Let's use a simple example to illustrate.

Imagine you want to buy a new sofa for £1,000 and you have the money in the bank to pay for it.

As you go to pay, you notice there is a 12-month, buy-now-pay-later interest-free deal, meaning you can finance the whole balance and pay nothing for 12 months.

You take advantage of the interest-free credit.

Knowing you don't have to pay back the £1,000 for 12 months, you seek out a fixed-rate savings bond that matures in 12 months when the payment is due. This pays you 2% per year.

This means at the end of 12 months you will have £1,020 – £1,000 to pay back the finance and £20 in your pocket!

At the same time, in the 12 months that have passed, inflation has been running at around 3% meaning that, in real terms, the value of the £1,000 you have to pay back is now only £970.

So in a roundabout way, you have made £50 off the back of the interest-free deal, assuming that your income has been increasing in line with inflation.

The interest-free debt ground rules

As with debt that pays you, interest-free debt comes with some rules:

> ALWAYS have a plan in place to pay off the interest-free finance at the end of the term.
> NEVER buy something just because interest-free finance is available. You should only use it for things that you would be happy to pay for anyway.

> ❯ NEVER spend more than you were going to, just because the finance is available. When you have a line of credit, there is the temptation to spend a little bit more than you might have otherwise. Shops often use credit deals to get you to upgrade your purchase. For example, a salesman might say: "Would you like to add leather upholstery to your sofa? It's only £10 per month extra." If you wouldn't have the extras if you were paying cash, don't have them if you are paying credit.

> ❯ ALWAYS check the debt is actually interest-free and that there are no other charges or fees to pay on finance.

Good debt #3 – debt that makes things cheaper

This is quite rare nowadays, but there are still some situations where buying on credit can make things cheaper.

The most common example is when buying a new car (only you can decide if a new car is actually a smart use of your money – used cars are often better value).

When you buy a new car, the dealership will be all too keen to sell it to you on finance, because they make more money if you do.

In order to incentivise people to pay on credit, you will often see a *dealer deposit contribution* mentioned as part of the finance deal.

This means the car dealer will pay some of the deposit for you if you take the finance deal.

If some cases, you can use this to your advantage – if you're smart.

Let's use an example.

Imagine you're looking for a new car and it has a cash price of £25,000.

You notice there's a finance deal available with monthly payments of £300, 6.9% APR and it comes with a dealer deposit contribution of £2,000.

You could just pay the cash price of £25,000, but you have a cunning plan and you take the finance.

The dealer pays the £2,000 deposit contribution and now you have £23,000 on finance.

If you kept the finance, you would pay a load of interest at 6.9%, which equals around £6,300 over the four-year term of the deal – way more than the £2,000 deposit payment.

But being smart, as soon as the finance is granted, you immediately pay off the outstanding balance of £23,000, incurring a £225 final purchase fee (this is quite normal when you pay off a car finance deal).

In this case, you've paid a total of £23,225 for your new car that should've been £25,000 – a saving of £1,775!

Care is required here as all deals are different and you should do the sums to make sure there is a genuine saving to be made.

As always, you should try to negotiate the best price for the car in the first place before you begin to have the conversation about credit.

The savvy way to use finance

By now, you will be expecting some rules:

> ALWAYS have a plan in place to pay off the finance immediately.
> NEVER buy something just because finance is available. You should only use it for things that you would be happy to pay for anyway.

> NEVER spend more than you were going to, just because the finance is available. When you have a line of credit, there is the temptation to spend a little bit more than you might have otherwise. Car dealers often use credit deals to get you to upgrade your purchase. For example, a salesman might say: "Would you like to add alloy wheels and metallic paint? It's only £20 per month extra." If you wouldn't have the extras if you were paying cash, don't have them if you are paying credit.

> ALWAYS check the small print of the deal and do your maths – make sure there is an actual saving to be made.

Good debt #4 – debt that's cheaper than inflation

If I was writing this book a decade or so ago, this section would not exist.

In this new world of ultra-low interest rates, there's some potential advantage to be had using something I call *inflation arbitrage.*

In simple terms, inflation arbitrage can be had when you borrow money at an interest rate lower than inflation.

At the time of writing, you can secure a mortgage that's fixed over 5 or even 10 years with an interest rate just over, or even below, 2%.

At the same time, inflation is running at around 3%. This means that the cost of living is going up by about 3% per annum.

In this example, you're paying 2% on a debt and the debt is shrinking (in real terms – i.e. in purchasing power terms) by 3% per annum, meaning you are, in effect, 1% per annum better off – not huge, but every little helps.

You can also use this same effect to make purchasing and investing decisions.

I could afford to pay most of my mortgage off now if I wanted to, but instead I choose to invest the money because I'm confident of getting a return of around 7% per year. This is much higher than the sub-2% interest I pay on my mortgage.

Even if I choose to use my investments to pay off the mortgage later on, I'm still better off to the tune of 5% per year because I've had the use of the money during that time.

Even in today's world, the benefit of inflation arbitrage is subtle and you should only use it if you are super disciplined.

Getting clever with your mortgage

You know what to expect now. Here are the rules:

> You MUST be able to fix the interest rate at a point that is below the current (and likely future) rate of inflation. If you can't fix the interest rate, it will probably go up as inflation increases, making the whole exercise a waste of time.
> You MUST keep the debt and the rate of inflation under review. If the inflation rate falls below the interest rate or the interest rate increases above inflation, you should repay the debt at that point if you can.

Good debt #5 – debt that lets you grow

The final type of debt that *can* be good debt. This is debt that helps you to grow as a person.

Perhaps there's a course that could increase your earnings potential, but you just can't afford it at the moment.

Maybe you need to invest in a piece of equipment to start a business but you just can't pull the money together.

In these cases, even if the debt has an interest charge, it can be worth taking the debt on.

The reason I believe this to be the case is that investments paying the highest rates of return are usually investments in you!

While you can earn 1% in the bank, perhaps 3% by buying bonds and 7% on the Stock Market, if you invest in improving your skills and knowledge, the returns can be as high as 100% or even 1,000%.

I've invested well over £100,000 in coaching and courses over the past four years, but this investment has paid itself back well over 10x already. If I'd not improved my own skills and knowledge, our business would probably not exist, I would not have an online knowledge website and even this book may not be in your hands right now.

There is a big BUT coming, though: you should only use debt to fund courses and knowledge acquisition if you can easily see a way to generate a return on that investment.

It's no use getting knee-deep in debt to improve your painting skills if you just see this as a hobby (by all means learn to paint, but increase your income to afford it first – see *Step 6*). You should only invest in courses and skills acquisition if there's a realistic and tangible return on the investment.

If you're convinced that your newfound painting skills could churn out masterpiece after masterpiece selling for £1,000 each, then by all means take the course.

I would only suggest taking on debt to fund new skills if you think that there's at least a 2x return on that investment within the first year (and that 2x projection should be on the more cautious end of your estimates).

When it's OK to take on more debt

No introduction needed. Here are the rules:

> ❯ NEVER take on debt for new skills that don't have a real prospect of generating a return on your investment. By all means learn new things for fun (in fact I positively encourage this), but don't get into debt over it.

> ❯ ALWAYS be realistic with your projections. It's always exciting to be learning a new thing and we can get carried away into thinking that the latest online marketing course will make us millions. Perhaps it will – but remember to be objective and make logical decisions.

> ❯ NEVER use high-interest debt or payday loans to fund courses or new skills – this is a slippery slope.

> ❯ NEVER use debt to learn something new just because you don't have anything better to do. I often hear of students taking on massive debts to take Master's courses in obscure subjects just because they haven't really figured out what they want to do in life.

So there you have it: two sure-fire strategies to clear troublesome debt and five ways to use debt to your advantage. You should now be a debt master and hopefully, if you have had problems with debt in the past, you can now put these behind you.

Snowballing to Success

The Debt Snowball in action

When I first arrived at James' house, I must admit I was impressed. Sitting on a quiet, inner London street, just minutes away from a bustling high street with boutique shops and restaurants galore, the location was certainly stunning. The house itself was imposing: a freshly renovated, pin-sharp exterior, with grey window lining and custom detailing in the brickwork.

On the driveway sat not just one but two high-end vehicles: a Porsche *and* a Range Rover. As someone who appreciates modern house design as well as cars, I must admit I was feeling a little envious.

As I entered the house, I was greeted by a vaulted, double-height hallway with an atrium landing suspended above. Clearly bespoke and high-end, the interior was arguably even more magnificent than the outside.

We sat down at the dining room table – 14 place settings in all – and started our meeting.

When I begin a meeting with a new client, I usually begin by asking a few simple questions: "What would you like to get out of the meeting today? What would make today's meeting a success for you?"

Having been in wealth management for over a decade now, I can usually read a situation. You can often tell by looking at someone's house, cars, interior design tastes and lifestyle how they will handle money.

In James' case, I was expecting him to ask how to maximise the returns on his burgeoning investment portfolio or how to invest some of his significant monthly income.

James ran a professional services firm. The business was worth millions, and his personal income was over £150,000 per year – that was net, take-home money. By all accounts, he was very well off – comfortably in the top 1% or 2% of income earners in the UK.

But James didn't ask me how to invest a seven-figure portfolio or how to maximise his estate for his children, as clients in his kind of house might do usually. No, what James said to me came as a surprise.

"Matt, I need you to help me get out of this crippling debt," he said.

I was a little taken aback. How can someone who clearly has so much income be in serious debt?

Lifestyle Inflation is the simple answer. Lifestyle Inflation that gets out of control equals debt – plain and simple.

You see, although James had an income of over £150,000 per year, he was living the lifestyle of someone with an income of £200,000 a year. On his income, he probably could have afforded *one* of those beautiful cars on the driveway, but not both. He probably could have afforded the slightly smaller house at the end of his road, but not this one he was currently living in.

He probably could have afforded to renovate his house to a really high standard, but just not quite to the point of a custom-made chandelier for the hallway with a price tag of £9,000!

Quite simply, he could clearly afford a very, *very* nice lifestyle, but he could not afford a lifestyle quite *as nice* as the one he was living – Lifestyle Inflation had him in its grasp.

The result of this Lifestyle Inflation was debt. A lot of it.

I got to work, summarising everything contained in the papers that James had set out on the dining room table. It was a good job it was big – there was a ton of paperwork here – and most of it contained details of James' burgeoning debt pile.

After what must have been an hour or so, we had a final debt summary table, very much like the ones contained in this chapter, summarising the balances, monthly payments, interest rates and terms on all of the debt.

The total was a rather sobering £74,000 of short-term consumer debt, plus another £1.8m or so on mortgages, most of which was at very uncompetitive interest rates given his poor credit rating.

After a lot of discussion and reflection, James agreed that something needed to change – and fast!

We talked over the options and decided the Debt Snowball would offer James the best hope of getting things under control.

The £74,000 odd of consumer debt was really scattered to the four winds. There were well over 10 credit cards, plus a few overdrafts and loans. The cards mostly had modest balances, but there were a lot of them, so we started there.

James was, to be fair to him, paying more than the minimum balance on most of the credit cards, so we had something to work with. We made the decision to reduce the payments on all but one of the cards to the minimum and divert all of the monthly budget to the smallest card balance, which was only just over £500.

By the end of the meeting, we had freed up over £500 of monthly budget, so that first card would be paid off the following month, and then CUT UP!

I went back to see James that following month and he felt a huge sense of relief as the first card went into his shredder. He could finally see a way out, a way to put things right.

Three years later, James' situation couldn't be more different. He stuck with the Debt Snowball plan we created almost to the letter and has now cleared all but one of the credit cards and loans.

What's more, as the smaller debts were repaid, his credit rating started to improve, meaning we could access a better mortgage deal for him that reduced his annual interest rate by over 1% per annum on average. That might not sound a lot, but on £1.8m, that's £18,000 of interest saved – £1,500 a month.

That additional monthly budget is now being directed towards the remaining loan balance, cutting the repayment time in half.

From small acorns big oak trees grow, and James can't believe the progress he has made since we paid off that first £500 balance.

The best part is he got to keep his house and those lovely cars on the driveway – he just stopped spending *more* money on unnecessary Lifestyle Expenses and used those funds to reduce his debts instead.

We are just about to begin a savings plan for James, meaning that for the first time, he will begin to accumulate a positive bank balance.

Although you might feel a little jealous of James' lifestyle and you might be wondering how someone with such a high income could get into so much trouble, do remember that all things are relative. Lifestyle Inflation is very sneaky, and it can happen to the best of us. It can happen to you too, even if your income rises exponentially.

Well done. You're making fantastic progress on your Journey. We just have one more step to complete before we get to the really exciting part (making more money). Before we get there, though, we need to work on building your Financial Resilience, so you don't get pulled off track along the way.

Summing Up

We have learned in this chapter how to eliminate that pesky debt once and for all and about the rare situations where debt could be a good thing:

> There are two main strategies for repaying debt: the Debt Snowball and the Debt Avalanche.
> The method that's best for you will depend on your situation and how disciplined you are.
> The Debt Avalanche is best if you want to maximise every penny.
> But the Debt Snowball is likely to be best for most people who live in the real world. It delivers the quickest win.
> When repaying debt, your mindset matters. Celebrate your victories (no matter how small) and don't give up.
> There are five types of good debt, all of which can be used by the disciplined to improve their financial situation.
> However, the five types of good debt are only for the most disciplined people – don't go there if you're likely to be tempted.

How quickly could you be debt-free if you implemented the strategies in this chapter?

---

1   www.independent.co.uk/news/business/news/credit-card-debt-household-bank-england-consumer-november-uk-economy-a8712271.html

Resources

The following tools and resources will help you learn more about the concepts in this chapter:

Debt Support

If you are really struggling with problem debt and you feel that there is no hope in getting out of the hole, then professional help might be in order. There are several organisations that can help people with significant debt, including:

Citizens Advice Bureau
www.citizensadvice.org.uk

The original and perhaps one of the best organisations to approach if you have problems with debt.

Step Change
www.stepchange.org

One of the UK's largest debt help charities and good people to speak with if you are struggling with debt.

Websites

Money Saving Expert
www.moneysavingexpert.com

Martin Lewis's website has some great comparison tools and 'best-buy' tables for finding low and zero-interest debt deals.

Step 5
Build Financial Resilience (So You Don't Get Pulled Off Track)

Before we start to focus on the final (and perhaps most exciting) step of our Journey to base camp – building new income streams – we're going to look at building what I call Financial Resilience.

Financial Resilience means you're ready to cope with any financial setback or emergency that might come along.

Perhaps your car needs an unexpected repair or a pipe bursts in your house. Perhaps you lose your job or get sick so you can't work.

The fact of life is that these things happen sometimes and it's best to be prepared.

Three Ways to Be Financially Resilient

There are three things you need to have in place to be Financially Resilient. The first of them is a healthy Emergency Fund.

Financial Resilience #1 – the important Emergency Fund

An Emergency Fund is a pot of money that's easily accessible, that you can draw on in an emergency or in any other situation where you need to get at money quickly.

An Emergency Fund is best placed in a simple, easy-access savings account. You probably won't earn much interest, but that's not really the point of the Emergency Fund.

So you may be thinking, *well, do I really need an Emergency Fund?*

The simple answer is an emphatic: YES!

If you don't have an Emergency Fund and your car needs fixing, how are you going to pay for it?

If you lose your job, how will you cover the bills while you search for a new one?

The answer in most cases is that people go into debt. They use their credit card to cover the grocery bill or pay for the car repairs. This can be a very slippery slope indeed and, in fact, most debt nightmares start with a simple emergency that people are unprepared for.

This is also the reason I don't recommend a credit card as your Emergency Fund. Although a credit card can be a vital source of funds in the short term, they can't be relied upon long term. Sometimes your credit limit gets reduced or, in extreme cases, the credit card company can cancel your card altogether.

As such, it's my strong recommendation that you keep your Emergency Fund in easily-accessible cash funds.

How much is enough?

So how much should you have in your Emergency Fund?

As with many things, there's no one answer to this question – just general rules of thumb.

If you still have debts on which you are paying interest, you should probably pay these off before you start an Emergency Fund. The interest on debt will almost certainly be greater than what you will earn on your savings.

The only exception to this rule is if you're using good debt in disciplined and advantageous ways like we covered in *Step 4*.

Once the bad debts are gone, then you can start an Emergency Fund.

I think that aiming for three months' worth of your expenses is a good place to begin.

When I first started saving, it felt great just having two weeks of money in the bank!

Once you have three months' worth, then try and achieve six months' worth of expenses as your Emergency Fund. This will be enough to cover almost any unexpected emergency and it also gives you up to six months to find a new job (or even better, start your own business or Side-Hustle) if you lose your employment.

Eventually, I would suggest you aim for up to one year's worth of Emergency Fund. Although some people would call this excessive, when you've been through the number of emergencies that I have (near-death experiences included) then you really appreciate the value of having that money behind you!

|||||||||||||||||||||||||||||||||||||||||||||||||||||||||||||||||||||||||||||||||||||||||||||||||||||

FACT
61% of Americans were predicted to run out of savings in 2020 in the midst of the COVID-crisis.[1]

|||||||||||||||||||||||||||||||||||||||||||||||||||||||||||||||||||||||||||||||||||||||||||||||||||||

With a nice 12-month Emergency Fund behind you, you can sleep easy at night knowing that even the most serious of financial emergencies is well and truly covered.

The final reason why having a strong Emergency Fund is great is it allows you to take advantage of any investment opportunities that might pop up.

Think about it, if you have no Emergency Fund at all or your money is tied up in investments, and then a great investment opportunity comes up, how will you take advantage?

If you have a healthy Emergency Fund to cover, say, 12 months, you could safely invest half of that money in an amazing opportunity and then replenish your Emergency Fund later on.

I've recently invested £20,000 in a friend's business in the AI space. This investment has the potential to 100x my money and I wouldn't have been able to take advantage if it wasn't for my healthy Emergency Fund.

Don't get me wrong – investments like this will always be risky, but that's the reason we have an Emergency Fund in the first place. If the value of your other investments falls, you have a safe pot of money to draw on until things recover.

With your Emergency Fund now in place, the next step in building Financial Resilience is making sure you have the right insurance in place.

Financial Resilience #2 – Goldilocks insurance (not too much, not too little, just the right amount)

Let me be clear: a lot of insurance is a total waste of money. The insurance industry loves to sell us overpriced insurance contracts that are almost impossible to claim on for things we don't really need.

With that said, it's also incredibly dangerous to have no insurance at all.

Certain things are worth buying insurance for, and others aren't.

Although everyone will have a slightly different set of circumstances, as a general rule of thumb, I only recommend you insure four things in your life. There's one other thing that's either vital or an optional extra (depending on where you live). For everything else, you can pretty much take the risk.

Four must-have insurances, and one for luck

The four things that everyone should always insure are as follows.

Must-have insurance #1 – you

When you do what I do for a living and you meet so many different people, you quickly learn about the impact that a death or a serious illness has on a family – not just emotionally, but financially too.

Though we all think of buying insurance for our homes, our cars, our pets and our cable TV boxes, it still amazes me how many people don't even have basic insurance for themselves.

||||||||||||||||||||||||||||||||||||||||||||||||||||||||||||||||||||||||||||||||||||||||||||||||||||||||||

FACT
Nearly 40% of Americans have no life insurance in place at all.[2]

||||||||||||||||||||||||||||||||||||||||||||||||||||||||||||||||||||||||||||||||||||||||||||||||||||||||||

You are your most important resource, and probably one of the key resources in your family as well.

When you go through a near-death experience as I have done, you quickly learn just how fragile life can be.

I think life insurance is vital if you have a family. But even if you don't, it can pay to have some cover in place. There are three main types of cover for you that I recommend:

A – life cover
Pays out a lump sum if you die.

You can also get so-called Family Income Benefit, which is still life cover, only it pays out a monthly income for a specified period rather than a lump sum.

B – critical illness cover
Pays out a lump sum if you suffer from one of a list of serious illnesses, such as cancer, stroke and heart attack.

C – income protection
Pays out a regular income if you're unable to work. This is *not* to be confused with PPI (Payment Protection Insurance), which can be a total waste of money.

Which of these covers you should have and how much will vary, but I have created some guidelines on what insurance you should have based on your family situation below. The following sections are numbered in priority order (i.e. you should have number 1 in place before you move to number 2, etc.):

Single, no children, no mortgage
1) Income protection to cover your monthly expenses if you can't work.

Single, no children, mortgage
1) Income protection to cover your monthly expenses (including mortgage payment) if you can't work.

Single, children, no mortgage
1) Family Income Benefit life cover to cover your monthly expenses, until the children are 25.
2) Income protection to cover your monthly expenses if you can't work.

Single, children, mortgage
1) Lump sum life cover to repay the mortgage.
2) Family Income Benefit life cover for your monthly expenses (minus the mortgage payment) until the children are 25.
3) Critical illness cover to pay off the mortgage.
4) Income protection to cover your monthly expenses (minus the mortgage) if you can't work.

Married, no children, no mortgage
1) Income protection to cover your monthly expenses if you can't work.

Married, no children, mortgage
1) Lump sum life cover to repay the mortgage.
2) Income protection to cover your monthly expenses (including your part of the mortgage) if you can't work.

Married, children, no mortgage

1) Family Income Benefit life cover to cover your monthly expenses, until the children are 25.

2) Income protection to cover your monthly expenses if you can't work.

Married, children, mortgage

1) Lump sum life cover to repay the mortgage.

2) Family Income Benefit life cover to cover your share of monthly expenses (minus the mortgage payment), until the children are 25.

3) Critical illness cover to pay off the mortgage.

4) Income protection to cover your share of monthly expenses (minus the mortgage) if you can't work.

Contrary to popular belief, life cover and illness protections don't need to be super expensive.

For the most basic life cover contracts, you can pay as little as £6 per month for a meaningful level of cover.

With all of these insurances, the younger you are when you apply, the cheaper the premium will be, so get to it.

You should also look for a policy with a guaranteed premium (meaning the cost stays the same for the whole policy) rather than one with a reviewable premium (where it will be a bit cheaper to start with, but the cost will go up over time).

Only you can decide how important it is to protect you and your family, but I spend about 2.5% of my income on protection cover.

In general, unless you have some expertise with this stuff, I'd recommend you go and talk to a high-quality financial adviser who can help you put the right protection in place.

Must-have insurance #2 – your home

You should also have full insurance for your home and its contents. The financial impact of your home burning down, for example, would be too big for most people to cope with.

As such, this is vital.

If you have a mortgage, the lender will usually insist that you have buildings cover, but many people skimp on contents cover. Ask yourself honestly: could you afford to replace every item in your home? Even if you could, would you want to? If not, buildings *and* contents insurance is a must.

Must-have insurance #3 – your travel

I recommend you always have good travel insurance for any trip you are planning to take outside your home country and even for some trips at home as well.

When I nearly died, I was on holiday in Las Vegas. My medical bill for my three weeks in hospital was almost £210,000!

I would have gone bankrupt if I hadn't had good travel insurance.

Enough said!

If you travel a lot, you can buy an annual policy to cover multiple trips. Otherwise, for less frequent travel, you can just buy an individual policy as you go along.

Must-have insurance #4 – your car

After your home, for most people, their car will be their next biggest asset. Most Western economies make car insurance mandatory for third-party claims (damage you do to other people's vehicles) so you don't have a choice in the matter.

The optional part of car insurance is whether you want to go for fully comprehensive (meaning your car would be fixed or replaced too if you had an accident).

There's no right or wrong as to whether you should pay the extra for comprehensive cover.

If you have a newer car, or one worth £5,000 or more, it's pretty much a no-brainer.

For cheaper cars that are not worth as much, you could find that the extra cost of comprehensive cover is not really worth it.

Nice-to-have insurance #5 – health insurance (highly recommended or optional)

If you live in the UK, we have the trusty old NHS to get us by if we need medical treatment. As such, private medical cover is strictly an optional extra and most people don't have this type of insurance.

That's not to say private medical cover is a bad idea if you live in the UK, but you should only have it if you can afford it and you value this type of cover. Despite our moans, the NHS is pretty good most of the time – and it's free!

Private medical cover allows you to be seen more quickly for non-urgent treatments than you'd be on the NHS and also gives you some more flexibility over which hospital and doctor you see.

If you live in the US or another country that does not have a state-sponsored healthcare scheme, then health cover is an absolutely essential insurance.

Americans spend a large amount of money on their health insurance because it really can be a life-saver – my £210,000 experience in Las Vegas is testament to that!

Other than this, I think most insurance is probably a waste of money.

You can get insurance for everything nowadays: your phone, Cable TV box, kettle, desk fan, anything.

Most of this is unnecessary and overpriced (unless you're *really* clumsy).

I'd rather invest the money for my future and then withdraw from my Emergency Fund if I need a new phone.

Emergency Room Emergency Fund

**The importance of a healthy Emergency Fund,
even where you have good insurance**
It's easy to assume an Emergency Fund is not necessary. I worked in Financial Services, so I was insured up to the hilt.

I always like to practise what I preach, however, and I don't like to recommend things to my clients that I do not have in place myself. As a result, I have pretty much all of the insurance listed above. High-quality policies with high limits on cover and generous terms.

With all of this protection in place, I could have been forgiven for thinking I didn't need an Emergency Fund. If all the big stuff that could go wrong is protected – my life, my house, my car, my travel – then what could I need an Emergency Fund for?

Well, my Honeymoon experience proved just why you need to have *both* an Emergency Fund and good insurance cover in place.

When I arrived at the Emergency Room in the US following my allergic reaction, they wanted a $6,000 deposit before they would admit me to the wards.

I honestly don't know what would have happened if we didn't have the money – I am sure a lot of people don't. Although we had really great travel insurance, phoning them up to start a three-hour phone call to make a claim is not really at the top of your priority list when you are laying on a gurney in a corridor in the process of dying.

Fortunately, we had the money in our Emergency Fund. Katherine was able to log in to our Internet banking, move some savings around and pay the deposit there and then. Any delay in making that payment could have cost me my life!

Although the insurance covered the $6,000 deposit *eventually* and we got every other penny we spent in the hospital refunded to us, that all took time (a lot of time). If it hadn't been for our Emergency Fund, I am not sure I would be here today, and that is despite us having some of the best travel insurance money could buy.

Don't get me wrong, our insurers were excellent – they took care of everything with no fuss. But it takes time. Sometimes, time is not on your side, so it pays to be prepared!

Financial Resilience #3

The third step on the way to Financial Resilience is to build new income streams. This third and final part of Financial Resilience is also a vital component of True Financial Freedom.

In fact, building more income streams is so vital and so important that it's a core part of the final *Step* on your Journey. Building multiple income streams is also a big part of *PART 3* of the book so you'll have to wait a little bit for that – but believe me, it'll be worth it.

So, what are you waiting for? Let's complete the Journey to the bottom of the mountain.

Summing Up

We have learned in this chapter how to build Financial Resilience so you don't get pulled off track on your Journey to True Financial Freedom:

> The first aspect of Financial Resilience is to make sure you have a well-stocked Emergency Fund.

> Although there's no hard and fast rule, you should begin by saving three months' worth of expenses, progressing to save a full 12 months' worth of expenses over time.

> Insurance is a vital and important component of Financial Resilience.

> You should insure your life, your home, your travel and your car.

> Some people may also wish to take out health insurance (depending on where you live).

> All other insurance is probably a waste of money.

> The final component of Financial Resilience is building multiple income streams – more on this in the next chapter.

How much difference would it make to your financial wellbeing if you had 12 months' expenses saved in the bank? Do you feel like you have the right insurance in place? Perhaps you have too much or not enough? What changes could you make to ensure you are in the Goldilocks insurance scenario (not too little, not too much – just right!)?

---

1 www.cnbc.com/select/americans-running-out-of-emergency-savings-in-2020/
2 www.marketwatch.com/story/nearly-40-of-adults-dont-have-life-insurance-these-startups-are-trying-to-change-that-2017-06-30

Resources

The following tools and resources will help you learn more about the concepts in this chapter:

Websites

www.comparethemarket.com

A good website for comparing life insurance deals – but only if you feel confident enough to do this yourself. Most people should get a financial adviser, see below.

www.unbiased.co.uk

For help finding a high-quality, fee-based financial adviser who can help you put the right life insurance and income protection in place.

www.vouchedfor.co.uk

As above – another website where you can read reviews of financial advisers from their existing clients. You might just find me on there as well!

Step 6
Get Your House In Order (And Maximise The Opportunities In Front Of You)

Now you've reached this final step of your preparation, it's important we have our financial house in order. Reaching True Financial Freedom is hard (really hard) and it's important we do all we can to take advantage of the little wins staring us right in the face – we often just don't see them.

Step 6 is all about making the most of what you have. It's about squeezing every drop of financial value out of every situation – you'll need to if you wish to reach True Financial Freedom.

Most people will begin this Journey as either an employee or the owner of a small business, so the following sections are reflective of that, showing you how to maximise your financial position as either an employee or a business owner.

This step is broken down into four paths as follows:

> *Path 6a* – Finding Financial Freedom as an Employee
> *Path 6b* – Maximising Your Financial Freedom as a Business Owner
> *Path 6c* – Finding Financial Freedom by Selling a Business
> *Path 6d* – Supplement Your Income Using Side-Hustles and Passive Products

There are reasons for these various paths. First of all, the financial actions you can take to improve your situation are very different for an employee when compared to a business owner, for example. As such, there's a different section for each set of circumstances.

In addition, you might want to work through the stages and maximise your financial success in each of them. Many employees go on to be business owners who then go on to sell a business, for example, so you might find that *Path 6a* is most relevant for you today, but you need to come back to *Path 6b* in five years' time when you start your own business, perhaps.

Path 6d is applicable for anyone who wants to increase their income and improve their chances of achieving True Financial Freedom. It doesn't matter whether you're an employee, business owner or whether you're building a business to sell; *Path 6d* should contain something for you.

I would recommend you read all the paths on your first go through the book (it's useful to see the journey you might go on in the future, even if it's not applicable to you right now). On your second read-through, pick which of the first three paths (*Path 6a, 6b* or *6c*) is most relevant to you and re-read that one, taking action and implementing the advice as you go.

Everyone should also re-read *Path 6d* on their second read-through to find any strategies in there you could use to improve your income.

Path 6a – Finding Financial Freedom as an Employee

In some circles (especially among younger people) being an employee has a stigma attached. When asked to think of an employee, many people will conjure up images of people working soulless jobs in little cubicles under artificial lights. They might think of working long hours for a boss they hate. They could think of sacrificing all of the fun in life just to run on the corporate hamster wheel. They could think of (heaven forbid) living to work.

Indeed, there are many employees doing these types of jobs right now. If that's you, my only advice would be to get out as fast as you can!

Life is too short for you to do work you hate for people you don't like.

Employment doesn't have to be this way.

There are companies out there offering employees great benefits packages, inspiring working environments and incredibly rewarding positions.

For some people, employment will be the destination; for others, it's just a stop on the journey. Whichever camp you fall into – that's fine – the only thing that matters is what's right for you.

So, can you find True Financial Freedom while being an employee?

The simple answer is, in my view, not really. But you can use your employment to get *closer* to True Financial Freedom.

You will never achieve True Financial Freedom by being an employee alone. If you're employed, no matter how good your employer, your fate is always reliant to some extent on factors outside your control.

What happens if your employer goes bust? What happens if you're made redundant, or you get sick? In most cases, no matter how fulfilling your work, employment will always carry these risks.

With all this said, if you currently love your job (note that I use the word *love* and not just *like* – I believe there's a lovable job out there for everyone), you can use your employment income to create your True Financial Freedom.

Whenever I hear someone say 'I can't wait until 5 o'clock' or 'how long is it until I can get out of here?' that just tells me that they're in the wrong job.

I am fortunate to LOVE what I do. When I get to the end of my workday, I'm sitting there wishing there were another four hours in the day so I can continue working on whatever exciting project I have on the go.

Some people might call that sad. Some would say I am obsessed with my work. Others still have told me I need to 'get a life'. But, if the alternative is getting up every day dreading the next eight hours and wishing my life away, I know which option I would choose every time.

If you don't feel the love in your current job, you're in the wrong job. Period.

We all have the occasional bad day – every so often I just want to go home and curl up in bed like everyone else. But if those days are anything more than the occasional exception, then you need to find a new job – plain and simple.

So at this point you might think I am being a little flippant... and I am!

Who's he to tell me to get another job? It's just not that easy, you might be thinking. *But I'm not that employable! I have a disability that makes it difficult for me to get a job!* Or perhaps, *I'm too old to get a new job!* Or, *What I enjoy could never be turned into a job!*

These are all very common reasons people give for why they simply can't do what they love.

|||||||||||||||||||||||||||||||||||||||||||||||||||||||||||||||||||||||||||||||||||||||||||

FACT
85% of people worldwide are estimated to HATE their jobs.[1]

|||||||||||||||||||||||||||||||||||||||||||||||||||||||||||||||||||||||||||||||||||||||||||

I'm going to be harsh here and say what many people call 'reasons', I call *excuses*. (I'm really hoping, for my sake, that you still remember the opening paragraphs of this book about not taking offence – this is tough, yes, but it's tough love.)

We live in a world where the limits of the human race are being pushed every single day. We live in a world where people who were paralysed learn to walk again. We live in a world where individual people – not governments (think Elon Musk and Jeff Bezos) – are sending rockets into space. We live in a world where the impossible is possible.

The Internet is now awash with people who've said goodbye to their dreaded 9–5 jobs and now follow their dreams – some of them have done so against incredible adversity.

Quitting your job to do something you love can be really, really scary. Sometimes it feels like it shouldn't be allowed. Work is meant to be dull and soul destroying, right? Wrong!

If you type FIRE (which stands for Financial Independence, Retire Early) into Google, you will come across hundreds and thousands of blogs by people who've done just what we are describing here (you may find my blog too).

If it's possible for us to send a man to the moon... If it's possible for people who were blind to start to see again... If it's possible for veterans who've lost two limbs in Iraq to break Olympic records... then it sure as heck is possible for you to walk away from a job you hate and follow your dreams.

It may not be easy. Your friends will probably think you're crazy; your family will wonder if you have a screw loose. It will be as scary as hell. But by gosh, surely you owe it to yourself to spend what little time you have on this earth doing what you enjoy?

So, from this point onwards, I'm going to assume that you do work you love. If not, start there. When passion combines with skill and expertise, your earnings will skyrocket way beyond what I can teach you how to do.

In order to be Financially Free, you will need to use your employment income to invest and create a Passive Income stream. We will explore both of these things in *PART 3*, but for now we're discussing your day job.

Believe it or not, there are loads of things you can do to optimise your employment to make your job work as hard for you as you do for it.

Eight ways employees can help themselves achieve True Financial Freedom

So, let's look now at some of the ways you can get on the path to True Financial Freedom as an employee.

1) Savings Rate

As an employee, perhaps more so than on any of the other three *paths*, you will need to really focus on your Savings Rate. Go back and re-read *Step 3* if you need a reminder.

In many cases, your capacity to increase your earnings as an employee will be limited (although I have a couple of suggestions for you below).

In the first instance, you should aim to increase your Savings Rate to as high as possible by reducing your expenses. Focus on basic expenses first so that you don't sacrifice too much of your lifestyle.

Once you've done this, there are a few other things that you can do to increase your Savings Rate really fast.

2) Ask for a raise

This sounds so obvious and so simple, yet few people actually do this on a regular basis.

Asking for a pay increase can be a really scary thing. There's the fear of rejection, the fear of your boss saying no – or worse – and always the possibility you'll lose favour with the management of your firm because you're being a pain.

In reality, however, most of these things tend to be in our own heads.

Especially in smaller companies (where the pay structure tends to be based on the owner's decisions, rather than a more bureaucratic structure) just asking for a raise can be enough to make it happen.

There are many strategies you can use to ask for a raise, but I prefer to use plain-old logic and justification.

Try to work out the value that you add to the company. If you're in a sales role, this is fairly simple – you can simply look at the volume of sales you are driving for the business and the profit those sales create, and then approach your boss with quantifiable reasons for that raise.

In other types of position, your value can be a bit more difficult to quantify in monetary terms, but try your best all the same.

Compare your **value** to your salary. Your value is the amount of income you generate for the company. In some roles this can be very easy to quantify.

If you sell stuff, then it will be the profit margin generated on your sales. (Notice I say profit margin and not revenue – if you sell a product, a part of the sale price is just paying for the manufacturing.)

If you are in a service role, you need to try your best to quantify the value you add to the company in monetary terms. Not always easy, but try your best.

You can also measure value by looking at your fellow employees doing the same job. If you're generating twice the results of the guy sat next to you, chances are you have a strong chance of getting that raise.

If, however, the guy next to you is achieving twice your results, you'd better optimise your own performance before you go demanding more money.

If your salary is higher than your value, you should probably be quite worried! I would suggest you hide under a desk and hope nobody finds you!

If your value is higher than your salary (and it really should be) then you can go ahead and ask for a raise.

How much you ask for will be heavily dependent on your industry or profession. In some software sales roles, where there's a massive profit margin, it's common to receive up to 50% of the total value that you generate.

Other businesses have far lower margins and if you work in a grocery store, for example, the profit margin on the sales you are making is probably far lower. You should do thorough research on your company and check how much money they are making and what their profit margin is.

If you work for a very large company, you can probably find this information in the company accounts, which will have to be published if your business is listed on the stock exchange.

For smaller organisations, you will have to either try to find out from someone in the know or make a best guess.

In the finance world, a lot of companies work on a system of thirds. This means the company should pay staff around 1/3 of their total value. This leaves 1/3 for a company to pay for space, heating, lighting and all of the systems they use and then 1/3 to allocate to profit. Of course, this will be very different indeed in other businesses.

You should also look at other jobs in your sector and compare what's on offer to your current package.

Many employers underpay staff, not because they don't value them, but because of apathy and inertia. If no one is complaining, why give them a raise?

How much you ask for in terms of a raise is really up to you, but just be aware that a raise of 10% or more is going to seem like quite a big deal to your boss. So if you're asking for more than 10%, make sure you have some really good data on your value to the firm and also your market worth.

Please don't tell them this, but if any of my current staff walked through my door and asked for a raise that was reasonable, I would probably give it to them (*I wonder how many of them will read this book and do just that?*).

Anything less than 10% and I reckon there's at least a 90% chance your boss will simply say yes. It can be really expensive to replace an employee and if you're a hard-working, valuable employee, then your boss will not want you to go. Of course, this depends on your boss being the ultimate decision-maker – in larger organisations, your boss might need to ask their boss, and so on.

The other thing to think about here is when you ask. Make sure you catch your boss at a time when they're going to be relaxed and receptive to your request.

Just after a major client has taken their business elsewhere? Bad time to ask. Right before they run out of the door on a Friday evening to head out for dinner? Bad time to ask.

Just after the company has broken a new sales record and they have the afternoon free? Great time to ask.

It also helps if you can manufacture a period of really good performance running up to your request.

Once you are armed with your value, your worth in the market and how much you are going to ask for and when, it's time to have the dreaded conversation.

There's no right or wrong way to have this conversation. Only you know your boss and how they are as a person, but I would generally say something along the lines of:

"Hi [insert boss's name]. I have been having a look at my value to the company and I feel that perhaps I could be a little better rewarded for my contribution. Last year I added [insert value you added to the company in £s if possible] in value to our firm and I was paid [insert current salary]. I was hoping that you would consider giving me a raise to [insert new salary] in light of my recent performance?"

Note: I wouldn't mention the other roles in the market in the first instance. Your boss may well say yes based on the above conversation without the need for any more information. Only if you get resistance, then you can pull out the market-value card if required.

If you work in a big company, you also need to get really comfortable with any bonus system and the method the company will use to decide on pay rises. These structures tend to be far more formal and rigid in larger organisations, so it may not be as simple as just asking the question as above.

You can't change the system and nor, most likely, can your boss, but what you can do is make it work to your advantage.

When I was working at the bank, the first thing I did was download all the documents about the bonus and salary-increase system so I could make the most of what was on offer. To this day, I'm amazed by the number of people who work the same job in the bank for years and don't even know these documents exist, let alone how to get the best advantage out of the system.

Very often, large businesses will pay bonuses for things that might seem unusual. When I was working for a big life assurance company, part of my bonus was linked to the number of people I signed up to their online portal, which was totally free to the client. Many people didn't make the most of this and missed out on a valuable bonus as a result.

3) Get a role in the Value Economy
OK, so if you've asked for a raise and maximised your earnings as far as possible, but you still want more, what can you do?

Well, you could look for a role in the Value Economy, where you are rewarded based on the value you add, rather than based on the number of hours you work.

To be clear, roles in the Value Economy that can be manipulated in this way tend to be in smaller or at least more dynamic organisations. If you're working for a rigid multinational (and really enjoy it) then you might want to skip some of this small section.

The most common example of this is in sales roles, where salespeople generally get paid in part or in full based on commission.

Of course, not everyone can or should be in sales. It simply doesn't suit some people, but there are other ways to create a role in the Value Economy.

Perhaps you could agree on some sort of additional payment with your boss based on production over and above the expected norm. This generally works very well if you're already a good performer in your current role.

Let's say your job involves generating planning application reports for clients. If we assume you're really good at this job (better than 90% of other people) and you already produce 110% of the reports that you're expected to produce, I would call this a pretty good employee!

At this point, you approach your boss and say you could produce additional reports for a fixed payment each time. This additional payment should be a portion of the value the company derives from the report and not just an extension to your hourly rate.

Let's say the company charges £1,000 for the report to a client and each one costs £250 to produce. At the end of your day, you could just go home (having already done 110% of your target) but instead you offer to do one additional report a day, after your traditional working hours, for a payment of £250.

The company now makes £500 from that report (which they wouldn't have had otherwise) and you make an extra £250. Sounds like a win-win situation to me.

Now, again, this is likely to work better in smaller, more entrepreneurial organisations and there must be the demand for the extra report. Larger companies won't generally have the flexibility to offer such a deal.

OK, so now we have optimised your earnings in the first place, how can we leverage your employment to get even better results for you?

4) Join your company pension scheme

I find it astounding how many people opt-out of their company pension plans. I know Einstein has his own definition of madness (doing the same thing over and over but expecting a different result) but this is mine.

How does this sound: if you pay £50 into a bank account, I will give you another £50 and the government will pay in £10 as well?

Sound like a good deal? Thought so!

This is exactly what a pension plan can do for you. When you join a company pension scheme, normally there's some sort of matching contribution from your employer. Let's use a simple example: say you earn £20,000 a year. Your employer might offer a 3% + 3% pension deal. This means that if you put 3% of your salary into a pension, the company will match that with an extra 3% on top.

That means that you pay in £600 per year, but your employer also puts an additional £600 in for you. This is an immediate 100% return on your investment – where else can you find that?

What's more, the government will then usually add further money in the form of tax relief, which could take your total to around £1,400 per year!

Many employers will also offer a matching contribution over and above the basic levels. So, with the above 3% + 3% example, the company might say you can pay in an extra 2% on top and we will match it, which could make a total of 5% + 5%.

Again, so long as you can afford to do so, you should snap up the deal like there's no tomorrow!

Finally, many big companies then have some sort of bonus contribution on top of that as well. When I used to work for the bank, we had a 5% + 8% pension deal (I paid in 5% and the company paid in 8%) but then you could add a further £250 per month and the company would top that up by 10% (note this is 10% of the contribution, so £25, not 10% of my salary).

Although this is far less generous than the matching contributions, it's still a great deal. Again, where else can you get an immediate 10% return on your investment?

Using these matching contributions is also a great way to get a leg up on your Savings Rate. Let's say you're aiming for a 50% Savings Rate, but you can only afford to save 10% of your income today. If your employer has a 5% + 5% matching pension contribution, you can take full advantage.

This means that you pay in 5% of your salary, your employer pays in another 5% and you still have 5% left to save in another vehicle like an ISA, giving you a total Savings Rate of 15% (even though you can only afford 10%!).

Add in the effect of tax relief and your total Savings Rate is probably closer to 16% or 17% in this example. Not bad going.

Now, pensions are generally going to take care of your longer-term savings, but what about the short term? What if you want to retire or reach financial freedom super early?

Well then you need the following.

5) Employee share plans

Some employers offer additional help beyond the pension scheme by offering an employee share scheme.

These are generally only offered by larger companies, but some smaller ones are beginning to follow suit.

Employee share plans come in all shapes and sizes, but all of them are generally a good idea as they often involve the purchase of subsidised shares in your company. They can have some generous tax advantages as well.

You will need to review the rules of the scheme on offer carefully (if your employer has one) as they will all be different. But assuming there's some sort of discount or matching shares offered by the employer, this is another great way to leverage your earnings.

Basically, the way they work is you may be able to pay in a certain amount each month to buy shares in your employing company. Then, you should receive some sort of discount on the share price (say 10%) or you might get so-called matching shares, where you might get, say, one free share for every three that you buy.

Usually you will need to be employed by your company for a certain period of time after the shares are purchased to qualify for the matching shares, if they are awarded, so you should think carefully about how long you are likely to remain with your company before going into the scheme.

Typically, the required time is three years. So if you start the share plan in year one, these shares will be released to you (and available to sell) in year four; a plan started in year two will be released in year five, and so on.

This is another way of effectively getting free money from your employer. If you buy three shares and you get one for free, that's a 33% bonus on your money on day one! I can't think of many other investments with that type of return!

My one piece of advice with employee share plans is that, although you should take advantage of them as much as possible, you should also sell the shares soon after they get released to you and you can dispose of them without penalty.

If you don't, you risk building up a large portion of your total wealth in shares in the company you work for. That's the company that you also rely on for your income.

This is very risky, because if your company gets into trouble (if the last few years have shown us anything it's that no company is too big to fail) then not only do you risk losing your job, but you also lose a big part of your wealth as well.

I saw this happen to a number of colleagues when I was working in the bank. Two guys in particular come to mind. Neither of them were big earners, but they had been diligently saving into every share scheme since they started work at the bank aged 16. Now, aged 63 and on the verge of retirement, by most estimations they were comfortably millionaires. The trouble was that all of their wealth lay in the shares of the bank that employed them.

When the crash hit, their million-pound fortunes were reduced to closer to £25,000. Their retirements were ruined and even in the 10 years that have passed since the financial crisis, the share price of the bank has never really recovered.

This highlights the risk of concentrating too much of your wealth (and your job) into one company. By all means keep a few of the shares, but once you're able to sell them, I'd recommend you sell most of the shares in your employer and diversify your investments elsewhere.

6) Work for a start-up

Most start-up companies won't have the advanced benefits packages, pension plans and other perks that come with larger employers. They simply can't afford them.

They might also not be able to pay salaries that are as decent as the larger employers.

What they can often offer, though, is shares in the company as a reward for your hard work and dedication.

While these shares may often be worthless to begin with, if the company grows very large then the shares could end up being worth millions. Just ask the early staff of Facebook how they feel about those worthless shares they received 10 years ago that have now made them multi-millionaires!

The other great thing about a start-up business is the working environment and the culture. There's something inherently exciting about working on something new and growing.

Yes, there are some challenges as well, but if you have not done so before, I would recommend that everyone does some work in a start-up environment at some point in their life.

7) Flexible benefits

Some of the larger employers (and often smaller ones as well now because of improving technology) offer a so-called flexible benefits package.

These come in all shapes and sizes, but the general idea is that you can buy discounted products and services by having deductions taken from your pay each month.

The different options available vary dramatically. Some employers will allow you to buy or sell your holiday days, which means either losing or gaining some salary in return for an increase or decrease in your holiday allowance.

Others will allow you to purchase discounted insurance or shopping vouchers. When I worked at the bank, you could buy supermarket vouchers up to a 7% discount, meaning you got an automatic £7 off a £100 weekly grocery shop. That's 7% more money to save or invest for your future financial freedom!

If your employer offers a flexible benefits scheme, I highly recommend you look over the details and figure out how it might work for you.

That's not to say every component of the scheme will be a good deal. When I used to work at the bank, you could buy home insurance through the scheme at a discount to the standard rates, but if you looked online, you could get a far better deal via a comparison website or by going direct to the insurer.

Do your homework, and flexible benefits schemes can be another great way to leverage your employment income.

8) Start a Side-Hustle

The final and possibly most impactful thing you can do as an employee to help you on your way to True Financial Freedom is to start a so-called Side-Hustle.

A Side-Hustle means different things to different people, but in my mind it's something you can do alongside your day job to earn a little extra cash.

A Side-Hustle can be brilliant, and in many cases the Side-Hustle is the difference between achieving financial freedom and not.

So, what exactly is a Side-Hustle?

A Side-Hustle is simply anything you do alongside your day job to earn some extra income.

A Side-Hustle job can take many, many forms and there are probably hundreds and thousands of examples (just Google 'Side-Hustle' and you will see).

Some people walk other people's dogs in the evening. Others make candles as a hobby and then start selling them on eBay or Etsy.

Some people use their work skills on the side and do a little bit of freelance work using websites like People Per Hour or Fiverr. This is a great option for people like graphic designers or copywriters.

The truth is, there are so many Side-Hustles out there it's impossible to summarise them all. But a simple Google, or a visit to my own blog, will give you loads of ideas you can apply almost right away.

You don't even need to have any special skills. There are people out there who need simple things doing and are willing to pay to have them done.

For example, a lot of entrepreneurs will hire people to transcribe meeting notes for them – almost anyone can do that.

Before we start talking about using Side-Hustles to achieve True Financial Freedom, I'm going to assume you are just about getting by with the income you earn from your day job. If you're not making ends meet with your day job income (and have already done all you can to reduce expenses) then you could argue an extra job is a necessity.

For the moment, though, let's assume you're just about managing on the income you have from your day job and you're pretty much breaking even on a month-to-month basis.

The beauty of a Side-Hustle is it can create extra income you didn't have before.

This is brilliant because you have probably trained yourself to live on your current level of income, so any new income is not immediately required in your monthly budget. This means you have a lot of freedom when you decide what to do with this newfound income.

||||||||||||||||||||||||||||||||||||||||||||||||||||||||||||||||||||||||||||||||||||||||||||||||

 It's reported that 48% of American Millennials now have a Side-Hustle from which they earn income at least once a month.[2]

||||||||||||||||||||||||||||||||||||||||||||||||||||||||||||||||||||||||||||||||||||||||||||||||

Three ways to use those extra pennies

There are three ways this new income could be used and I would suggest you approach this in the following order:

1) Pay off bad debts

Extra income on the side can really speed up the process of debt repayment. If you have any bad debts, I'd suggest that any Side-Hustle income you can generate should go here first, save perhaps a tiny something for yourself as a reward for your extra work. After all, it's a Side-Hustle.

2) Increase your Savings Rate

Side-Hustle income is, by definition, income you didn't have before – therefore it's very likely you managed to survive without it.

As such, any new income you receive is surplus to requirements and can be added to your savings (once bad debt is paid off). This means you can increase your Savings Rate and add more money to your investments.

3) Treat yourself

If there's a special purchase you've been thinking of, but you can't really afford or justify from your usual income, a Side-Hustle can be the perfect way to get it. If you're planning a nice trip or a special experience you just can't really afford, a Side-Hustle can be a great way to save the extra money you need.

The added benefit is that the Side-Hustle allows you to generate the extra income you need without hurting your usual monthly budget.

I'd try to focus on saving some of the money as well, but a Side-Hustle is what I define as *extracurricular* work and so there should be some fun allowed as well!

All in a day's work

So there we have it. There are so many ways that you can use your employment to help you on the Journey to True Financial Freedom.

For some people on this quest, their job is all they need. Perhaps they have a great income and love their job. Perhaps they have a great employer who offers complete autonomy and unlimited holiday.

An increasing number of people will decide at some point that long-term, full-time employment with one main employer is not for them.

If this is you, the next task is to use one of the other strategies in the following chapters to escape the 9–5. For some people, setting up their own business will be the destination; for others it will just be another stop on the Journey.

If you're not going to be employed, the next logical step for most people is to start their own business of some description. So, without further ado, let's get started.

Summing Up Path 6a – Finding Financial Freedom as an Employee

We have learned in this chapter how to leverage your employment to achieve True Financial Freedom much faster:

> Most people don't take advantage of all the generous perks and bonuses their employment might offer.
> Larger employers are more likely to have a structured benefits package including things like pensions, matching share schemes and bonuses.

> These perks and bonuses can often be worth many thousands of pounds each year if you make good use of them.
> Smaller employers or start-up companies might not have those types of perks, but they often make up for it by offering shares in the company or by providing greater working flexibility.
> In all cases, just asking for a raise can secure you that much needed extra income, but make sure you do your research before you ask.

Do you think you could use some of these strategies to improve your own financial position? Why not research the options your employer offers and note down how much you could make or save each year if you maxed out all the perks offered to you?

---

1 https://news.gallup.com/opinion/chairman/212045/world-broken-workplace.aspx
2 www.bankrate.com/pdfs/pr/20190605-side-hustles-survey.pdf

Resources – Path 6a

The following tools and resources will help you learn more about the concepts in this chapter:

Websites

Workplace Pensions

www.workplacepensions.gov.uk

Information about your workplace pension rights and contribution limits.

Employee Share Plans

www.gov.uk/tax-employee-share-schemes

Information on employee share plans and how they are taxed.

People Per Hour

www.peopleperhour.com

Freelance working website where you can sell your skills on a per project or per hour basis.

Fiverr

www.fiverr.com

Another freelance working website where you can sell your skills on a per project or per hour basis.

Path 6b – Maximising Your Financial Freedom as a Business Owner

Many people dream of having their own business one day. There are so many attractive things about it. You get to be your own boss, control your own time and perhaps most importantly, control your own earnings and get rewarded for the value you create.

Get it wrong, though, and your business can do the opposite of these things. It can be a drain on your time and freedom, it can become the boss of you and it can cost you money (all of your money if you let it).

Yes, being a business owner is one of the best things in the world but, like all good things, it must be treated with care and respect. So many people go into business thinking it will be easy.

I can assure you it's not. If it were easy, everyone would do it. I know you've heard that saying many times before, but it's quite true.

Even when something looks really easy, it often isn't. In fact, sometimes the things that appear the easiest on the surface, hide the most sacrifice, blood, sweat and tears underneath.

When you look at someone like PewDiePie earning millions playing video games from their bedroom, it looks so simple. Behind the scenes, though, I can guarantee there's a ton of hard work and learning that has happened. Success in business is not earned overnight.

It requires dedication, perseverance, resilience and determination.

Many ways to achieve financial freedom

Starting a business will not be for everyone. It may not be for you and that's totally OK. There are many other ways to achieve financial freedom and we're in the process of exploring all of them.

Again, you need to tell the truth and be honest with yourself here. If you don't have a burning desire to start a business, you probably shouldn't.

For those who do have that flame, though, and are willing to commit, the rewards can be incredible.

Where to start?

A lot of people know they'd like their own business. What's often not so clear is what that business should do. It's easy to decide that being your own boss is right for you, but then people often struggle to decide what they are going to be the boss of.

Ask yourself:

> What's the big idea?
> What service or product will you create?
> How will you add value to other people's lives?
> How will you be better than the competition?
> How will you market your business?

These questions are much harder to answer!

1) Love, love, love
I would suggest you begin with something you're passionate about. People often get jealous of those who've turned their hobby into a business – it's for good reason.

If you can make your hobby into something you do for a living, it can make your work one big game. I'm fortunate that I love the world of money and finance. I don't know why (and I know it's very sad) but I do. This is brilliant, though, because it means I love my work.

"If you love what you do, you will never work a day in your life."

This is a quote often used (and perhaps sometimes abused) but it's true. Don't get me wrong, starting a business will be hard work, but you probably won't feel like it is.

It's far easier to get up in the morning when you love what you do, than when you dread another eight hours sat in a cubicle under artificial lighting.

As such, the first place I'd look for business ideas is in your current hobbies and passions.

> If you're currently a black belt in martial arts, could you open a school and become an instructor?
> If you love to bake cakes and decorate them with elaborate icing, could you open a bakery business?
> If you're super passionate about the health of the planet, could you create a business that builds a greener earth?

You get the idea: do something you love.

For me, a love of money came at an early age. It's always been my destiny to work with money and I'm very lucky to have had things become so clear to me at a young age.

Since the age of about eight, I've been fascinated with money and the role it plays in people's lives. I set up my first business of sorts at that age – rounding up a few kids on my street to wash cars with me. At eight, any money looks like a lot of money and so I think I paid them about £2 an hour (good job there weren't any employment lawyers living on my street!).

They were happy to have the money but, most importantly, they were happy to have someone willing to knock on doors and ask people if they wanted their car washed. That is the part that no one wants to do because it's as scary as hell (especially at eight years old). Because of this fear, people often work for much less than they should because they're not willing to go through the pain of asking for more.

My car washing business lasted all of about two weeks and it was pretty clear that car washing was not my passion. What was my passion was the money I had amassed – at the end of those two weeks – about £50 in total.

It might not seem like much now, but at that tender age, £50 spelt financial freedom to me. I felt I could do anything I wanted – and I could, for a tiny while.

I had tasted what financial freedom could be like for just a few weeks and I wanted more, much more!

It wouldn't be until much later that I could turn my love of managing money and helping people with their financial freedom into a career, but this has always been my path.

I know from experience that many people do not find it easy to recognise what they truly love to do.

First, find your passion

There are whole books dedicated to the subject of finding your purpose and passion and I won't attempt to list them here. But what follows are the first tiny steps to finding your calling in the world.

I'd suggest you have a think about the things you really love to do. We all have them. These are the hobbies and passions that make us come alive.

Write them all down. On this list could well be your new business idea.

Be sure to only put down things you really love to do. Things that you just *like* won't cut it here, however attractive they look compared to your 9–5.

This is a process that comes easily to some people, but I know others really struggle. If you're finding it hard, here are some questions you could ask yourself. I'd suggest you have a pen and paper handy at this point to capture any thoughts the process generates.

Consider the following:

> What did you dream of being when you were younger? We all have something we wanted to be (think spaceman, fire fighter, ballet dancer, etc.). As we grow up, we tend to write these dreams off as silly, childlike or unrealistic, but I do believe almost anything is possible. Write down anything that comes to mind.

> What are you doing when time just seems to fly? When you're having fun, time disappears – when this happens, chances are you're doing something you love. For example, I get to the end of my working day and think, *where did all the time go?* I wish I had another few hours to continue working on this project (some people will call me incredibly, incredibly sad, but what I think is really sad is working 10 hours a day in a job you hate for 30 years just wishing for the weekend).

> Ask your friends what they think you're really good at. What special skills do they think you possess? There could be some surprises in their answers.

> If you had all the money in the world, how would you choose to spend your time? The answers might give some insight into what you most love to do.

Dr Katherine Benziger, author of the book *Thriving in Mind*, has suggested that when you're doing the thing you are born to do, you only use 1% of the energy you'd use to do something you weren't born to do.

I can see some truth in that statement. When other people look at what I do in my working day, they think I'm mad. They ask how I could possibly cram all that activity in. The thing is, I don't really notice it. I come away from the day buzzing and full of energy. Perhaps this is because of the 1% rule!

Dr Benziger also suggests that people who work for too long outside of their natural tendencies can develop something called 'Prolonged Adaptation Stress Syndrome' (PASS for short). PASS has been shown to cause fatigue, depleted immune system, memory impairment and self-esteem problems, among other things.

So, the importance of doing what you love is not just because it makes life more fun, more enjoyable and easier (although those reasons are good enough for me), there could also be health benefits in doing the work you were meant to do.

You must spend time here to determine what your business should actually do. This could be nothing at all to do with your current work or skill set.

Once you have the area or niche you wish to target, you need to do some real, honest thinking.

Second, spin it your way

Remember way back in *Step 1* where we had to *Tell the Truth*? This is another of those moments. It's really easy to get so wrapped up in the excitement of a new idea, that we forget to really consider whether it's a *good* idea.

You have to ask yourself if you can truly bring something new to the table. What does your idea have that's unique, not shared by other businesses in that field? Why would people choose to work with *you* instead of the competition?

To be clear, the existence of other businesses or individuals in your chosen field is usually a very good thing. It proves there's a market for what you want to offer.

The key here is you must be able to do something better, faster, cheaper or with a better customer experience (or a combination of these four) than the competition. If you can't, why would anyone use you?

If you've chosen a sector where there are already a lot of large multinational businesses (think fast food, clothing, etc.), doing things cheaper is likely to be very difficult. Even if you could undercut your competition, they often operate on such a large scale they might cut prices further in a race to the bottom. Chances are you will run out of money before they do!

Financial Planning is actually a fairly unique example here, where some of the larger players offer an inferior service AND they're more expensive. In our world, there's actually a lot of room for service-driven, boutique firms to do very well indeed.

In most businesses, though, the big boys are hard to beat. If you're planning on making burgers and fries for a living, you'd be hard-pressed to beat McDonald's on price, for example – or speed for that matter.

What you can do is create a product that's better than anything else out there. If you're super passionate about food, perhaps you can create the best burger and fries people have ever tasted. That's something people will pay a princely sum for!

There are now a ton of small and medium-sized gourmet burger restaurants popping up to cater for people who want a great burger.

That's not really to say these businesses are competing with McDonald's directly – they serve very different markets – but what they do very well is a good burger.

Now to be clear, this is not a book about how to start a business. What we're looking at here is financial freedom. However, a business can be a vital tool to help you achieve that financial freedom and so I include it here for completeness.

Below you'll find some brief advice from my years in the business trenches in the hope it helps you on your Journey – or perhaps helps you avoid some of the disastrous mistakes I've made along the way.

I will recommend several other books and resources you can use to help you if you decide to start on your own business journey.

2) Research, research, research

One of the things I probably didn't do very effectively before I started the Financial Planning business was market research.

Before we launched, I spent hours and hours dreaming up a really inventive new charging structure that was different to anything else in the Financial Planning world at that time.

I spent days thinking about it and then created a beautiful two-page document to explain how wonderful my new idea was.

I paid a graphic designer to create a lovely colourful table to explain to clients how our radical charging system worked and why it'd be so great for them.

After all this work, I launched the charging system to the first client and... they HATED it!

They were not alone; client meeting after client meeting ended in despair. They didn't even understand the new charging system I'd spent so long perfecting, let alone want to sign up to it.

My prized creation was one, big, massive flop.

I'd tried to re-invent the wheel and it turns out my clients actually liked the wheel just the way it was. *Why fix what's not broken?* was their response.

Back to the drawing board for me.

If I'd done even the most basic of market research before I jumped in head first, I probably could've saved myself hundreds of hours and thousands of pounds of wasted time and money creating something no one actually wanted.

A couple of hours speaking with prospective clients about my plans would've very quickly revealed what a bad idea it was and saved me all the agony in the process.

Oh well, lesson learned!

Test it out
Once you have an idea, concept or prototype, you really must do your research to ensure your idea has wings.

You need to research and test your concept until it hurts. The more feedback you can gather, the better.

Most people begin this process with their friends and family. While they will no doubt provide a good sounding board while you're fleshing out an idea, they can NOT (repeat NOT) be relied upon for any sort of meaningful feedback.

Though you can ask your friends and family to be as honest as possible, human nature says people who like you won't want to upset you. As such, I'd take any sort of feedback from friends and family with a big pinch of salt.

What you should begin with, if possible, are real-life prospective customers of your product or service.

Now, you might be wondering where you'll find these people and why they would help you.

On the first count, I can't be much help I'm afraid. Where your potential customers will congregate will depend massively on your chosen product or service.

If you're planning on launching a dog grooming business, go to a dog show. For a yoga class, go to a health festival. If you think about it hard enough, the vast majority of interests, hobbies and activities have some sort of event or conference you could attend to see where your prospective customers congregate, what they like (and don't like) to do and where they spend their money.

Ask 'em

When it comes to getting people to help you I have one very simple solution: you just ask them.

This is like in the TV show *The Apprentice* when candidates think up a new product or service and then go and ask people what they think about it in a focus group. The point here is to get real-life feedback from real-life people on your product or service idea. The only problem with *The Apprentice* is they tend to do this once the product is already finalised. Now, what's the point in getting feedback when you've already finished the product? That's just plain silly.

What you're looking to do here is kind of similar, but just way more logical. You want to get feedback from as many people as possible while you're still at the **idea stage**, not once you've already spent a load of time and money on prototyping and developing an idea (just as I did – doh!).

Most people when asked are naturally inclined to help. So long as you ask in a humble and appreciative way, you should have no problem. Even asking random strangers what they think of your idea, I'd put money on at least 50% of them stopping to help.

Now add a pinch of salt

Now, once you have your feedback, you need to add a very large pinch of salt.

Despite all the good things you've no doubt heard about your idea from prospective customers, you need to apply a filter to the information received.

You see, numerous studies have shown people are far more gung-ho saying they'll buy something when they're presented with a hypothetical situation. As soon as actual money is involved, the response often changes.[1]

This has even been proven in studies where a sale is first pitched in a hypothetical sense ("If X product were available at a price of £15, would you buy one?") and then followed up with a real-life opportunity to buy the product ("As it happens, we actually do have X available today for £15, would you like to buy one?").

It might surprise you to learn that fewer than 50% of people who say they'll buy something hypothetically will actually do so when presented with the opportunity.[2]

As such, I'd be inclined to play it safe and assume that only 25% of your market research group that said they'd be interested in your idea would actually be willing to part with money for it.

I'd suggest you continue to develop and refine your idea, pricing and strategy until you're in the position where 10% of your potential customers would be willing to buy your product. This means that, using the above 25% rule, you need 40% of people to say yes during your market research – which will boil down to 10% of them willing to pay in real life.

Check you are ready to launch

Once you have refined your idea to this point, you're ready to launch. Although it's tempting to continue testing and improving the idea almost ad infinitum, there comes a time where you must take the leap of faith and launch something.

This point is usually where you feel like you have 80% of something figured out. If you spend too long worrying about the remaining 20%, you may never get anywhere. It's often better to just launch something and figure the rest out as you go.

With that said, let's get going...

3) Go, go, go (but slowly though)

Once you have sufficient confidence in your idea, you're ready to launch.

My recommendation is to launch your new business as a side business (as opposed to a Side-Hustle, which tends to refer to casual jobs you can come and go from, rather than a fully-fledged business) and avoid quitting your job. The vast majority of businesses can be started this way.

Although it's tempting to throw caution to the wind, quit your job and put everything into your new business venture, this can be a risky strategy – although when starting a business there will always be a measured degree of risk.

Despite everything I've said about doing something you love and leaving behind boring and soul-destroying jobs, if there's one thing worse than a soul-destroying job, it's financial stress.

If you go ahead and quit your job to follow your dreams without the right financial backing, you could end up struggling to pay your rent or mortgage, which is much worse (believe me, I've been there).

Better to put up with the job just for a few more months or even a couple of years until your new venture is off the ground. If you find yourself in this situation, the job always seems a little better anyway because you know deep down inside that you're already working on your escape plan.

In a few select situations, there will probably be no other option but to quit the day job.

If you are a super-deluxe coffee connoisseur and you're planning on setting up a new coffee shop, for example, you probably need to be there full-time. A coffee shop that's only open between 7pm and 9pm is probably not going to go so well! Do give me a call when you open, though, and I'll be your first customer!

Most other businesses you can start as a side project in your spare time and with very little expense, and then build things from there.

If you want to start a dog grooming business or be a yoga instructor, these ideas can be started with just a laptop, a phone line, a basic website or Facebook page, some basic equipment and a space in which to operate. This is probably the way most businesses should be started.

The beauty of this approach is it allows you to test and improve your idea without putting everything on the line.

Once the business is gaining some traction (and after you've made some of the early mistakes) then by all means you can quit your job and give everything to your new baby.

Once you're up and running, you will probably be able to celebrate some early wins. Nothing beats the buzz of a new business and it's a wonderful feeling to wake up in the morning full of excitement and anticipation (rather than boredom and trepidation!).

Be warned, though, there could be some tough times ahead. Being a business owner is a wonderful thing, but only the worthy are allowed into these hallowed grounds.

In fact, I believe that in order to be a business owner you have to pass through what I call *The Proving Ground*.

There will be some long, lonely days ahead and I believe it's only true belief and passion that pull people through these times.

It would be unfair of me to tell you all the advantages of being a business owner without explaining the process you have to go through to get there. Enter The Proving Ground... if you dare.

4) The Proving Ground

This is the no-man's land that no one likes to talk about. It's the graveyard where many businesses sit, lifeless and empty. However, if you want to enjoy the rewards that are on the other side, you must pass through The Proving Ground. There's no other way to the other side.

How long you will be here will depend on your business, your marketing, your industry and many other things. But you must know you'll arrive here at some point on your business journey (from my discussions with business owner clients and in my own experience, this is usually around 12 months in) and it will be very tempting to give up.

We all know the statistics that say that four out of five new businesses fail and most of them do so within the first year. My own view is that four out of five new business owners give up too soon.

When you arrive at The Proving Ground, you will generally have started a new business around 12 months earlier. As I wrote about in *Step 2*, when you first start a new business, there always seems to be a honeymoon period where everything goes smoothly.

This is easy, you think, and then it happens.

The money stops flowing in quite like it used to. The phone stops ringing. Your friends will start to say things like, *I knew it was a bad idea.*

I believe this happens for a variety of reasons, but the main one is that when you start a new business, there's always the tendency to go for the low-hanging fruit.

You will do business with your friends and family and your existing network of contacts first. Past colleagues and people you used to do business with in an old job might be customers for a little while too.

But then, around the end of the first year, this business seems to dry up. The novelty of the new business has worn off (I think secretly people admire those who are brave enough to start a business, so they'll often give support in the early days). This is about the point where you have to go out into the world and win new customers.

This is where things get tough.

Having waxed lyrical about how great it is to start a business, you might be wondering why I'm now spouting all this pessimism.

The reason is most definitely not to deter you from following your dreams. It's simply to prepare you for what is to come and to paint an honest picture of what you must go through to make it in business.

If you're not willing to go through this period of pain, starting a business may not be for you. I suggest you skip this section and look for another route.

When you enter The Proving Ground, things will get tight. You might have to cut back on your lifestyle for a while. You might be eating into your savings to get the business off the ground. You might not be able to take that holiday you were hoping for.

When I started my business, we had to cut back on all sorts of things. In some months it was a struggle to pay the mortgage. Other times we had to cancel events and days out as we simply didn't have the money.

The reason for me telling you all this is to let you know there's light at the end of the tunnel – and when you get there, the view is incredible!

This Journey is not unique to me. In my Financial Planning business, I often deal with successful business owners and they almost always report the same story. A (roughly) 12-month honeymoon period, followed by The Proving Ground period of 12–18 months.

The reason I mention this now is to re-enforce the point: your business needs to be something you're truly passionate about and that you deeply believe in.

You could have the best idea in the world, but if you don't have the passion and belief to see it through, you won't make it through The Proving Ground.

If you've had an epiphany and figured out how human teleportation works, but you've no passion for travel or transport, I'm sorry but the business probably isn't going to work.

It's where skill and passion combine that true riches lie.

5) Read widely

This is a point I'm going to re-visit in later sections as well because it's so important.

I believe books are one of the most valuable yet most underutilised resources in business (and in life).

As you develop your business, there will no doubt be things you wish to learn about and improve. Books can provide the answer.

Nowadays, there are fantastic books on almost any subject and in almost every niche.

First of all, there are books that apply to business in general. Some great examples are *Traction,* by Gino Wickman, and also *The E-Myth,* by Michael Gerber. In *Traction,* Gino writes about the 'Entrepreneurial Operating System' or EOS. This is a fantastic way to run any small business and I wish I'd applied the lessons much earlier in my business.

These books are about business, and their teachings can be applied to almost any business at almost any stage of growth.

There will also most likely be several great books that apply specifically to businesses in your niche. I can name at least 10 titles that have helped me hugely in my Financial Planning business.

Books are brilliant because they're both cheap and accessible. For £10–£15, you can benefit from years of the authors' accumulated knowledge and teachings. This information is worth thousands, if not hundreds of thousands of pounds. What an incredible return on investment.

I can directly attribute well over £250,000 of earnings just to things I've learned in books.

For a start, there's the book *The Soul Millionaire* that was written by my first business coach, David Scarlett. That book gripped me so hard that I read it all in one sitting. Much to the detriment of my performance the following day, I stayed up until 4am just to finish every last page. I just couldn't put it down. This book is a parable of David's own life and the process he went through to start his own coaching business.

That book led to me appointing David and we continue to work together to this day.

Then there are titles like *Lighting The Torch* by George Kinder. This book revolutionised the way we run our first meetings with clients and it increased our new client take-up rate by over 50%. It shines a whole new light on what Financial Planning can do for clients by focusing on their life, rather than their money!

Given the breadth of reading available at a very low cost, there's really no excuse not to learn and improve both yourself and your business.

Before we move on to the next path, there's one more thing you simply must do if you want to be successful in business.

6) The one thing (apart from books)

The preceding pages contain a high-level overview of some of the steps I recommend you take if you're thinking about starting a business. I hope this acts as a catalyst and directs you to the further reading and research that you really must do before you take the leap of faith.

For a start I would recommend you read *The 4-Hour Work Week* by Tim Ferris, *The E-Myth* by Michael Gerber and *The Lean Startup* by Eric Ries. These books will give you a great foundation in business and allow you to start with the end in mind. If you speak to any business owner, they will tell you there are things they wished they'd known before they got started. These books will let you in on some of those mistakes and hopefully set you off on the right track as you begin your business journey.

As with this book, you must also do the exercises and thinking tasks included in them if you want to make the most of them. Just reading a book is all well and good, but it won't drive any change in your life. You need to implement the teachings of the book as well – you must take action.

I would follow up these excellent reads by also consuming three further books from those who already run successful businesses in your chosen field.

The world contains millions of different business types and models and it would be impossible for me to give (or claim to give) advice on the vast majority of these. If you're planning on starting a Financial Planning firm, though, do give me a call – that's one thing I do know a little bit about!

For all other business types, please re-read and apply the advice and guidance on the past few pages. These tips stem not only from my own journey, but also from the experience of the many businesses owners and entrepreneurs I work with in my Financial Planning firm and whom I speak to in my various coaching groups.

The above guidance might not seem like rocket science (and it certainly isn't) but it could well save your business, your marriage, your house and your life from what can quickly turn into a big disaster.

A business is a bit like fire: used well, it's immensely powerful, but in the wrong hands, a lot can go wrong!

There is, however, one tip that trumps all of the others hands down. This one thing has probably been by far the biggest contributor to my own business success. In fact, if it weren't for this one thing, I might not be where I am today. I probably wouldn't be on the Journey to True Financial Freedom and I probably wouldn't be writing this book right now.

What I'm about to recommend will seem totally counterintuitive – in fact, it could well seem downright crazy.

Making this decision could well be the most difficult thing you do on your business journey.

Relationships and marriages will be tested. Everyone will tell you you're totally mad.

But, please hear me out. I put much of the success and happiness in my life down to this one decision we made five years ago.

So, here it is.

Appoint a business coach

I can hear the groans already. For some reason business coaches have a bad rep. Many people in business will be familiar with the saying 'those that can, do, and those that can't, coach'.

This is true in part: there are many business coaches who've never had any other form of business (other than coaching) or who've tried to do something, then failed, and decided it makes them somehow qualified to coach others in their field.

These people should be avoided like the plague.

While they're no doubt lovely people, they probably can't help you get where you want to go in business or in life.

There's a second breed of coaches, though, and these are the people you are looking for.

These coaches will generally be walking the walk as well as talking the talk and if not, they will have already had a successful business in your chosen field that's been sold on (I generally say *sold* because otherwise it means the business failed – and that's not good for a coach).

Appointing a business coach is one of the most illogical things I've ever done in my life. As I mentioned earlier, we spent £18,000 of our final £19,000 in savings on our first coach. But that decision changed my life.

In the search for the business coach that's right for you, there's no magic formula. There's no recipe book for success. What I will say, though, is when you find the one, very much like dating, you just *know*.

When you're courting your potential coaches, if you find someone who you think you might like, my first recommendation is to read all the books they've written (they have written a book, right?).

By reading their material, you can quickly get a feel for how your relationship might work. If you start reading and by page 6 you're wondering what on earth they're on about, you should probably continue your search for a business coach romance a bit longer.

If, however, you find a page-turner you simply can't put down, then you may have found the one for you.

As I mentioned, I stayed up until 4am reading *The Soul Millionaire* – and those who know me would tell you how important getting enough sleep is to me – so this really was quite unusual indeed.

I remember that night so vividly because it was the night I decided I needed to work with David. This decision was most likely the single inflexion point that made the difference between my business failing or thriving.

The right business coach can help you to do all sorts of things. If you've picked someone from your own industry (preferably someone who has or did have a successful business in your chosen field), they should be able to help you not just with the big picture stuff like strategy and marketing, but also the day-to-day practicalities of how to set up your website and hire staff.

To say all of this, though, does great coaches a huge injustice. If you've found a truly excellent coach, they should be helping you with more than just *stuff*. They should be helping you with far bigger issues like figuring out *why* you're in business in the first place. (What's your purpose and how are you going to serve your customers at the highest level?)

Possibly the biggest thing a business coach can help you with, though, is building the most important business muscle of all... confidence.

7) The art of the possible

Have you ever noticed how your mindset before a big event often dictates the outcome?

If you've ever had to give a big presentation, for example, how you thought about it in your head beforehand probably had a big influence on how things actually unfolded.

If you had visions of sweaty hands, fluffed lines and an embarrassing trip off the stage, chances are some of those things became a reality.

If instead, you pictured a confident talk, rapturous applause and the result you were hoping for at the end, then chances are the real thing went much better – even if it wasn't totally perfect.

There's a huge amount of science to back this up. Professional sportspeople often picture crossing the finish line in first place before the race even starts. Racing drivers picture the trophy in their hands before they even leave the starting line.[3]

The science behind why this works is beyond me (although you can no doubt read a book all about it) but what I do know is your level of confidence has a direct correlation to your level of success.

If you believe that you can do something, if you believe in yourself, then you'll be amazed by what you can achieve.

If you don't believe you can do something, then why should your prospective clients believe you can either?

When you start in business, it's very easy to get caught in the trap of thinking success is something that only happens to other people. To those who are special or gifted in some way. *Normal people like me don't get* [*insert desired outcome here*], is often the narrative going on in your head.

This is where I was the day I appointed David as my coach. After the initial early successes, I was stuck in a rut. The phone had stopped ringing and we were struggling to gain any traction. We were surviving, but we certainly were not thriving.

David helped me to see the art of the possible. He showed me previous experiences of normal people who had made it in Financial Planning. He helped me to restore my confidence and believe in myself.

The funny thing is that confidence is exponential. As soon as you start to gain some confidence and you experience some wins, you can build on this and very quickly you believe you can take over the world (OK not quite, but you get the idea).

Put simply, building your confidence is the single best thing you can do to make it in business.

There's a difference between confidence and arrogance. What you're looking to develop is a steely, inner strength that makes you believe you can achieve what you set out to achieve.

That's not to say that you can't be humble, polite, courteous and all of these other nice things. Indeed, I would suggest that a generous helping of the above attributes will be needed to help you on your way to business success.

8) The end game – your goals

Before you begin your business it really helps to (as Stephen Covey so beautifully put it in his book, *The 7 Habits of Highly Effective People*) 'begin with the end in mind'.

You should have a written goal and a vision that you're going to shoot for. Otherwise, you are just meandering aimlessly through the world of business, meaning you're far more likely to get stuck in The Proving Ground and find yourself in the business graveyard and not the business hall of fame.

Goals have layers

Your goals are just that: yours. But given we're hoping to use our business to achieve True Financial Freedom, there are a couple of things that I believe should feature in your vision.

These goals are like layers, with one sitting on top of the other, and I urge you to build these things into your plan somehow.

Layer 1 – Generating enough income to support your current lifestyle

For most business owners and entrepreneurs, this will be the first hurdle: getting the business to a point where the income it generates will support your current standard of living. Sounds simple, but the execution can be anything but.

If you can reach this point, you deserve a pat on the back. The vast majority of businesses never even reach profitability, so getting this far is a massive step.

While getting this far is no doubt an accolade that you wish to celebrate, to achieve True Financial Freedom, you must go further.

Layer 2 – Increasing your income to improve your savings rate

When you have enough to cover your current lifestyle, I would then focus on improving your Savings Rate. We should be shooting for the fabled

50% Savings Rate where you can save half of your income. Although this might seem like a stretch, as a business owner, you're now at a huge advantage because to some extent you can control your earnings.

You can do all sorts of things to improve your income and therefore increase your Savings Rate. For example, you might:

> Improve your offerings.
> Sell higher value services.
> Employ staff to take some of the strain for you.

There are many, many options available to you in business to increase your income.

Layer 3 – Increasing your income further still to live your perfect life

Now that we have your Savings Rate under control, you can improve your income further still up to the point where you can start living your Perfect Life. Remember your Budget Spreadsheet from *Step 2* where you mapped out your Perfect Life? It might help you to pull that out and refresh your memory.

As you increase your income further still, try to stick to the 50% Savings Rate. You can achieve this using the Spend Half, Save Half method we discussed earlier. An example might help.

Let's say that your current lifestyle costs £50,000 a year.

You have first built your business to cover your current expenses. Well done!

Next, you went further so you could achieve a 50% Savings Rate, meaning that your income became £100,000.

Let's imagine your Perfect Life will cost £75,000 a year – £25,000 more than currently.

Most people would simply assume they needed to increase their income to £125,000. That would give them the extra £25,000 alright, but it would also mean that their Savings Rate would fall below 50%.

In order to maintain the Savings Rate, we need to continue to employ the Spend Half, Save Half method. This means that for every £10,000 of extra income, half can be spent and half is saved.

Let's imagine in the first year after you begin this process you achieve £110,000 of income – £10,000 more than the year before.

You can now add £5,000 to your spending, making a total of £55,000 and add £5,000 to your savings, also making a total of £55,000 and maintaining that magic 50% Savings Rate.

You would continue in this way until your total income was £150,000. This means you can now spend the £75,000 while saving the remaining £75,000 (living your dream lifestyle AND ensuring your future financial freedom – the best of both worlds).

Layer 4 – Building a self-managing company

Once you have the income to live your dream life, you may well decide that you want to work less or have a better balance. You might need some more free time to do what you have planned, perhaps. Maybe you want to go travelling for six months or spend eight weeks overseas helping others.

The way to achieve this is to build what Dan Sullivan of Strategic Coach calls a 'self-managing company'.

I'm not going to say too much about that here. The self-managing company concept is the intellectual property of Dan Sullivan and the Strategic Coach and I believe that intellectual property should be respected.

I will say, however, that a self-managing company means you can leave your company for an extended period of time and it will still continue to operate in exactly the same way without you.

Clearly, this is not an easy endeavour, but it's possible. I would highly recommend you join the Strategic Coach to find out more.

Layer 5 – Removing yourself from the company (optional)

Some business owners will reach *Layer 4* and still want to expand their freedom further. They might wish to remove themselves from the business completely or start to tackle another project.

Unlike in *Layer 4*, where you could take extended time away from the business, but ultimately you were still working in the business some of the time, in this *Layer 5* we're talking about never working in the business ever again. A clean break, if you will.

In this case, you could consider exiting the business.

The most obvious way to do this is to simply sell it, but that's not really the focus here (more on that in *Path 6c*).

The other option is to employ other people to run the business for you. What I'm talking about here is a situation where you effectively become only a shareholder in the business and have nothing to do with the day-to-day operations or management of the company.

This way, you can hopefully still receive an income from your company in the form of share dividends, but without the need to actually work within the business.

You will notice in all of the above situations, we're looking to generate an income from our business to support our dream lifestyle and allow a high Savings Rate.

I have intentionally not said much about the prospect of selling the business for a big lump sum of capital because I believe this is a totally different game.

We often hear stories of companies (especially tech companies) being sold for multimillion-dollar valuations just a few short years after they've been launched. These businesses are called 'Unicorns' (a term for a tech company that reaches a $1 billion valuation) and for good reason: they're very rare. However, for certain individuals, this could be their path to financial freedom.

So, without further ado, let's explore if giving birth to a Unicorn could be right for you...

Summing Up Path 6b – Maximising Your Financial Freedom as a Business Owner

We have learned in this chapter what it takes to be a business owner and how to establish if you have a great business idea.

> Building a business can be a great way to enhance your earning power in order to bring you closer to True Financial Freedom.

> But a business is a little like fire. Used wisely, it can be very powerful, but in the wrong hands, it can cause a lot of damage.

> Before you even think of launching a business, it's vital to do thorough research to ensure there's a market for your product or service and that you can turn a profit.

> When you first launch, try to run the business as a side-project in your spare time if you can. This massively reduces the risk and stress involved with quitting your day job before the business is really off the ground.

> There are so many things that you can do to increase your chances of success in business, but reading widely and appointing a business coach might be some of the best.

Do you think that starting a business could be for you? Do you have a hobby or passion you could turn into a business opportunity? Do you think you have the resilience and determination to see your new venture through The Proving Ground?

---

1 www.jneurosci.org/content/31/2/461
2 https://pubmed.ncbi.nlm.nih.gov/11373840
3 www.entrepreneur.com/article/242373

Resources – Path 6b

Books

There are a ton of books that will teach you invaluable lessons in business and in life. These are just some of my favourite general business books as well as some from the Financial Planning world specifically:

Thriving in Mind: The Art and Science of Using Your Whole Brain

Katherine Benziger, KBA, 2004

The 7 Habits of Highly Effective People: Powerful Lessons in Personal Change

Stephen Covey, Free Press, 2004

The 4-Hour Work Week (Expanded and Updated)

Tim Ferriss, Harmony, 2009

The E-Myth Revisited: Why Most Small Businesses Don't Work and What to Do About It

Michael Gerber, Harper Business, 2004

Lighting the Torch: The Kinder Method of Life Planning

George Kinder, FPA, 2006

The Lean Startup: How Today's Entrepreneurs Use Continuous Innovation to Create Radically Successful Businesses

Eric Ries, Currency, 2011

The Soul Millionaire: True Wealth is Within Your Reach

David Scarlett, Summertime, 2012

Traction: Get a Grip on Your Business

Gino Wickman, BenBella, 2012

Other

Strategic Coach

www.strategiccoach.com

Path 6c – Finding Financial Freedom by Selling a Business

In *Path 6b,* we spoke about building a business with the primary aim of generating income to increase your Savings Rate. What was intentionally overlooked, back then, was the prospect of selling a business for a big lump sum, which you then invest to generate your True Financial Freedom.

I have given this gnarly topic a whole section of the book because building a company with the intention of selling it on is very different to building a company to generate significant income for the owner.

Building a sellable business

This idea of building a company (often a tech company) and then selling it for millions (or billions) a few months later has been romanticised by a few high-profile stories in the media – think Facebook, Twitter, Snapchat, etc.

While the idea of working your socks off for 18 months to build a tech monster and then selling it and sailing off into the sunset has an obvious appeal, you must be aware that these stories are very much the exception and not the rule.

There are far more tech companies in the business graveyard than in the business hall of fame. Most tech businesses fail within around 12 months, having usually cost the owner (and often their investors) a bucketload of money with a capital B!

Even the tech companies that do manage to secure venture capital funding (this means a professional investor sees enough potential in the company to put their money on the line), 75% still fail.

This is a game with very long odds indeed. The success stories are amazing, but very much the exception.

What I'm really getting at here is that for the vast, vast majority of people reading this book, this will not be the path for them.

Most people who become wealthy do so the boring way: spend less than you earn, focus on a high Savings Rate and invest your excess income.

I include this step here for completeness because there are a few exceptional businesses that get sold for a lot of money and I'm fortunate to have a tiny number of such people among my Financial Planning clients.

For a start, the majority of businesses that are capable of growth at this scale and speed are going to be tech businesses. It's generally Internet-only businesses that have the ability to reach very large-scale, very quickly.

If you know nothing about computers, programming, AI or anything similar, then this option probably isn't for you.

I know nothing about these things and accept this path is not for me.

Who it is for, however, is one of my best friends. I mentioned earlier that he'd recently started an artificial intelligence business and secured some significant investment funding.

I invested in his business because I believe he is one of the rare few people who have the ability to build a Unicorn.

For a start, he's a computer genius (and far more intelligent than I will ever be). He deeply understands the field of artificial intelligence and his company was one of the first to enter the AI market.

All these ingredients are definitely needed to grow a tech company fast, but even they are no guarantee of success.

I can't offer a great deal of advice about how to start and scale up a tech company. It is not my area of expertise and it would be wrong of me to profess to be able to help you with this.

As with many things, however, there are hundreds of books dedicated to this topic and I suggest if you think you might have what it takes to start a Unicorn, then read widely before you dive in.

What happens next?

What I can provide some advice on, however, is what to do once you have sold a business. In fact, many people come to see me for the first time having recently sold a business.

For a lot of business owners, the sale of the company is the first time they've had any real money in the bank since they started the company.

Now, to be clear, it shouldn't be like this. If you start a business you should be focusing on your Savings Rate the whole way through, just like we spoke about in *Path 6b*.

The sad reality, though, is that a lot of businesses are cash-eating monsters that barely survive, and it's only the sale that provides any real reward to the owner.

The problem with this (and yes, there's a problem with making too much money too quickly) is that these business owners are unprepared for the big lump sum of cash heading their way. They don't really know how to handle it and very often things go wrong.

Money quickly gets spent on fast cars and bigger houses and within a few short years the ex-business owner finds themselves back at square one. The capital that was supposed to last a lifetime has disappeared in just a few short years.

I've seen this story play out a couple of times from afar and it's not fun for anyone involved.

So, if you're lucky enough to sell a business for a few hundred thousand, millions or even billions, how should you handle the money?

I'm glad you asked... because we are going to explore this in detail in *PART 3* of the book when we look at investing to generate Passive Income – more on that later!

Summing Up Path 6c – Finding Financial Freedom by Selling a Business

In this chapter we have learned how to determine whether you are one of the rare few people who has what it takes to build a Unicorn company.

In doing so, you would have appreciated that most people don't get wealthy this way – I certainly won't, so I don't try.

> A Unicorn is usually a tech business that has reached a $1 billion valuation.
> Although we hear a lot about them (think Facebook, Snapchat, etc.) these businesses are the exception rather than the rule.
> For every Unicorn, there will be literally thousands of failures.
> Starting a business to sell is not for the faint-hearted.
> You have to decide if this is really something for you.
> For most people, this will not be the right path to True Financial Freedom.
> If you receive a large lump sum from a business sale (or anywhere else for that matter), don't do anything until you have read *PART 3*!

Do you think starting a Unicorn could be for you? If so, do you really have what it takes to make it a success?

Resources – Path 6c

Websites

www.hrmguide.co.uk/sme/unicorn-startup.htm

A great guide to see if you have what it takes to build a Unicorn company!

Path 6d – Supplement Your Income Using Side-Hustles and Passive Products

In addition to all the other tactics we've spoken about over the last few chapters, there's one thing you can do that'll have a larger impact on your progress towards True Financial Freedom than anything else. What's so special and appealing about this method is you don't need to have loads of money in order to pursue it and you can do it in your spare time to begin with.

What I am talking about here is starting a Side-Hustle or Passive Product business.

Side-Hustle success

A Side-Hustle is something you do to earn money on the side of your normal job, as I said before. Side-Hustles are usually casual jobs or tasks you can do to earn a little on the side and they come in all shapes and sizes. Perhaps you love dogs, so you could do some dog walking for your neighbours a couple of times a day, or you could do some online user testing for other people's websites and get paid for your comments. You could be a great proofreader and get paid to check other people's blogs, articles or books. The possibilities are endless.

The beauty of a Side-Hustle is you're generating new money on top of what you've been generating before. Let's imagine you are just about making ends meet. You're not saving a great deal, but your income is just about covering your expenses.

Let's imagine you take your neighbour's dog for a walk (just an example) for an hour a day at £10 an hour. Now you have £10 you didn't have before.

You were managing just about fine before you had that £10, and so now you have £10 of surplus income. But, that £10 was earned in just one day. If you did that five days a week, that's £50 a week or around £200 a month! Now imagine if you started saving and investing that £200 a month. Imagine how quickly you could build up an Emergency Fund or start saving for a house deposit. Imagine how much difference that money would make if it were invested for your future.

There are literally thousands of things you could do as a Side-Hustle. Just do a Google search for 'extra income ideas' or 'Side-Hustle ideas' and you will get lists with a ton of things you could try.

When I was struggling for money, I used to do online user testing. Basically, this is where companies who are trialling a new website want to know what you think of the pages and navigation before they go live with their new idea. You sign up as a tester and then, when your profile fits what the company is looking for, you get an invitation to do a test. The tests usually last 15 minutes and you simply browse around online on the site and talk your thoughts into your webcam as you go. I did a couple of these a day and got paid around $8–$10 (£6–£8) a time. On some days, I'd do three or four of them to earn even more.

Now, don't get me wrong, income from user testing was never close to what I was earning from my job, nor was it ever very consistent (some days you could get five tests, other days none at all) but it really made a difference to my Savings Rate at a time when I didn't have much cash to spare.

To be clear, there's a big difference between starting a Side-Hustle and starting a business like we talked about in *Path 6b*. Although both sound similar, there are some big differences. A Side-Hustle is usually very casual work, which you can come and go from as you please. It doesn't tend to come with big commitments, and you can usually dip in and out of this work as your circumstances allow. Side-Hustles don't tend to be started with the intention of *replacing* your 9–5 job, more as a supplement to it. Although, of course, you'll find many stories online of people whose Side-Hustle became so successful it eventually replaced their full-time job.

Though you also might work on a new business in your spare time, the intention from the start is always to build something bigger that will replace your full-time job. It's a subtle difference, but an important one.

Unlike starting a business, where I recommended months of research and preparation before you even get started, a Side-Hustle can usually be started today or tomorrow. Want to walk dogs on an evening off? Well, make some calls or knock on some doors and you're away. Want to do some proofreading? Just post a job offer on Fiverr and you might receive offers of work within 24 hours. A Side-Hustle is a quick-start, fairly easy way to make a little extra on the side. Starting a fully-fledged business, on the other hand, is a much bigger deal.

The other thing you could consider is starting a Passive Product Business. Now, I know that this might appear to contradict what I've just said, and to a certain extent it does, but a Passive Product Business sort of sits in both camps. You can have a Passive Product that's definitely a Side-Hustle, or you could make it into a business. A Passive Product is kind of like a Side-Hustle on steroids, if you will.

A Passive Product Business – the Side-Hustle on steroids

A Passive Product Business is the natural extension of the Side-Hustle. I guess I'd define the difference like this: a Side-Hustle tends to focus on short tasks that can be completed individually and you get paid per task completed. (Think dog walking, online user testing, taking a marketing survey – all things that take no more than an hour and you get paid for each task completed.) A Passive Product Business, on the other hand, is something you're trying to build. This is going to be a longer-term project but will normally be something you're passionate about. Most Passive Product Businesses start out as hobbies or side-projects, but they do have the potential to become full-time jobs/businesses – if you want them to.

So, what the heck is a Passive Product?

Passive Products are things that, once you've created them, can earn more money with very little (sometimes zero) ADDITIONAL effort. Don't get me wrong, they often involve a LOT of effort up front, but once completed, the effort to continue to earn money either significantly drops or is eliminated completely.

You're holding a Passive Product in your hands right now. Although writing this book was a ton of hard work, now that it's done, I can sell multiple copies with very, very little (if any) additional effort for each copy sold.

Unlike most work, which operates in the Time for Money Economy, Passive Products are the definition of the Value Economy. You get rewarded based on how valuable your product is to other people – not based on how hard you work or how many hours you spent on it.

Books are probably the oldest and best-known example of Passive Products.

Don't get me wrong. I'm sure that JK Rowling put a lot of hard work into writing the first Harry Potter book. It took her six years, after all. What I'm getting at here is that *creating* a Passive Product can take a lot of work – in fact, the creation phase is not that passive at all. BUT, when it's finished, then you can sell multiple copies of the product with little to no additional effort – that's the passive part!

Now that it's done, it can earn money almost indefinitely. In fact, with each new Harry Potter merchandise item, film sale, book sale and so much more, JK Rowling will be earning a cut, while doing almost no work at all.

It's reported that Mariah Carey earns over £600,000 every year from the royalties on just one track – *All I Want For Christmas Is You* – and she made that record in 1994!

Good old Mariah doesn't have to lift a finger to sell another copy of that track. Just wait for Christmas to come along (and it has a habit of doing that around once every year) and the radios start playing the song and people start buying it again.

Passive Products are pretty incredible and you don't need to create anything on the scale of JK Rowling or Mariah Carey to really help you on your Journey to True Financial Freedom.

There are simply hundreds of underground stars of the Passive Product world. People like Brendon Burchard and Natalie Bacon and Amy Porterfield. People you've probably never heard of before now, but who have online followings of hundreds of thousands of people and earn seven-figure sums from products and resources they created many years ago.

The world of Passive Products has fascinated me since I realised its potential around four years ago and I've been infatuated ever since.

It was this fascination that led me to write my first book on estate planning, which so far has sold a few thousand copies, netting me £12,000 in the process – and it only launched 18 months ago. What's more, you can use a Passive Product to support your career or business as well.

I wrote my first book on estate planning because:

a) It's a subject I enjoy and am passionate about.
b) My clients want to read about it.
c) If people read my book, they're more likely to want to do business with our Financial Planning firm.

Now, this is a specialist book on a niche topic. I self-published the book and have had no formal marketing, yet it's still on track to make me around £8,000 this year alone.

The best part is, once the book is completed, I barely have to think about it. At the end of the month, I log in to my account, see how many I have sold and then Amazon just sends the royalty payment to my bank account. What could be better than that!?

Over time, you can build up a library of Passive Products and they have a habit of multiplying and compounding. There are now seven Harry Potter books that have spawned eight movies and every possible highly-priced merchandise item you can imagine (£18 notebook anyone?).

Every time any one of these items gets sold, JK Rowling gets a cut, and I would hazard a guess she's taking home more than £8,000 a year on the back of her Harry Potter franchise!

What's even better about Passive Products is that they tend to be related to something you love.

Though I don't know her personally, I'm pretty sure JK Rowling wrote the Harry Potter books because she loves writing. Most writers earn very little and there's almost zero chance of hitting the big time. She wrote the books because she loves writing them, then she happened to get lucky and strike the jackpot.

This is not to take away from her writing skill – the books are incredible – but the point I'm making is she would've written that first book for the love of writing. Most new authors don't make millions of pounds like she eventually did.

Passive Products can take many forms. The obvious examples are books and music tracks. But there are also online courses, printable worksheets, workbooks, blogs, software, apps, websites, subscription services, podcasts and much more.

We're going to look at each of the main Passive Products in turn and see which of them might be right for you.

What's also brilliant about Passive Products is that, in almost all cases, you can create a Passive Product for very little (if any) money.

My first book cost around £400 to produce and that's only because I hired a professional editor to do the final editing and proofreading. I could've done this myself, but I just didn't have the time.

You can create a website nowadays for less than £10 a year. It costs nothing to write a book and there are loads of free tools you can use for designing worksheets or coding apps.

What's even better, you can create a Passive Product alongside your main job or business. No need to put everything on the line. When you look at many of the successful full-time Passive Product producers, the vast majority of them would've started their venture part-time and only progressed to their Passive Product Business full-time once they were sure it was earning money.

The final thing I love about creating Passive Products is you can pick them up and put them down. If I'm in the middle of writing a book (as I am as I write this book) and I want to go on vacation for a month, no problem. The book will wait patiently for me until I get back and my existing book will sit happily on Amazon selling copies, which Amazon ship for me.

Unlike a more traditional job or business where we have bosses, colleagues, customers and clients who all want a piece of us, making it very hard to just leave, a Passive Product business will normally sit quite happily by itself and no harm will come of it.

All these reasons – and more – make Passive Products one of the most exciting developments in the world of True Financial Freedom for ages.

The Internet and technology make things even better. A couple of decades ago, if you wanted to publish a book, you had to go and find a publisher. You would have to write them all letters and proposals, most of which would get rejected. Only if you were lucky (really lucky) then one of the publishers might agree to take your book and publish it.

Nowadays, you can self-publish a book using Amazon or any of a number of similar companies. All of this can be done yourself, from the comfort of your computer screen. At this point you may need to get the assistance of a proofreader and a cover designer and then you're ready to send your book to Amazon. A few days later you have a beautiful, printed book in your hands. Pretty cool, in my book!

In fact, technology allows you to create almost any of the Passive Products we have discussed here with very little up-front cost or investment (apart from time and passion).

Passive Products do come with a little health warning, however...

When you look at them from the outside it all just looks so easy. Just write the next Harry Potter book and launch it into the world and make millions – simple, right? Wrong.

Passive Products can be very deceptive. They're a little bit like icebergs in that what you see is only a tiny portion of the whole operation. Take an online course, for example, from the likes of which Amy Porterfield now makes millions of dollars a year.

It all seems so simple. She films a course on a topic she knows intimately and... hey presto... she makes $2 million.

The Long Haul

Amy Porterfield appears on screen to greet her followers (now running into the millions) and she appears calm, confident and self-assured. She's in the process of launching her latest online course (about how to create online courses), which will go on to generate more than $2 million on the first launch. She will go on to launch the course many more times in the future with little additional effort.

It all seems too easy, and it's natural to wonder, *how could that be me?* It's also easy to resign yourself to thinking, *that will never be me! She must be special!*

The thing is, by her own admission, Amy Porterfield is not special. She's actually a fairly shy person who doesn't see herself as having any special gift or ability.

What she does have is drive and determination and an ability to face her fears.

It all looks so easy on screen, but there's a lot you don't see.

Her latest course discusses the 10 years spent creating content and adding value to her community in order to build an e-mail list of people to market to.

When she started, Amy had an e-mail list of zero, just like everyone else. In fact, she made life harder for herself by putting off building an e-mail list until later on in her online business journey.

You also don't see the first course launch she did which only made $247. You don't see the millions of dollars she has put on the line buying Facebook ads to make her campaigns a success.

You don't see the long nights of work to get the business off the ground or the missed holidays and time with family.

Although Amy would be the first to admit that online courses have changed her life for the better, it has taken years of hard work and sacrifice to reach that point.

You see – although you might not see it as clearly – all successful Passive Product Businesses hide the usual sacrifices you would expect from any successful business owner. When you make it in the Passive Product Business, the rewards are perhaps better than any other. But it takes a ton of hard work to get there.

Yes, Passive Products can be the key to your financial freedom. Yes, Passive Products can make you money while you sleep. Yes, you can sell 100,000 Passive Products with little more effort than it would take to sell 100.

But (this is a big BUT) creating a Passive Product, like anything else in the world that's worth doing, takes a lot of hard work and dedication. If it was easy everyone would do it and everyone would be a success.

When you first launch your Passive Product into the world, it might feel like no one is listening (and they may well not be) but you have to stick at it. Be persistent and eventually, slowly but surely, your product can begin to gain traction.

I'm going to explore each of the kinds of Passive Products at a very high level in this book so you can decide which of them might be right for you. The strategies and processes involved to create each of these different types of Passive Products would require a book in itself (and indeed, there are many good books to read for each of them – which I list in *Resources* – so we won't be delving into huge detail here).

What I would like to do is give you enough information to decide which (if any) of the Passive Products could be for you and then I'll signpost further books, tools, courses and help-sheets at the end of this section to get you started. Most of the resources I recommend to help you learn about creating your own Passive Products are Passive Products themselves – books, online courses, etc. There's an irony in there somewhere!

So, without further ado, let's begin with perhaps the oldest Passive Product of all: books.

Books

Books are one of the oldest and most-popular Passive Products on the planet, and for good reason. They have the potential to inspire, educate and entertain in equal measure.

There's a lot to think about if you'd like to write a book and we'll only be able to scratch the surface here, but when I think about writing, my first thought is:

What's the purpose of this book?

Three reasons to write a book

I believe there are three main reasons you might want to write a book. Which of these reasons applies to you will determine the amount of time and money you'll want to invest in it.

1) Lead Magnet

Some people write a book (usually an e-book) to use as a so-called Lead Magnet to attract people onto their e-mail or physical mailing lists.

You might well have signed up for a Lead Magnet or two in your time without really noticing. Whenever you sign up for a free e-book, report, PDF, cheat sheet or basically anything else free on the Internet, you will usually give your e-mail address in return for the freebie.

Once they have your e-mail address, the individual or company in question will usually then send you e-mails and other marketing material in the hope you'll go on to purchase something in the future.

If you're looking to create a book to act as a Lead Magnet, it means you likely have another business or enterprise that will benefit from collecting e-mail addresses.

Books created as a Lead Magnet will generally be fairly short (perhaps 20–30 pages) and will be produced with a very small or non-existent budget.

If this type of book is for you, then you'll probably not want to spend more than a few days writing it. It probably won't be responsible for any direct revenue creation.

If this is for you, it'll probably be obvious, so I won't say much more about it here.

Books in this category are almost always non-fiction – they'll be about teaching someone something valuable enough to warrant the freebie request in the first place.

Since these types of books are not focused on direct revenue generation, I'll say no more here.

2) Business Reputation Builder

Some people also create what I call a Business Reputation Builder book. These books tend to be created by business owners and the topic of the book will be related to the business they run.

The purpose of the Business Reputation Builder book is either to sell it or give it away to build trust and favour with potential clients. It's sort of like a printed business card.

So, What's the Difference?

At first glance, this might seem similar to a Lead Magnet, but there are many differences. A Lead Magnet will generally be a short book, produced with reasonably little time and effort, designed to get people to hand over their contact details in exchange for a copy.

Once the business has your contact details, they can then communicate with you about other products and services, in the hope that you buy something else from them – it's the special *something* that generates the revenue here.

With a Business Reputation Builder book, you're writing a book to allow you to build trust, confidence and reputation with prospective clients so they do business with you on the back of the book alone (no follow up marketing or e-mails required). The difference is subtle, but significant.

A Business Reputation Builder will usually be a proper book, and could run to several hundred pages. It will generally be available in printed (as well as e-book) versions and will generally have a higher production quality and might require some outlay for editing and design services.

My estate planning book falls into this category. I run a business that offers estate planning services to clients. I want them to know, like and trust me and so I wrote a book on the topic to help them along the way.

We sell the book online and at our seminars and events, which in itself makes some small amount of revenue, and then a percentage of people who buy the book will ask us to work with them on a one-to-one basis.

Books in this category might not make huge volumes of money by themselves, but they can have a transformative impact on the business as a whole. As I said, my estate planning book is on track to generate about £8,000 of revenue in its own right this year alone, but the additional business we have done on the back of the book will be many times that amount.

If you're looking to create a Business Reputation Builder book, you should allow for much more time and effort. I spent almost two years writing my first book on and off and, though you could write something a lot faster, you shouldn't underestimate the work that goes into it.

Books in this category will again almost always be non-fiction. They will generally be related to the business in which the owner operates.

3) Stand-alone book

This is the book many people dream about writing: *The Sunday Times* (*The New York Times* for my US readers) best-selling masterpiece that takes the world by storm.

If you're writing a stand-alone book, you could choose to write about anything or anyone, so long as there's a sufficiently large audience for your book. Now, sufficiently large does not have to mean millions and millions of people. You could write a book on a fairly niche subject (as I have done) and then sell a number of copies in that market – *but,* these kinds of books are unlikely to be bestsellers.

If you're looking to have a multimillion-selling title, then it goes without saying that you'll need to be writing something with mass appeal.

You don't need me to tell you about the range of different things you could write about.

Stand-alone books could be non-fiction (like this one) or fiction. My understanding is that fiction books generally make less money on average; however, the ones that do make it big, make it REALLY big. Non-fiction books tend to make more money on average; however, fewer of them make it big time.

When you set out to write a book, you should make sure you understand what you're committing to. I'm sure there are millions of half-finished books out there sitting on people's hard drives and in their note pads. They were probably started with the best intentions (and most things are) but life got in the way.

The thing is, life will get in the way. It has a habit of doing that. If you're not committed to your book in the first place, chances are it will join the millions of others in the half-finished book pile.

I actually have two unfinished books on my computer as we speak. I forget the specific reasons they were left unfinished now, but I suspect it was a lack of commitment and a lack of prep work.

Before you set out to write a book, make sure you're writing something you're passionate about. If your book does not fill you with joy, it will probably not get finished – simple at that!

You also have to be prepared for your first book not to sell that well. Of course, some authors' debut works do go on to sell millions of copies, but these are very much the exception.

Writing, like anything else, is a skill that must be practised and perfected over many years. You should expect there to be some failures and frustrations along the way, but that's all part of the learning experience.

The key is to write about things you enjoy and then keep at it. Even if your first book is not a *Sunday Times* bestseller (mine certainly wasn't), don't give up. Even a book that sells a handful of copies has the ability to make you a decent side-income, but you have to put the same amount of energy into marketing and promoting your book as you did writing it.

Remember the iceberg that I spoke about earlier? A book is just like that. Looking at things on the surface, when you watch a book fly onto the bestseller list, it looks so easy.

Write a good book = become a bestseller – simple, right!

Well, not so much.

What those high-profile book launches hide is years of hard work and sacrifice (most authors earn very little while they're writing and therefore have to live on very little). They hide all the promotion and effort put into marketing the book. They hide the early starts and the late nights.

I'm not saying this to put you off – writing a book is one of the most amazing things I've done, but you have to be prepared for what you are undertaking.

Six tips for a winning book
A book can be hard to write and it's harder still to sell.

Before you commit to writing a book, I have some tips for you:

1) Make sure writing a book is really for you – do you actually have the time, energy and inclination to write a book? Would one of the other Passive Products be better suited to your current situation?
2) Write about something you love. If you don't, you probably won't finish the book. My two half-finished books are testament to that!

3)   Do it as a Side-Hustle first time. Although the idea of quitting your job to sit in a café all day writing the next Harry Potter masterpiece is alluring, it's also incredibly risky. One of the best things about writing a book is that it can be done in your spare time. I suggest writing on the side in the first instance and then by all means quit your job once you're on the bestseller list!

4)   Be prepared to put the work in. Writing a book can be hard work and marketing the book can be harder still.

5)   Don't get too down if your first book is not a runaway success. Writing, like anything, is a skill that must be mastered. Use your first book as a learning process and keep at it!

6)   A book must be written for one or more of the following reasons: to inspire, support, inform or entertain.

Who Again?

Tim Ferris was relatively unknown until he launched a book called *The 4-Hour Work Week*. That book launched him into relative stardom and was on *The Sunday Times* and *The New York Times* bestseller lists – eventually selling more than 2 million copies.

Before this – nothing. Tim Ferris reached fame and fortune seemingly overnight.

Before writing the book, Ferris founded and then sold a reasonably successful sports nutrition company, but he was not famous as a result.

I'm not sure what rocketed his book so quickly into the bestseller lists (most new authors don't get so lucky with their first book). Perhaps it was just the right message at the right time.

The reason I mention Tim Ferris is that it shows what's possible when you write a book. Please don't get me wrong. I'm sure he had a lot of good luck, a great marketing team and a supportive publisher, but it proves that a first book can, just sometimes, be a big success.

Now, your book doesn't need to sell 2 million copies to make a huge difference to your life. My book has sold a few thousand copies and has had a huge impact on my finances and my business. What's more, it's incredibly satisfying to be able to pass on my knowledge and expertise in the form of a book.

Online courses

An online course is exactly what it says on the tin. It's a course, that you take online, to learn something. Both professional and amateur teachers film content and then upload it to one of many online course platforms (this is a website that has all of the tools and features you need to host an online course) such as Teachable, Udemy or Kajabi.

Courses range from just a couple of hours to days or even months of content. Prices range hugely too. Many teachers will offer a free course of some description to hook you in, but the most expensive offerings can run well into the thousands of dollars.

I was actually taking an online course around three-to-four years ago when I first realised the potential of Passive Products. In fact, I think that moment was probably the first time I started using the term Passive Products in the first place.

I was taking a course on how to run a successful client meeting in a Financial Planning business. I was paying £97 per month for access to the online course. And then I learned that 500 other people were as well.

I paused for a second to do the maths. £97 x 500 = £48,500 per MONTH!

Now, the cost of this particular course platform was only around £200 a month, meaning that pretty much all of the revenue being generated was profit!

OK, now I was interested. That moment was the catalyst for a lot of learning about this brave new world of Passive Products.

That moment is probably the reason I wrote my first book (and this one) and it's the reason I'm now working on my own online course to share my knowledge with the world.

Online courses can be about almost anything (how to can food, how to pickle cabbages, how to make a potato gun – these are all real online courses – I do mean anything) and they can be created by almost anyone. They can be short *How To* courses or comprehensive systems to change your whole life.

I believe that pretty much everyone has something they could teach using an online course. You might think you don't have anything unique to share with the world, but you do. There are courses about almost everything. You name it, you can create a course about it. *How to sound better on camera, how to cope with stress at work, how to start a yoga business.* They have all been done and they're all successful courses.

It seems no matter how seemingly niche or strange your topic, there are people out there who want to learn about it. If anything, a niche topic is better. It's far easier to market to a niche, rather than targeting everyone with a scattergun approach.

There's a little saying in the online marketing community – the riches are in the niches!

Even though you might think no one wants to learn what you have to teach, I'm almost certain there's a group of people out there just like you who'd love to listen as you teach what you know to the world.

There are now loads of platforms where you can set up and host your online course, and they make it super easy to get started. You can also create an online course without a load of expensive equipment. Most of the filming that happens for online courses is done with a smartphone or webcam.

An online course basically involves you filming yourself (or a voiceover on top of a slide deck) teaching what you know to your audience. It can be intimidating for some people and so this option might not be for everyone. Alternatively, some online courses are all written or take the form of audio files or workbooks.

Five tips for a winning online course

If you think an online course might be for you, then I suggest you follow the five tips below and check out the tools and resources that follow.

1) The riches are in the niches – if you are thinking of creating a course, don't try to be all things to all people. Focus on a niche – the tighter the better. You will have far more success talking to a specific group of people rather than trying to speak to everyone.

2) Don't go too big to start. When people begin thinking of creating an online course, they often get caught in the trap of thinking they have to teach everything they know about a topic right out the gate. You can start small. Perhaps consider a mini-course on a small part of your overall topic. For example, if your course is on True Financial Freedom, then you could do a mini-course on just budgeting.

3) Be patient. Like all good things, a successful online course business will take time to cultivate. You need to commit to it for the long term. As you build an audience online, you may well feel as if you're talking to no one when you start out (and you won't be). Just stick at it. An online following is like a snowball. It will be very small at first, but it will get exponentially bigger as time goes on.

4) Feel the fear and do it anyway. When you're creating an online course, there'll be moments that push you way out of your comfort zone. Despite talking in front of hundreds of people a month at

our seminars, I was really nervous the first time I did a Facebook Live. It didn't feel natural at all! You have to push through the pain barrier at times like these. The fear of doing something is usually worse than just doing it, so go ahead and do it!

5)   Validate your idea before doing all the work. Just because you think your course will be a sell-out success doesn't mean it actually will be. Make sure you fully validate your idea with at least 10 people who fit your target demographic before you charge full steam ahead into creating your course.

The Near-Death Experience

Sitting upside down in a car at the age of 19, Brendon Burchard asked himself three key questions.

> Did I live?
> Did I love?
> Did I matter?

The answers to these questions led him to create and launch the world's largest online training business and allowed him to become the globe's highest-paid performance coach.

Only a few years earlier, Brendon had been sleeping in a spare room and was on the verge of bankruptcy. From that single bedroom, he wrote his first book, which catapulted him to relative stardom in the online world.

Now Brendon comfortably generates a seven- or eight-figure income from his myriad of online courses, live events, books and other resources.

All of this started with nothing. Brendon will be the first to admit that he started with nothing. He sees himself as 'just a normal guy' and yet he's achieved all this!

Brendon is now arguably the world's most successful online course creator. In addition to a whole range of online courses, he's also written several best-selling books, presented at ginormous live events and even been involved in coaching celebrities and former presidents!

Start a blog

You would be surprised at how profitable a blog can be. If I told you there are several bloggers who you've never heard of before but are earning more than a million dollars a year, would you be surprised? Thought so!

A blog can either be a stand-alone business or it can act as the portal to other parts of your online world.

Many people who create online courses will also have a blog as a way to attract and build a relationship with their prospective customers, who might then go on to purchase their courses and other online products.

In fact, I run a blog at www.millennialmutiny.com, which serves exactly this purpose. I use my blog as a way to add value to my community of potential customers.

Before you start a blog, you need to decide if you are using it as a stand-alone business or whether it will be a window into your online world to help sell other products.

Which of the routes you choose will massively affect how you go about starting and running your blog. The strategies and tools you need are far beyond the scope of this book, but I will direct you to some great tools and resources to get you started at the end of this section.

Just like with an online course, you can blog about almost anything. There's a ton of different blogs and websites out there that cater to all sorts of different niches and interests.

Some niches are easier to monetise than others and if you're treating your blog as a serious business, you should give this some consideration before you get started.

Alternatively, you can start a blog as a hobby that might also earn you a tidy income on the side. Importantly, make sure you blog about something you enjoy. As with all of these Passive Products, what you see on the surface of a successful blog often hides years of hard work and so you need to make sure you're enjoying the ride to ensure you go the distance.

There are so many ways to monetise a blog – it really surprised me when I started to learn about it all. You can make money from ads (when you see adverts on the side of a webpage), affiliate marketing (where you recommend other people's products and services), courses (if you also decide to create an online course) and other products you can sell to your blog subscribers (think PDF worksheets, podcasts, etc.).

When you get started with blogging you'll discover a whole new online world full of opportunities and excitement.

Five tips for a winning blog

If you're planning to start a blog, I have five tips for you:

1) Decide on your niche before you start – the most successful blogs have a tightly defined niche that is clearly targeted towards a certain type of person. If you try to speak to everybody, you often end up talking to nobody.

2) Before you begin, make sure you're setting off in the right direction. Is your blog going to be a hobby, a stand-alone business or a window into your wider online world? The answer to this

question will define how you set up your blog, the platform you use and your whole strategy.

3) Commit for the long term. For the first six months of blogging, you'll probably have a very small number of readers. But, if you follow the right marketing strategies, slowly they will start to appear. You have to stick at it and keep going when things seem like they are not working – success is probably just around the corner.

4) Be consistent. People will grow to know, like and trust you if you show up with new content at the same time each week.

5) Blog about something you love – it's the only way you will stick with it.

Passive takes patience

Like anything worthwhile in this life, getting up and running with your own Passive Product will take time and persistence.

If you're planning on writing a book or starting a blog, you have to be prepared to stay the course. It's very romantic to think if you build it they will come, but the reality is they probably won't.

Building an audience online takes significant time and effort and it can be tempting to give up at times.

For the first six months after I started my blog, I had essentially zero readers. It was really tough to keep writing and posting content every week when no one was listening. But, just around the six-month mark, things started to change.

Where before there was no one, now there was someone. Only a couple of people to begin with, but over time that number grew to tens and then hundreds and it's well on its way to thousands. My blog is still very much in its infancy, but I'm consistently getting upwards of 1,000 visitors a month.

There are many ways to grow your blog traffic – you could consider paid advertising on Google, for example, but this gets expensive. The best way is to reach out to the blogging community and collaborate with other bloggers. I've been invited to write guest posts for other bloggers (where you write an article for their blog) which means I then get access to their audience. In return, I will offer the opportunity for them to guest post on my blog and they can access my audience – a win-win situation!

Don't get me wrong, the traffic I get to my site is tiny in comparison to some of the bigwigs of the blogging world, but I don't need to speak to everyone. That's the beauty of the Internet. You just need to speak with your tiny little niche to make it work.

When you first start with any new venture or Passive Product, it takes some time to get off the ground. You have to do some learning and make some mistakes before things really take off, but that's all part of the experience. Just like in a physical business, you must pass through The Proving Ground in the online world as well before you can make it big.

But, for those who persevere, the rewards are potentially life changing! Keep at it and you'll get there. I promise.

Another thing that takes patience (and a lot of it) is building a Passive Income stream. Now we have finished our Journey through the *6 Steps,* we're ready to start the final ascent. We have arrived at base camp. Now is the time to take a little breather, check our equipment and get ready for our climb towards the summit. The summit of the mountain is the ultimate destination on our Journey, what I call the *Hallowed Ground:* and it's called Passive Income.

Summing Up Path 6d – Supplement Your Income Using Side-Hustles and Passive Products

In this chapter, we have learned about Passive Products – products which, once created, can continue to earn revenue with little additional work.

> Passive Products take lots of different forms.
> You could write a book, create an online course, make a music track, write a blog or many more.
> Passive Products often look easy on the outside, but they hide a lot of hard work and dedication.
> Once you get them going, though, Passive Products can be a fantastic way to create True Financial Freedom.

Do you think you could create a Passive Product? Do you have any special skills or abilities you could teach to the world? Do you have a passion you could write about in a book or blog?

Resources – Path 6d

Books

What better place to start than books about writing books! Here are some excellent reads that could help you to craft your literary masterpiece:

Release The Book Within

Jo Parfitt, Summertime, 2007

It would be remiss of me not to mention the book by my book mentor and editor, Jo Parfitt. This step-by-step guide will walk you through the process of writing a book from idea to finished article!

The Essential Guide to Getting Your Book Published

Arielle Eckstut and David Henry Sterry, Workman, 2010

It does what it says on the tin, really. It is one thing having a great idea and writing a book, it is another thing entirely to get it published. This book gives you the inside track.

DotCom Secrets: The Underground Playbook for Growing Your Company Online

Russell Brunson, Morgan James, 2015

Expert Secrets: The Underground Playbook for Creating a Mass Movement of People Who Will Pay for Your Advice

Russell Brunson, Morgan James, 2017

Russell is the famous chap who created a how-to DVD on making a potato gun and managed to turn it into a huge business. Russell's books give you the low down on establishing yourself as an expert in your niche and attracting your ideal clients.

People to Follow

John Meese, Platform University

www.platformuniversity.com

Not just about writing books, but also about creating an online platform to get your content (books included) noticed. There are lots of great articles and free resources to be found here.

Georgia Kirke

www.writebusinessresults.com

Although the content is focused on business books, it can be applied equally to most kinds of books. Definitely worth following if you are looking to write any kind of non-fiction book.

Michelle Schroeder-Gardner

www.makingsenseofcents.com

Michelle has built a blog with millions of readers which generates millions of dollars in revenue. Who better to learn the art of blogging from? Michelle even has a really great 'how to start a blog' course and the best part is it's free!

Grant Sabatier

www.millennialmoney.com

Grant was a millionaire by the age of 30, mainly due to the success of his blog. He has loads of great content and articles to help you start building an audience in the blogging world.

Online Courses

The Book Publishing Academy

www.bookpublishingacademy.com

Now the two worlds are colliding! This is a step-by-step online course about book writing and publishing. Usually available for a 30-day trial at a cost of £1. I suggest you make full use of the trial period and see if this is for you before continuing your subscription. As with many online courses, it is easy to start and then give up on something but keep paying for it. Make sure you only pay if you are using the content.

Some good online courses that teach you how to be successful creating online courses (confused yet?):

Amy Porterfield

www.amyporterfield.com

Amy is known as the queen of online courses and for good reason. She has created and launched several 7-figure plus online courses and is well known in the online marketing world for being the master of using online webinars to sell online courses. Amy has several courses from beginner to advanced. As with many of these options, I suggest you sign up for some of her free content first to see if you will be a 'good fit'.

Brendon Burchard

www.brendon.com

Brendon might have been one of the first people to successfully create an online course. In the past decade or so, he has built what is arguably the world's largest online course and coaching business, which has spawned many other products and even live events. Definitely worth checking out!

Online Course Platforms

Nowadays, you don't really have to be that techy to run an online course. In the old world you had to understand coding and HTML and all that stuff. Now, there are a ton of ready-made online course platforms that do a lot of the hard work for you:

Kajabi

https://kajabi.com

I run my whole online business on Kajabi, including my website, blog, online content and e-mail list. It is simple and elegant – how online platforms should work. If you are looking for an all-in-one online business solution, this is it!

Udemy

www.udemy.com

Udemy is not as fully featured as Kajabi but offers up a simple and easy to use system to get a course online quickly. This is better for smaller and cheaper courses. If you are planning a £1,000 change-your-whole-life type course, then Kajabi would probably be a better bet.

PART 3
THE HALLOWED GROUND – PASSIVE INCOME

Building and growing your Passive Income streams so you can be truly free

The
Hallowed
Ground

We have arrived at the final step on our Journey. We stand at base camp looking at the mountain peak, all the way up there in the clouds. As we begin this last PART of the book, I have some good news and some bad news.

The good news is that everything up until this point has been preparing you for the final leg of your Journey. This *PART* could well be the most exciting, rewarding, life changing thing you've ever done!

The bad news is that this final *PART* (like the *PARTS* that went before) requires some hard work. There's no such thing as a get-rich-quick scheme and there's no such thing as a get-rich-easy scheme. If these things existed, everyone would be rich.

Even things that seem really easy (let's use PewDiePie in his bedroom playing *Minecraft* as an example) often disguise years of hard work and dedication.

While your dream of True Financial Freedom is achievable (and probably achievable far faster than you believe possible), it won't happen overnight.

This final stretch of the road is the most difficult to travel. Like any good story, there's a challenge to overcome and a mountain to climb to reach your happy ending. But when you get there... by gosh is it worth it!

Ready for the final ascent?

Let's go!

Financial Freedom vs True Financial Freedom

You may have noticed as you read through the book that I use the terms *financial freedom* and *True Financial Freedom* seemingly interchangeably. However, where these terms are used, they're used intentionally.

Although similar in nature, these two things are different, and one generally comes before the other.

Although they both belong to the same club, financial freedom and True Financial Freedom have some differences that, although subtle, are very significant.

Financial freedom means that you can live your Perfect Life all day every day, doing what you love along the way.

You can achieve financial freedom as an employee, as a business owner, with a Side-Hustle or with any combination of these things.

I believe that once you're living the life you want to live, doing the work you enjoy, in the time you enjoy doing it, you can call yourself Financially Free.

If you've made it that far, you're probably among less than 1% of the population who can genuinely say that they are doing what they really want and love to do when they get up in the morning. The remaining 99%, to some extent, are doing things because they feel they have to – big difference.

But, this is not True Financial Freedom because you are still working to support your Perfect Life. It may be the best work in the world, work that you truly, dearly love, but it's still work – and the thing about work is we reach a point where we don't want to do it. Sometimes we don't want to do work *at all,* ever, and sometimes we just want to work at *something different.*

How about if you wake up one morning and decide you don't love what you used to? How about if you stop feeling like you want to go and do the work that filled you with passion and purpose five years ago? Humans, much like politicians (they're a different species, right?), sometimes decide we have changed our minds!

Things that we enjoyed previously no longer interest us in the same way (just ask my mum about the graveyard of myriad sports uniforms in our house as I was growing up!).

If this happens, you don't want to lose your financial freedom now, do you? Certainly not! This is where True Financial Freedom comes in. This means you can continue to live your Perfect Life even if you're not working at all – sounds good, right?

Like anything worth having, True Financial Freedom does not come easily and you must be prepared for a big journey ahead.

The Milestones on Your Journey

Just like any big trip, the Journey up the mountain to True Financial Freedom has many milestones and landmarks to look out for along the way – seven to be precise. No one goes from broke to True Financial Freedom in one go. (Unless you win the lottery, but that's actually a really bad way to get rich – most lottery winners end up broke again because they've not been through the learning process to be Financially Free. They haven't earned it – both literally and figuratively.) There are many hard miles ahead and it's good to stop every so often and pat yourself on the back for the progress you have made.

Look out for these seven milestones on your Journey up the mountain to True Financial Freedom:

1) Short-term emergency independence

It's a sad fact that over 30% of Americans don't have any savings at all and a further 25% have less than $1,000 saved up. This means that the vast majority of people are totally unprepared for even the most minor financial emergency.[1]

It could be an unexpected car repair, a higher than anticipated utility bill or some minor medical treatment. Any of these things could easily derail someone's finances if they have no savings at all.

The problem is, if there's no Emergency Fund in place, how do people pay for the emergency?

The answer is usually to turn to credit cards! This is a very slippery slope indeed. If there wasn't enough money to pay for the emergency in the first place, adding a load of credit card interest on top of your monthly expenses won't do anything to help matters!

As such, the first step on the Journey to True Financial Freedom should be to get your beginner Emergency Fund in place like we talked about in *PART 2* of the book. Aim for one month's worth of expenses in the first instance.

When you have your beginner Emergency Fund in place, not only have you taken the first step towards True Financial Freedom, you're also far less likely to be pulled off track.

2) Consumer debt independence

Once you have your short-term Emergency Fund in place, the next step is to tackle any consumer debt. I'm talking credit cards, overdrafts, personal loans, car loans, etc.

Many people feel trapped by their debt and they probably are. The problem is that most people go into debt in the first place because they're either living beyond their means (spending too much) or they have a short-term emergency they're unprepared for (see above).

This creates a seemingly never-ending debt spiral, which is really hard to get out of, but it can be done!

The key (as with most things) is to start making tiny steps towards the goal of being debt free.

Head back to *Step 4* if you need help.

3) Medium-term emergency independence

Once you've repaid any consumer debt that you had, give yourself a big pat on the back. Getting out of debt is arguably the hardest step on the Journey to True Financial Freedom so you can give yourself a massive cheer on getting this far.

Once the debt is gone for good, the next step is to establish a longer-term Emergency Fund. What if your car needs replacing or you need some more serious medical treatment?

A medium-term Emergency Fund allows you to cope with these mini-disasters with ease. Most importantly, having just repaid all the debt, it stops you having to go back to the credit cards when something goes wrong – which it will, that's just life!

My advice is to try and save 12 months' worth of expenses at this step in the process.

4) Cashflow independence

When you're cashflow independent, you have all the money you need each month to comfortably cover your expenses. This is more than *making ends meet*. This is more like *making ends overlap!*

At this point, it doesn't really matter where the money comes from – it could be your job, a business, a Side-Hustle or consulting gig – so long as the money you're earning (after tax) more than covers your expenses.

This is important because it means you're far less likely to fall back down the ladder to the previous steps. If your income is more than your spending, you no longer need debt and you'll consistently be able to save and invest more money.

Things just get better because as you save and invest money this then makes more money, which improves your monthly cashflow position even further and so it continues. It's a virtuous cycle!

5) F-you Money

I'm not sure if he invented it, but it was JL Collins who introduced me to the term 'F-You Money' and I like it.

F-You Money means that you can say 'F you' whenever you want to. This will most often apply to employed people, but you could equally apply the principle to self-employed people or business owners.

F-You Money is great because it allows you to stop doing something immediately if it's making you unhappy or damaging your health.

Although others might disagree, I think you should aim for two years' worth of expenses in the bank to say you have true F-You Money. Saving a year's worth of expenses sounds great (and it is), but 12 months is not that long and time flies when you're having fun.

The principle here is that if you have two years' money in the bank, you can just walk out of pretty much anything and you then have time on your side (and no financial pressure) to work things out.

If you've just walked out on a job you hate (or been fired or made redundant) then having a full two years to figure out what you want to do next can be incredibly empowering.

Although some will see spending the two-year savings pot as a step backwards, I think this is one situation where it's OK to take a small step back or tread water for a while if it allows you to find longer-term happiness and fulfilment.

Money is meant to be a tool to help us, after all!

6) Financial Independence

I think Financial Independence is where you have enough saved or invested that the income from your investments covers your *current* cost of living. This means you could stop working to earn income and you should see no changes at all to your lifestyle.

That's a pretty cool place to be!

Even people who are about to retire will very rarely have enough money to continue living the exact same lifestyle as when they were working, and I think it's a real shame.

If anything, I would like to have *more* money available when I retire than beforehand. After all, in 'retirement' (I have to use scare quotes because I'm not sure I ever want to retire in the traditional sense), I will have a lot more time to fill with amazing experiences and fun activities.

There are plenty of arguments against it and some disagree with the maths, but the 4% rule is a good place to start when working out how much you need to achieve Financial Independence.

7) True Financial Freedom

This is the big one. The Hallowed Ground.

When you achieve True Financial Freedom, you'll have saved and invested enough money so the return on your investments is enough to cover the lifestyle you really *want* to live – your Perfect Life.

Not the lifestyle you think you should be living or the one that your friends think is sensible: the lifestyle *you* really, truly, *want* to live.

Want to travel for six months of the year? You got it!

Fancy flying 1st Class? Add that to the list!

Would you prefer to hike everywhere and live in a tent? Then add that to your list.

This is *your* Perfect Life and *you* get to decide what it looks like.

Once you've figured out how much your ideal lifestyle will cost, you can work out how much money you need to achieve True Financial Freedom, like we did in *Step 2*.

The number might scare you at first (it certainly did for me), but this is why we have the seven milestones along the Journey.

You don't go from £0 to £4 million overnight (unless you win the lottery – but that's not a reliable path to reach True Financial Freedom). It takes a lot of time and effort and persistence. Just like anything else worth having in life.

The Happy Ending

It was January of 2017 when it hit me.

Only two years earlier we'd been struggling to pay our mortgage. We had started a new business and reached the end of our honeymoon period. This is the period after starting a new business where everything seems to go your way. You're winning clients and money is flowing in freely. But then, it all stops. Things got hard – really hard!

Looking back, this time is exactly what I call The Proving Ground for business owners. Only the entrepreneurs with the grit, determination and perseverance to keep going reach The Hallowed Ground on the other side and, on that January morning, it occurred to me we'd finally made it.

There was no fanfare. No drumroll, no big announcement. Just a bank statement through the letterbox (yes, we still got paper statements back then) which showed the previous month's income for our business.

At this point, finally, we could consider ourselves Financially Free. Our business was generating all of the money we needed not just to survive, but to thrive. We had all the income we needed to start living our Perfect Life.

What this means is we didn't have to do anything different for the rest of our lives and we could live our Perfect Life. Our business was generating enough income to pay all our foundation and basic expenses AND allow us to live our Perfect Life – all while maintaining a Savings Rate around (and in some cases above) the magic 50% number.

We had a healthy Emergency Fund in the bank, our investment portfolios were growing nicely and we were even in a position to help our friends and family members in times of financial need. How cool is that?

So, how can you achieve the same in your life?

I'm glad you asked.

Let's get started...

Two Paths to True Financial Freedom

There are two main *paths* you can take up the mountain to achieve True Financial Freedom. Each of them is equally valid. Each of them may be equally tough. Whichever one you choose (and you may actually decide to use both *paths* at different points in the journey), know this – you can reach True Financial Freedom.

In my work, I deal with clients from all walks of life, all of whom have achieved their own version of True Financial Freedom.

Some of my clients have enjoyed six-figure salaries, but some of them have achieved freedom (and seven-figure investment portfolios) while never earning more than £20,000 per year.

In fact, one of the first clients I saw when starting the Financial Planning business was in this exact situation. He'd been a mechanic his whole life. His income at the point he retired was around £21,500 per year and this was the highest his income had ever been. But he'd managed to accumulate an investment portfolio worth in excess of £1.6 million!

When I asked him how he achieved this incredible feat, his answer was as simple as it was humble: "Well I just lived within my means and invested the rest." It sounded so simple.

Now, of course, when something sounds this simple, it's rarely the case. The achievement of True Financial Freedom is rarely done overnight. It takes small actions, applied often and with discipline.

When I probed further, the real sacrifice became clear. He'd lived an incredibly frugal lifestyle. There'd been little in the way of family holidays or trips out. He'd not seen much of what the world had to offer.

In order to save money, he'd managed his investment portfolio himself, even as it became larger and larger and would've benefitted from professional input.

In fact, despite their apparent wealth and obvious financial freedom his wife burst into tears as he was telling the story of how the £1.6 million was made and how he now managed it.

When I asked her what was wrong (passing a tissue) she explained that despite achieving an impressive investment portfolio, her husband had become obsessed with managing it. He was spending six hours a day in the study tinkering with his investments. They were spending no time together as a couple and they certainly were not enjoying what a Financially Free life should look like.

He'd become obsessed with the means and not the end.

A few years later, I met Annie and Paul, a young couple in their early 40s. Having worked for some of the large corporate employers, they'd both left their jobs a few years earlier to pursue their passions.

During their corporate lives, they'd both been earning fairly average money. Neither of them had a salary above £30,000 a year. They had saved and invested diligently – preferring Property Investments to the Stock Market – and they now had a rental portfolio worth in excess of £1 million. While they were accumulating their property portfolio, they'd also set aside some money to travel and experience the world. Their photo reel was full of awe-inspiring views from exotic locations around the world.

They lived in a nice property in London, close to their burgeoning property empire, and they seemed relaxed and at ease with life. Having quit their corporate jobs a few years earlier, Paul was running a delivery firm and Annie was using her skills to do some consultancy work part-time in other businesses, while still looking after the rental portfolio. Even now, neither of them have what might be perceived as big or powerful jobs or businesses. But Annie and Paul are two of the most contented people I have come across, and two of the most comfortable around money.

They save and invest and make sure they're on track for a great future. But they also live for today – making sure they fill their scrap book with memories each year.

I tell these two stories for a couple of reasons:

1)   To show that you can achieve True Financial Freedom (and a seven-figure investment or property portfolio) without a huge income. In both cases, the people involved were earning something around the UK national average income. Neither had six-figure salaries or were born into wealth.

2)   To show that if you're not careful, the pursuit of that seven-figure portfolio can become the end and not the means. Then you know you're in real trouble. This is what happened to our mechanic friend. He'd become obsessed with the accumulation of his pot of gold and even more obsessed with not losing it. He'd become so obsessed, in fact, that he'd forgotten the reason he probably started saving the money in the first place – to be free!

If you're not careful, this could be you too. Although you must remain focused on your overall goal, please don't let it become an obsession. Remember the guidance in the previous chapters about saving for the future *and* living for today. Remember the Spend Half, Save Half rule. Please, whatever you do, try to be more like Annie and Paul than my mechanic friend – you will thank yourself for it later on.

Some of my clients have inherited money; many of them have actually given money away. Some of my clients have sold a business for seven figures; most of them have not.

The point here is that no matter your income, no matter your employment position, no matter your starting point, True Financial Freedom is possible for you.

What we're going to explore in detail in the final part of the book is Passive Income. So... what is it, how do we get it and just why is it so darn good?

Passive Income

There are only a very few ways to achieve True Financial Freedom and generally this is going to involve having so-called Passive Income.

Passive Income means you're earning money while you sleep. It means that you can be sitting on a beach somewhere while your bank account fills with money each and every day.

The words can be quite dangerous. There's a mysterious allure to this so-called Passive Income, and for that reason everyone's keen to sell you a method or a secret to get some of it, and fast!

There are millions of web pages dedicated to getting you Passive Income. Most of them are a waste of time. To start with there are the out and out scams, which, of course, should be avoided like the plague.

There are people who promise to give you their proprietary market trading secrets meaning you can beat the Stock Market every single day. Believe me, if these people really could beat the Stock Market, they'd be multi-trillionaires and wouldn't need to sell you anything above and beyond this in order to be rich.

Guaranteed returns?

Then there are the investments that offer guaranteed 15% returns per year. There's no such thing. If you see the words *guaranteed* and *investment* in the same sentence you should be very wary at best, and run a mile at worst.

Then you have those who are looking to sell a get-rich-quick scheme, or should I say a get-Passive-Income-quick scheme? Again, these are at best a waste of time and at worst a complete rip-off.

These people generally mean well. They *think* they've discovered the fountain of eternal wealth. Generally, though, they've got lucky.

They had the right idea or bought the right stock at the right time and it paid off big time. While this sounds very alluring, in most cases these things are million-to-one shots. Luck like this doesn't come around very often and (I'm really sorry to say) it probably won't happen to you.

Passive Income doesn't come easily. I believe that there are only two reliable and consistent ways to achieve truly Passive Income.

In order to find The Hallowed Ground of True Financial Freedom *and* Passive Income, you must become an investor.

If this is all a bit much to take in, please don't worry. We're going to walk through each of the methods to generate Passive Income in detail in the following chapters.

The majority of people begin this Journey from the beginning, so what better place to start with than the first step?

Ready? Let's go...

Enter True Financial Freedom (With a Bit of Help From His Buddy, Passive Income)

True Financial Freedom means you can continue doing all of the things you love to do, continue living your Perfect Life and stop doing the things you don't like. Just like that, at the drop of a hat.

True Financial Freedom means you could be sitting on a beach in Tahiti somewhere and still your bank account is filling with the money you need to live your Perfect Life.

Sounds pretty good, huh?

This is where we need some of that Passive Income I was talking about earlier. This is what this Passive Income thing is all about.

As I warned earlier, Passive Income does not come easily. There are plenty of people trying to sell you the dream of achieving Passive Income in record time, but it almost always takes a lot of hard work and dedication.

If you ever meet someone massively successful who didn't lose a ton of blood, sweat and tears, you can be sure the luck that person experienced was so rare it may never be repeated again.

The secret of Passive Income

The formula to generate reliable Passive Income is actually very simple. There's no secret or magic recipe as some people will tell you.

In fact, the rules of how to generate Passive Income are almost as old as money itself.

The paths that lead to them are not that exciting. There's no overnight transformation. Usually, a series of simple, small steps are taken that allow you, day-by-day, month-by-month, year-by-year, to build up a stream of Passive Income.

The best thing about Passive Income, though, is that once you get it started it's like a snowball.

The first part is always quite tricky, but as you continue to roll it gets bigger and bigger, until eventually it reaches critical mass.

The first bit of Passive Income can be re-invested to generate more Passive Income. That Passive Income can be re-invested again... (you get the picture).

Passive Income can be generated in a couple of different ways – that's what this next section of the book is all about.

Ready to have some of this Passive Income for yourself? Then join me one last time as we explore it in detail...

The Final Ascent –
Finding True Financial Freedom as an Investor

The vast majority of people who find True Financial Freedom do so as an investor.

The reason for this is simple: investments make money, with little to no work, even while you sleep. For this reason, they're the best and most attractive way to secure your True Financial Freedom.

All the other strategies in this book will require a fair bit of work on your part – even the Passive Products in the previous chapter take a lot of work in the first instance to get started.

Investing is different. Once your investments are set up, you can genuinely be sitting on a beach somewhere while your bank account fills with money.

The only challenge with investing is you need money to get started. Not a lot, necessarily, but some. This is why I've been banging on so much about your Savings Rate and putting money aside. Only by doing this can you begin investing and only by investing can you generate true while-you-sleep money.

Don't get me wrong, investing will take time to work its magic. But slowly and surely, your interest starts to earn interest. Dividends start to grow and earn more dividends and your tiny little investment snowball starts to grow larger. Eventually it becomes unstoppable to the point where many of my clients have investment income many times what they need – even for their Perfect Life.

The beauty of money is that once you have some, other people are willing to pay you handsomely for it (to borrow or have use of it, that is).

This manifests itself in many ways. The most obvious example is lending money to the bank. I say lending money, because when you deposit money with a bank, you're in effect lending your money to that bank. A lot of people are put off investing money because they don't understand it or say 'it's all smoke and mirrors'. So I think it's important you gain a basic knowledge of what investing is and why it works before we go further. I'm going to put my teacher's hat on for a moment and give you a little lesson in how a bank works.

How Banks Work

The main function of a bank is to make money. They like to tell you that they're 'there for you' and they spend millions creating all sorts of caring-sounding marketing slogans, but really they're there to make money. (There's nothing wrong with this; I believe in capitalism. I just think we should be honest about it.)

A bank makes money by either charging interest on loans or by investing money. In order to make loans or invest money, you need money to lend or invest in the first place and so, for that reason, the bank wants *your* money.

The bank wants to use your money (generally to lend to other people, ironically) and so they'll pay you an interest rate to borrow your money from you.

The bank will then invest this money or lend it to someone else (and in some cases both – the banking system has lots of strange ways to make the impossible possible). They hope that in doing so they can earn more on their investments or charge more in interest than they're paying you in interest.

Let's use a simple example:

You deposit (lend) £10,000 to your bank. They pay you an interest rate of 1.5% per year or £150.

The bank lends all your money to a local business that needs funding, but they charge that business 5% per year or £500.

At the end of the day (assuming no bad debts) the bank has made a profit of £350 on your money. Not bad really!

It's for this reason that, as a rule of thumb, you want to be a **lender** or **investor** and not a borrower. Lenders receive interest, borrowers pay interest (unless you have good debt like we spoke about in *Step 4*).

Although saving money with a bank is the most obvious example of investing money, it's also usually the worst example.

We all know that banks are paying record low-interest rates at the moment and they have been since the financial crisis – all the way back in 2008!

Many people see saving money at the bank as a safe and secure way to keep their cash, but the only real certainty when you put money with your bank is that you'll lose money. Or should I say, lose purchasing power.

You see, the rate of inflation usually outstrips the interest you'll earn on money left at the bank.

If you're earning 1% on your money, but inflation (the rising cost of goods and services) is running at 3%, in effect you're losing 2% of your money's purchasing power each year.

The bank is useful for storing the money you need for your Emergency Fund and any expenditure you plan to make in the next couple of years, but that's about it.

Any funds you have in excess of this should be invested in order to generate a better return. This is how you really start to grow your wealth.

The Stock Market is the first thing that springs to most people's minds when we talk about investing, so what better place to start than the best wealth-building tool of all time...

Investing in the Stock Market

When we talk about the Stock Market, a lot of people get a little clammy.

The idea scares them. *What if I lose money? What if it goes down? What if it goes wrong?*

These are all perfectly normal fears, but they're totally unfounded in reality, so long as you do your investing the right way.

Most people acquire their views on the Stock Market from the media and this is perhaps the worst place to go to get your financial advice.

For a start, the media reports on the negative events in the Stock Market about a trillion percent more than the positive events (OK, I exaggerate just a little, but I'm close).

This is totally ludicrous when you also consider that the market goes up about three times more than it goes down. (Research has shown that the market goes up around three years out of four.)

|||||||||||||||||||||||||||||||||||||||||||||||||||||||||||||||||||||||||||||||||||||||||||||||

 Over the 189 years to 2013, the US Stock Market, measured by the Dow Jones Industrial Average, went up in 134 years – or nearly 71% of the time.[2]

|||||||||||||||||||||||||||||||||||||||||||||||||||||||||||||||||||||||||||||||||||||||||||||||

This overly-pessimistic media coverage is often peppered with high-blood-pressure-inducing words like 'panic', 'turmoil', 'carnage' and, my personal favourite, 'bloodbath'. We're talking about the Stock Market, for goodness' sake!

All of this unfounded negativity means that many people miss out on the best wealth-building tool of all time: the Stock Market.

The Stock Market has made more people wealthy than anything else, I would bargain. But probably not in the way you're thinking.

When people think of the Stock Market, they might conjure up images of very, very (very) stressed people shouting at phones, each other, staplers and anything else that can be shouted at on trading room floors.

Indeed, this is a part of the Stock Market, but certainly not the part we wish to be a part of.

This is called **trading**. Those people on the trading room floors who look as if they're on the verge of a heart attack (many of them probably are – I'm serious) are trying to make money by buying and selling stocks, bonds and other financial instruments over very short periods of time. We're talking days, minutes, seconds and (in this computer driven world) sometimes milliseconds.

For you and I (and most of them too) this is a loser's game. It's a get-rich-quick scheme and they don't work. They'll make you get poor quick alright, but rich, not so much.

Some suggest that over 95% of people who practise so-called day-trading lose money.[3]

I invest other people's money for a living and I can't make money day-trading.

I tried it once and failed miserably. This was in my younger and more naïve years. I funded a trading account with £10,000 and tried to play the game. *I can do this*, I thought, *I invest money for a living, I can beat the market, I can be the 1% who make it in this game.*

Within about six hours I'd lost pretty much all the £10,000 and added around 10 years to my age in the process!

The only saviour – the £10,000 wasn't real money.

Fortunately, I was sensible enough to try this out in practise mode before doing it for real and I'd used a demo trading account.

There are plenty of online platforms where you can try out trading with fake money. I'm so glad I had the good sense to fail with fake money rather than real money.

Despite the fact I was using fake money, it was probably one of the most stressful days of my life. It certainly did my blood pressure no good!

Very quickly my usually calm, rational self became a nervous wreck. I was making bigger and bigger bets each time to make up my hypothetical losses.

If you ever think you're one of the 1% who can make it by trading, then I strongly suggest you open one of these dummy accounts and practise with fake money first. If you don't, I can almost guarantee you'll lose a lot of money very fast.

And when I say practise, I'm not talking about trying it for a day, getting lucky and then thinking you can hand in your notice and become a trader. I'm talking about years and years of consistent, successful, practise. Only then should you try this with real money (but you probably just shouldn't so let's move on!).

But I don't get it!

Many people mistakenly believe the Stock Market is really complex and scary. Naturally, people don't want to invest in something they don't understand (and you shouldn't).

The Stock Market (and all the associated financial markets) can be very complex and indeed parts of them are. There's all sorts of jargon floating around. Margin, alpha, beta, Sharpe, Sortino. In fact, the Stock Market pretty much has a language of its own.

The good news is you don't need to worry about any of that. At all!

Stock Market investing can actually be beautifully simple and I'm going to make it as simple as can be for you.

In a few pages, I'm going to show you the single thing you need to invest in to have a simple investing life.

Where I have to use jargon (and I will sometimes) I'll always explain what I am talking about – promise.

So what are we talking about here?

When I talk about the Stock Market, I'm talking about the thing that's created more rich people than anything else. This is *investing,* not *trading.*

Investing means we buy good companies and hold on to them for the longer term. It's over periods of years and decades that the Stock Market works its magic.

So what are we talking about when we say the 'Stock Market'? Well, put simply, a stock (or an *equity* if we use the lingo) is a share in a company (hence they're often called shares). If you buy a share in Apple you actually own a tiny, iddy bit of Apple.

You own a bit of all their spaceship-like buildings. You own a bit of their very clever design process, you own a bit of the App Store and, most importantly, you own a bit of the money that Apple makes. In case you've been living under a rock for the past decade, Apple makes a lot of money – A LOT!

The best wealth-building tool – EVER!

Despite all the negative media that surrounds it, the Stock Market makes money – a lot of money.

If we look at the FTSE 100 for example (that's the 100 biggest companies in the UK collected together into what we call an *index* so we can track how they're doing), it started at a figure of 1,000 in January 1984.

This year is significant because it was roughly when the first Millennials were being born (depending on the definition you use, but we'll go with it for now). I was born in 1987, so not long after the FTSE 100 came into existence.

At the time of writing, the FTSE 100 is at around 7,000. This means the value of the top 100 companies in the UK has grown seven times (or 700%) during the past 34 years – that's pretty impressive growth!

In fact, this represents growth of around 20% per year. Wow!

Presented with these facts, you might be wondering why few people invest in the Stock Market – good question. I often wonder the same thing.

I suspect the main reason is because of volatility. Volatility means temporary swings in value. The word *volatility* should not be confused with *loss* – they're two very different things.

Volatility means that the value of a share goes up and down over time. Volatility is perfectly normal in Stock Market investing.

Losing money means you've lost money – very different.

On its continuous march upwards, the Stock Market can and often does go through periods of significant volatility.

Let's take the financial crisis of 2007–09 as a great example. During this time, the FTSE 100 fell over 50% from peak to trough.

But, and here's the amazing thing, within about three years it had recovered all of that fall and was heading on to break new-record highs.

There's a simple fact about the Stock Market in general: it always goes up. It does so with periods of volatility but, over time, it always goes up. When it goes up, it often does so spectacularly.

Note when I mention the market always going up, I'm talking about *the market* in general. This refers to hundreds or thousands of companies at a time.

If you hold what I call a *market portfolio* (a portfolio of investments in hundreds or thousands of different companies across several different countries) then it will always recover from these temporary dips. Hundreds of years of Stock Market history have proved as much.

As we'll see a little bit later, these temporary dips in the market can actually turn out to be your best friend over time.

Anything you can do, I can do better!

Many people think they can beat the market – and this is where things go wrong. Spectacularly wrong.

Some people believe so strongly a particular company is set for greatness they put *all* their money into shares in it.

Putting all your money into the shares of one company is very risky indeed. I mentioned this in the previous section when we spoke about employee share plans.

You don't want to build up a ton of wealth in the shares of a single company. Like my ex-colleagues, this can make you go broke very quickly.

Other people will select a couple of companies to invest in, but it's still just a couple. A couple of firms can and do get into trouble and cost you a lot of money in the process.

So how do we avoid these problems?

Enter diversification

The answer to this problem is what we call in the investment world *diversification*. Put simply: don't put all of your eggs in one basket.

In investing, we don't want all of our wealth invested in the shares (basket) of just one company.

We want to spread our assets over a range of different companies so if one gets into trouble, it doesn't sink our whole ship.

When you have a selection of companies in your portfolio, if one has a bad year or a bad decade – or even goes bust – chances are there's another one having a great year to make up for it.

This is diversification: when one goes down, the other goes up and vice versa.

The best thing about diversification is that you can reduce your risk substantially *without* reducing your returns. This is one of the very rare times where you can have your cake and eat it!

Diversification is easy to get wrong, though.

Let me explain: when people put together a portfolio of shares, they're influenced by their own internal biases.

The most obvious of these is what we call *home-country bias*. This means you're more likely to invest in shares of companies based in your home country.

If you live in the UK, you're likely to invest more than you should in the UK. If you live in the US, you probably have too many US shares – you get the picture.

Investing all your assets in shares in one country will give you *some* diversification, but not a lot of it.

Sometimes an event impacts the Stock Market across the whole of a country. Think Brexit, for example. This has had a massive impact on the UK market, but not so much on the US.

For this reason, we want to invest not just across different shares, but across different countries as well.

We can take diversification one step further by investing in different *asset classes,* as they're known. An asset class is just a type of asset. A share is one type of asset, but property would be another, bonds another still, etc.

In the same way that events can impact on one country differently from another, the same is true for asset classes.

If there's a problem in the property market, this will not always have an impact on shares. A problem with shares could be good for bonds, and so on.

So how do I know what to invest in?

Put simply, you don't!

Sorry to sound so harsh, but it's very true.

As an individual investor, you have to appreciate you probably don't have a clue which shares or bonds you should be investing in.

If you did, you'd be a trillionaire by now – and if you're reading a book about financial freedom I'm guessing you are not a trillionaire.

I've tried investing in individual shares and to pick winners, but over the years I've reached the conclusion that I simply can't.

I invest people's money for a living. I have a ton of investment qualifications. I understand how the market works and how to play the game, but I still can't pick individual shares with any consistency.

Sure, I've had some really nice winners, but I've had my losers as well. Over time, the two have near enough cancelled each other out and I've been left with pretty much the average return in the market.

A good chunk of people who invest on an individual basis lose money. The bulk of the rest of them underperform the market (that is to say, in trying to *beat* the performance of the market, they actually end up doing *worse*).

A select few will outperform the market, but I suspect this is more to do with good luck than judgement.

There's a whole fund management profession dedicated to making investments for other people. These are individuals who get PhDs for fun. They are super, super intelligent. They're way smarter than I will ever be, but they still get it wrong at least half of the time. (Recent studies have concluded that professionals get it wrong just over half of the time.)[4]

So how do you actually get started in investing?

Well, the answer really is very simple.

First of all, you will want to invest in **funds** rather than individual shares. When you invest in a fund, you're investing in tens or hundreds of individual companies, meaning you have significantly reduced your risk. A fund also means that a fund manager is making all the decisions behind the scenes, saving you the time and bother.

Two investment strategies

The next thing you have to decide is what you believe about investments. In investment management, you have two main strategies to choose from:

1)   Actively managed fund
2)   Passively managed fund

1) Active management

Active managers will buy shares they think will outperform the market. They're trying to pick the winners and avoid the losers.

To be clear, many of them fail in this endeavour. They have all the tools they need, they have expert teams behind them doing countless hours of research and analysis, and yet the majority of active managers still underperform the market they're trying to beat.

The vast majority of academic research supports this assertion: most active managers underperform the market, especially over longer periods of time.[5]

However, as always, there are exceptions to the rule. A select few exist who seem to consistently outperform their markets over a long period of time.

The big question is whether you think you can pick these managers. In the Financial Planning business, we spend thousands of pounds and hundreds of hours each quarter researching which fund managers to hire to run money in client portfolios, and even then we don't always get it right.

We do a good job, but we're not perfect.

Active management also tends to cost more in fees. Fees will eat into your investment money and damage your returns over the long term, so it stands to reason that if you're paying fees, you need to be getting value in return.

As such, if you're going to be paying a bigger fee, you want to be darn sure you're getting additional value for your fee.

Let's say we have Fund A and Fund B that charge 1% per annum and 2% per annum, respectively. At first glance you might pick Fund A because it's cheaper. However, it could be that Fund B is performing at an average of 10% per year, whereas Fund A is only growing by 5% per year.

The problem is, the charge is a known future-cost and the performance is an unknown future-variable. The figures you get shown (and on which you make a decision) are based on the past and not the future. Because of this, it's hard to tell if you'll get additional value by paying more.

If you're not sure you'll get additional value and you don't have the time, expertise, knowledge, inclination or experience to do the research, then I suggest you look at passive investments.

2) Passive management

Passive investments are designed to track a particular market or index. If you buy a FTSE 100 tracker for example (a **tracker** is another name given to a passive investment fund), you're looking to track the FTSE 100 index. Remember, the FTSE 100 simply represents the biggest 100 companies in the UK. The fund will be managed by a computer to track the relevant Stock Market index – in this case the FTSE 100.

This means the fund does whatever the index is doing, and the index does whatever the market is doing.

For example, if we buy a FTSE 100 tracker and the FTSE 100 goes up by 5%, we'd expect our fund to go up by very nearly 5%. (The increase will be a bit less to account for fees, but fees are much smaller on passive funds.)

If the FTSE 100 falls by 5%, we'd expect our fund to fall a bit more than 5% (again to account for fees).

With a passive fund, you basically get what the market is doing. You get the average.

Getting average might not sound great, but when investing it's actually really good.

Returning to my previous example of the FTSE 100 and its growth since 1984, we determined that the average was around 20% per annum in simple terms.

If 20% per annum is average growth, then sign me up right here.

It's not to say that 20% will continue to be the average. When we are dealing with investments, past performance is no guide to the future. But even if we say the average return going forward will be half this amount – 10% a year – it's still pretty darn good!

Heck, even if we only get a quarter of the past return – 5% per year on average – that's still *fairly* good in my book. It certainly beats the measly 0.1% we'll earn in the bank at the moment!

For most investors, average performance will be better than the success they'd have trying to beat it.

Research has shown that the vast majority of people who try to beat the market fail miserably, so (you won't hear me say this very often) why even bother?

So, get to it – what should I invest in?

At this point you need to make a decision. You need to decide if you're an investor who knows what they're doing or if you simply don't have a clue.

Now let me be clear, there's a big difference between thinking you know what you're doing and *actually* knowing what you're doing.

I meet personal investors all the time who've made a bit of a mess of things. They think they're doing the right thing. They've done the research and read the books, but they've still put together a bad portfolio.

It's not because they're bad investors, or unintelligent. It's simply because they're human beings.

Human beings are riddled with biases and emotional behaviour, which makes them pretty bad investors by default.

Unless you can identify, acknowledge and then remove these biases, you'll make a hash of investing too – just like everyone else.

These biases become more prevalent when we're investing our own money. As a result (and I know this is tough to admit) you'd do a better job investing your friend's money than your own.

(P.S. Never, *ever* invest someone else's money – unless you don't really want to be friends with them anymore.)

If you know what you're doing you don't need me to explain how to build a well-diversified investment portfolio that sits on the efficient frontier of investments, and I'm not going to.

No, I'm not talking about *Star Trek!* If you don't know what the efficient frontier is, then might I be cheeky to suggest there's a possibility you don't know what you are doing?

If you've decided you don't really know what you're doing (and most people don't – so that's fine), you've a choice to make and I think the option you go for will depend on how much money you have.

You have two options here:

Option 1 – hire a professional to help you decide

You can hire professional help, like a Financial Planner, to build your portfolio for you. Of course, I've a large amount of self-interest in recommending this option so I thought I'd get it out the way.

A professional Financial Planner can help you figure out your objectives, find out your Freedom Figure and build an investment portfolio to help you get there. If you already have a Financial Planner and they're not doing all this for you (and much more), then you need a new Financial Planner!

The main objective of a good Financial Planner should be helping you identify what you want to do with your future, helping you discover the amount to achieve that and then building a robust Financial Freedom Fund to make this vision a reality – acting as your critical friend and keeping you on track along the way.

If your Financial Planner focuses only on investments, without doing all of this groundwork beforehand, then you probably need a new Financial Planner.

I'm a firm believer you should hire experts to do things that are potentially dangerous or damaging if they go wrong. Investing is a case in point. The stakes are high (your life savings and your future True Financial Freedom) and the damage if you slip up can be severe (think bankruptcy-and-losing-your-home-and-family severe).

I know nothing about teeth, so if I needed a filling or a tooth removed, I'd go to a professional dentist who knows what they're doing. There's no way you'd dream of attempting your own root canal, is there?

That's not to say I won't Google what's wrong with my teeth and research all possible treatment options before visiting the dentist, so I'm better informed. But when push comes to shove, it'll be the dentist's advice I follow – and it'll sure as heck be the dentist doing the work. I'm squeamish enough around teeth as it is to even imagine a DIY extraction with string tied to the doorknob!

I know nothing about most things. And because I don't, I call an expert for help.

Even when it comes to DIY, I'm utterly hopeless. Katherine will delight in telling you that when I aim to fix something around the house, I not only end up breaking whatever it is I'm trying to fix, but myself and the rest of the house in the process as well.

As a result, I call in an expert.

The same is true with investments. If you do them badly, you can do a lot of damage and lose a lot of money.

The good news: investing is one of very few things I do know a lot about. I've spent the past decade of my life dedicated to the subject. I've taken dozens of exams and have a Master's Degree in Financial Planning. As such, it's one of the few topics in this world where I do feel I know what I'm talking about.

The only problem is that Financial Planners are expensive (rightfully so) and if you're just starting out on your investment journey, you might have to find another way. The fees a Financial Planner needs to charge simply might not add value for you at the beginning of the True Financial Freedom process, or you might not be able to afford them.

Although many Financial Planners now operate without a minimum portfolio amount (the amount of investments you need to have to work with them), they will generally have a minimum fee level.

As a rule of thumb, you'll really benefit from the input of a good Financial Planner when your portfolio reaches around £100,000 or more. At this point, the fees of many Financial Planners will represent good value for money.

You might be thinking this means you have to do the whole thing without any help. That you have to go out and build a well-diversified portfolio by yourself, picking all of those funds and stocks and bonds.

The good news is there's a range of funds that have done it all for you and will make the start of your investing journey easier than you can imagine.

Option 2 – the done-for-you multi-asset fund

Before we get started here, I want to make clear that if you can afford a Financial Planner, you should go and hire a really good one. This will always be the best option and research has shown that people who hire a good Financial Planner are far more likely to achieve their goals, and retire much richer.

|||||||||||||||||||||||||||||||||||||||||||||||||||||||||||||||||||||||||||||||||||||||||||||||||||||

 People who receive Financial Planning advice retire on average £47,000 better off than those who don't.[6]

|||||||||||||||||||||||||||||||||||||||||||||||||||||||||||||||||||||||||||||||||||||||||||||||||||||

However, there's a sad reality in the UK, the US and most other markets that financial advice is expensive. Due to the rising cost of regulation and protection schemes (both a very good thing), Financial Planning has increased in cost over time. If you can't (yet) afford to hire an adviser, please don't fret – help is at hand. Enter the multi-asset fund.

A **multi-asset fund** is a single investment fund that does everything we've spoken about for you. It means you can buy a single investment fund and have a globally-diversified portfolio across shares, bonds and property with a few mouse clicks. What could be easier than that?

Three investment types

Before I go any further, let me explain the three main types of investment:

1) Shares – A share is a tiny bit of a company, like Apple, and we've discussed this in detail over the last few pages.

2) Bonds – A bond, in this case, is a loan. It could be a loan to a government (usually called *gilts* in the UK) or a loan to a company (usually called *corporate bonds* in the UK). Basically, you're lending the government or company money and, in return, they'll pay some interest and you'll get the original capital back at the end of the loan term.

3) Property – In this context, I'm talking about commercial property (i.e. shops, warehouses, offices, etc.) and not residential property (which we'll cover in detail in the next section).

There are several providers that offer these types of multi-asset funds – I like Vanguard or Legal & General if you'd like a passive fund and Prudential if you'd like an active version.

If you're just starting out, then Vanguard does a nice range of funds called LifeStrategy.

There are five LifeStrategy funds and each of them has a percentage attached to them – 20%, 40%, 60%, 80% or 100%.

The percentage refers to how much of the fund is invested in shares (the rest is in bonds). As you climb the spectrum you have more shares in your portfolio. As a result, you have a greater potential for long-term returns and a greater potential for short-term volatility (which we now know isn't a cause for concern).

You can buy these funds from a whole range of brokers or 'platforms' as they're known online. We don't need to concern ourselves with what these things mean at this point. You just need to know these are the providers you need to visit to buy these funds.

If you're looking for a place to build a portfolio of several funds or investments, I suggest you take a look at AJ Bell YouInvest. We use the advisory arm of AJ Bell in the Financial Planning firm and recommend them to clients, and we're very happy with them as a provider.

If you want a super simple way to buy the Vanguard funds, though, you can go to Vanguard themselves. They have a simple and low-cost online service, which you can use to buy the LifeStrategy funds in either an ISA or a General Account.

I'm trying not to be too UK-centric in this book, so it can benefit people all over the world, but I'll include a brief explanation of the difference between an ISA and a General Account at the end of this chapter in the *Resources* section. For the moment, if you have an ISA allowance available, you want to be using the ISA.

Just visit www.vanguardinvestor.co.uk (or .com for those in the US) and click on 'get started' – the system will walk you through the rest.

Just for full disclosure, I don't have any referral or commission arrangement with Vanguard or any of the other providers mentioned. I do not get a bean if you do business with them. I mention them only because they've done a good job for me and my clients. They're financially stable businesses and have a good track record in their field.

If you're in your 20s, 30s or 40s

I'd suggest you look at the higher end of the Vanguard LifeStrategy fund spectrum (the 80% or 100%) versions. You've time on your side and you could be investing for many years to come. If the market has one of its frequent temporary dips at some point (and it will) then you've plenty of time for it to recover.

When you get to your 50s, 60s or 70s

You might want to be a little more cautious, but not too cautious – being conservative is one of the biggest reasons people don't reach True Financial Freedom! Even at this stage in life, I'd probably plump for the 60% or 80% version, so you've a little more in shares than you do in bonds.

The riskier your portfolio, the greater the returns will be. But as we've just seen, it's not really risk at all – just temporary periods of volatility. As I've alluded to, these periods can be your very best friend. Here's why...

Pound Cost Averaging

Oh no, more jargon!

Pound Cost Averaging means we're buying into the market at all sorts of different points in the cycle. Sometimes we'll buy when the market is high, sometimes we'll buy when the market is low.

When we talk about Pound Cost Averaging, we're talking about a simple concept (like many things in the investment world) with a complicated name.

Pound Cost Averaging is your friend if you're investing on a regular basis – and let's face it, most of us will be.

Very rarely we might be lucky enough to have a lump sum to invest – from a bonus at work or the sale of that rare painting you bought for a pound at a boot sale (no, me neither) – so when you can afford to, you'll begin investing on a regular basis.

If you do have a lump sum to invest, though, hold your horses – more on this in a moment.

When you're investing regularly, you'll be investing in dribs and drabs when you have the money.

If you've followed the previous steps, you should've been focusing on your Savings Rate and have a pretty good idea where it's at and what you'd like it to be in future.

Having already built up your Emergency Fund and followed the other steps on Building Financial Resilience, you're ready to start investing.

Let's assume that you're going to invest £100 per month. I'm not saying this is any sort of target (you should be saving more if you're serious about True Financial Freedom) but it will keep the following example simple.

How Pound Cost Averaging works

It's when the market is low that Pound Cost Averaging works its magic. Let me explain.

Let's say we're looking to invest £100 per month for three months (I told you this was going to be a simple example). As an alternative, we could invest £300 in the first month as a lump sum payment.

Pound Cost Averaging – A simple example, over three months

Let's say in month one that a share in our fund is worth £1.

a)   If we're investing monthly – we buy 100 shares (£100/£1) in month one

b)   If we invest our lump sum, we buy 300 shares (£300/£1) up front

In month two, the share price of our fund has fallen to £0.50. *Oh no,* you think. *I've lost money!* Not so fast...

In month two, if we're investing monthly, we can now buy 200 shares (£100/£0.50). In our monthly investing example, we now have 300 shares.

In month three, the share price in the fund has gone up to £2.

In our monthly investing example, this means we can buy 50 shares (£100/£2).

So where does this leave us?

In the lump sum example, we now have 300 shares worth £600 (300 shares x £2 per share) – not too bad for a £300 investment!

However, in the *monthly investing* example, we have 350 shares worth £2 for a total of £700 (100 shares + 200 shares + 50 shares = 350 shares x £2 per share = £700) – a whole £100 more!

The reason for this is the fall in value in month two. It meant we could buy more shares for our money, which went up in value later on.

Clearly, this is a very extreme and simplified example. It's incredibly unlikely that anything you'll be investing in will be that volatile (if it is, you've probably invested in the wrong thing) but hopefully you get the point.

If you're investing for the long term (which you will be) and you're investing regularly (which you'll also be) then the temporary falls in the market can be your best friend.

In fact, when the market falls by more than around 20% from a previous high, I try to increase my Savings Rate just a little bit more. The Stock Market is on sale and I want to buy as much as I can at a low price!

When you're investing money on a monthly basis, you should Pay Yourself First – the direct debit to your investment provider should always be the first to leave your account after payday.

So, what if you have a lump sum to invest? Then how should you do things?

Investing Windfalls

If you have a lump sum of money to invest, you need to think carefully about how this money will play a role in your future.

It's not very often these lump sums come along, and they should be cherished.

It could be you've received a bonus at work or you've sold a business. Perhaps you've lost a loved one and received an inheritance.

In any case, lump sums are often a cause for confusion for many people.

There's a lot to think about when you have a lump sum of money. Should I go and blow it on a nice holiday? Should I pay off my debts? Should I save or invest this money?

The answer could well be some or all three of these things.

Of course, how you choose to use the money will first of all depend on the size of the lump sum. These things are all relative, but if you have a lump sum that's, say, 2x your usual monthly income, it's no doubt a significant sum of money, but probably won't mean reaching True Financial Freedom right away.

On the other hand, if you've just inherited £2 million from your great aunty Flo, this could be a life-changing sum of money.

Invest the 90/10 way?

There are no hard and fast rules, but I like the 90/10 method for managing lump sums.

When I receive a big lump sum of money, I tend to use the first 90% to pay off bad debts – if I have any – and if not to invest for the future.

The remaining 10% I do whatever I want with. Go on holiday, buy a car, go for a fancy meal. It doesn't really matter. Life is for living so go and have a little fun!

You can, of course, create your own set of rules, but I think the 90/10 split is a good place to start.

So how to invest a lump sum?

When people are thinking of investing a lump sum, many of them will think about Pound Cost Averaging into the market.

Let's say you have £120,000 to invest (lucky you).

You could put all of it into your chosen investment fund(s) in one go.

Alternatively, you could invest £10,000 per month for 12 months, hoping to even out the price you buy in at.

Whether or not you should Pound Cost Average the money into the market is a topic for debate.

When you're investing on a regular basis (as most people are), Pound Cost Averaging is hard-baked into the process – you have to do it because you're investing regularly out of your income.

With a lump sum investment, you have the choice. *Do I invest it all now, or drip-feed the funds into the market over time?*

There are many schools of thought on this subject. My suggestion is to invest the money as soon as possible.

It might seem counterintuitive and contradictory, but there are good reasons why you'd want to invest all the money right away as follows:

1)   The market goes up roughly three years in four and it goes down roughly one year in four. For Pound Cost Averaging to work, the market has to go down during the period in which we're investing.

If we're investing our monthly excess income over periods of three or four decades, the market's bound to go down over that period of time at some point.

Over a single year, however, the odds are in favour of the market going up.

As such, if we invest all the funds on day one, we have a nearly three in four chance of being better off a year from now.

2)   Money that's invested earns dividends. No matter what's happening with the capital value of your investment, most companies pay dividends – or income – each year. The earlier you invest, the earlier you can get your hands on some of that income.

3) Money that's not invested is being eroded by inflation. If we put money in the bank in the current environment, the only outcome we can expect is that we lose buying power.

Given the ultra-low interest rates currently on offer and inflation (which is running at a higher rate), if we leave money in the bank, we're simply asking to make a loss. This is not an issue with monthly investments out of your income, because you don't actually have the money until you have it paid into your account each month. With a lump sum, things are different. If you don't invest it right away, the money will just sit in the bank gathering dust (losing purchasing power because of inflation) – and you might just spend it.

Unlike market losses, which are actually temporary periods of volatility, losses due to inflation are real and permanent.

Hopefully these reasons will convince you to invest any lump sums all in one go, but if not, then go ahead and *average in* to the market. The most important thing is that you invest the money in your Financial Freedom Fund and that you don't fritter it away!

Having now looked at the Stock Market in detail, we move on to consider the other big wealth-building tool: property!

Investing in Property

When I look at my clients in the Financial Planning business, almost all of them have built up their wealth either using the Stock Market or property – or both.

These two things are, by a massive margin, the main source of Passive Income for most of my wealthy clients. And for good reason: they work.

Investing in property can mean different things to different people, but most will picture buy-to-let property. Basically, this means buying a house or a flat and then renting it to someone else.

You benefit from the rental income that's produced and any uplift in value in the property over time.

Unlike the Stock Market, which is an open and widely-traded market, with second-by-second deals and valuations and (generally) very good liquidity (meaning you can sell your investments when you need to), the property market operates on a deal-by-deal basis.

There's no main exchange that brings buyers and sellers together. Each deal is negotiated as a separate event and the process is usually concluded by the buyer's and seller's respective solicitors.

Property has made a lot of people very wealthy. In the UK, especially, we seem to have an infatuation with property and seem to believe it will go up in value indefinitely.

Over time, property in the UK (and indeed in many other countries) has enjoyed impressive growth. However, as with all major markets, the property market can and does go through downturns.

In the financial crisis of 2007–2009, UK property prices fell by around 30%. Although property has generally gone up in value over time (and impressively so) it's not so immune from falls in value as you might have thought.

The reason people often think of property as this ever-increasing pot of money is that when the value falls, you don't really feel it as much, unless you happen to be trying to sell at that moment in time.

As I said, the Stock Market is valued on a second-by-second basis. Usually you'll have online access to your portfolio so you can see every little up and down, every single day. I'm a huge fan of technology and apps, but when it comes to Stock Market investing, I'm not sure they are actually a good thing.

When making investments in the Stock Market, one of the main mistakes people make is checking the value too often. The Internet just makes this 100 times easier.

In the property market, on the other hand, when the value falls, you don't always know about this. Although you may hear anecdotal stories on the news, you never really know what a property asset is worth until you try to sell it. Only then will you figure out what someone is willing to pay.

I think for this reason, some people find property a little less high-blood-pressure inducing than the Stock Market, but this shouldn't really be the case.

A lot of people ask me which is better: the Stock Market or Property Investments. My answer is usually: "It depends."

Property is a very different animal than the Stock Market; however, it can be a very powerful wealth-building tool.

Looking at the returns of the whole Stock Market and property market over time, the Stock Market generally delivers a slightly higher return on average, but this doesn't tell the whole story.

When making Property Investments, you have far more influence over the process. Which property will you buy? Will you do any work to it? What area is it in? Is the location likely to experience a boom? All of these things and much more will determine your success in the Property Investment game.

Although I'm not a property investing expert (you can buy many books from people who are), I've advised hundreds of clients on their Property

Investments. At this stage I think it's useful to summarise the differences between Property Investments and investing in the Stock Market.

Individual assets

As mentioned above, each property is an asset in its own right, which is distinct and separate from all other properties. Even two houses right next to each other can be very different in terms of their space, price, state of repair, decorative style, etc.

For some people this is a blessing – for others a curse.

Some people love the fact they can pick a specific property in a specific location that's in need of a bit of TLC and do some work to the property to add value – others will want an investment that's as hassle-free as possible.

Speaking of work...

Improvements and works

If you invest into a share in a company or a fund, you don't really have any influence over the value of that company (unless it's a company you own, but we already know this is different from investing in the Stock Market).

Let's say you buy shares in Amazon. Other than what you personally buy on Amazon (which I can assure you is totally insignificant in the context of Amazon's total revenue), you can't change how the company works or how much money it makes.

With a property, however, you can change a lot of stuff. You could simply give it a lick of paint to make things seem a bit fresher. Perhaps you want to put in a new bathroom or change the kitchen. You may even want to add an extension to the property.

If you're doing work to your own home, you're generally aiming to create something you like. Although money will be a consideration, of course, the general objective is to make the house somewhere you want to live and create a space where you enjoy spending time. When you're doing work on an investment property, however, the aim is to make money.

You could be aiming to increase the rental value of the property. This could be achieved using any of the above improvements. Or you might be looking to add to the capital value of the house. A worthwhile piece of property work will achieve both!

The mistake I see so many people make is they work on their investment properties in the same way they work on their own home – they focus on things they like. This is dangerous as it means making money is not the focus.

When it comes to interior design, there are loads of expensive things out there that could take your fancy. These could be great in your own home, but they're probably not suitable for an investment property.

When you're doing work on an investment property we're looking for maximum impact with minimum cost. *How can I achieve the look we're aiming for with the lowest possible spend?* – this should be the aim.

People also often assume they need to do a property up to an ultra-high standard to secure a tenant.

Although this might be true in some locations, in most places you don't need 5-star luxury to win over a tenant. Clean and simple will do the job in most cases.

Make sure you look at the competition. Check out what other rental properties in the area look like and what work has been done. Perhaps even be cheeky and go and have a look at some of them. This will all give you valuable insight into the level of work (and the amount of money) you actually need to put in and could help prevent you from getting carried away.

Repairs and renewals

Unlike an investment in the Stock Market, which does not need any looking after (from you anyway), a Property Investment can create all sorts of unexpected drama.

Perhaps the roof starts to leak or the boiler breaks down. As a landlord, it's your responsibility to arrange repairs for these things and to pay for them!

This is a major unknown because property repairs are unexpected. They don't work on any sort of schedule.

In addition to the repairs, you'll need to service and maintain the property each year, just like you would with your own home. Perhaps the boiler will need servicing, the gutters need clearing, etc. All of this must still be done with a rental property.

Unlike a Stock Market investment, which is very unlikely to cost you more money once you've made it, a Property Investment almost certainly comes with an element of future cost ¬– some of this will always be unknown.

Even new-build properties have their problems, and though they might not need much in the way of maintenance, they often have service charges or other costs that need to be taken into account.

Location, location, location

We all know how important location is when choosing a property to live in. It's certainly no less important when picking an investment property.

When you're choosing a home, the location will generally be important because of the amenities and transport links and local jobs – these are things important to everyone. When picking your own home, you might also be influenced by other factors unique to you. Perhaps your mum lives down the road or you want to be right next to your favourite café.

When picking an investment property, you're looking to choose an area likely to increase in value. Just like the Stock Market, the property market can't be predicted with any certainty. But you can look at some factors to see if an area is up and coming or down and out.

Think about whether there are new transport links going into an area, or whether a high-quality school is about to open. These factors are likely to increase the value of nearby properties.

Of course, you need to try to keep ahead of the curve. It's no good buying in once everyone else has already done so. You need to keep your ear to the ground and take your time. Once they've decided to buy an investment property, some people get too excited by the whole thing, rush, and make a mistake.

Leverage

When people buy a property, many do so with a mortgage. This means you're borrowing money to fund an investment.

In the Stock Market, this would be considered very risky. In the property world, it's commonplace. I'm not sure why we've become so accustomed to borrowing money to fund investments (in property) in this way, but it's a feature of the buy-to-let landscape and one that needs some further analysis.

When you borrow money to invest you're using so-called *leverage* or *gearing*. Quite simply this means you're using someone else's money to make an investment in your own name.

When making an investment, using leverage usually increases your possible gains (as you're investing more money) but it also increases your possible losses (because if the property goes down in value, you'll still owe the bank their money). As such, it's a tool to be used very carefully.

When people take out a mortgage to fund an investment property, they're hoping the rental income will be more than enough to cover the interest payments on the loan. Until recently, in the UK, there were generous tax breaks on mortgage interest payments, but these have mostly been pulled away.

If an asset is growing at a higher rate than you're paying on the mortgage interest, using leverage will generally make you better off. But you have to appreciate that, in doing so, you're taking on more risk.

Let's look at some simple examples. Imagine you have £50,000 to invest. You could invest this in the Stock Market without using any leverage, or you could use the £50,000 to put down as a deposit on a property worth £200,000, using a mortgage to cover the remaining £150,000.

For simplicity, we can assume that both the Stock Market investment and the Property Investment generate capital growth of 5% per year and income (dividends or rental income) of 4% per year.

Finally, we can assume that the interest rate on the mortgage is 3% per annum.

(Please note these are not assumed or historical returns on these assets, just numbers we're going to use for this example.)

Ten years later, you wish to sell your investments and realise your gains.

With the Stock Market investment (assuming you re-invest those dividends) you will have a total of £122,567 – not too bad!

With the property, you've been collecting a rental payment of 4% of the property value each year (£8,000), but you've been paying 3% interest on the mortgage of £150,000 a year (£4,500), meaning you have £3,500 left. If we assume you're also paying around 20% of your rental income for repairs and services (which is fairly typical), this takes another £1,600 out of your rental income, meaning you're left with £1,900 per year.

Over 10 years, this means you've collected £19,000 net rental income.

The property is worth around £329,000 at the end of the 10 years and you go ahead and sell it. You still need to repay the mortgage of £150,000, meaning you have £179,000 left. I'm going to assume the costs of sale are £4,000, leaving you with £175,000.

If we add back in the £19,000, we're left with a net figure of £194,000.

At first glance, you might come to the conclusion that the Property Investment is better – in this artificial example, it is!

What this doesn't take into account, however, is the uncertainty of the market. Perhaps your property does not go up by 5% per year (it could fall in value). Perhaps your tenant moves out and you can't find a new one (more on this in a second). Perhaps you have a larger-than-expected repair bill because the boiler has broken down.

All these things and much more can eat into your profit margins.

Perhaps the biggest risk of all, though, is interest rates. If the interest rate goes up on your mortgage, the cost of borrowing the money gets higher, which means you have less left over from your rent collections each month.

In the above example, if the 3% interest rate climbs to 4%, you're now paying £6,000 in interest each year, meaning you only have £2,000 left. Deduct the £1,600 for expenses and you only clear £400 at the end of the year.

You don't need me to tell you that if the mortgage interest rate goes to 5%, you're left with a negative return each year!

Because of this additional risk, you should *expect* a higher return on a rental property if you're using leverage, but be aware that things can and do go wrong.

Leverage is a tool that's made a lot of people very rich. It's also made a lot of people very broke!

Void periods

The final main difference between Stock Market and Property Investments are so-called *void periods*. This is simply a period when you don't have a tenant. No tenant = no rent – simple!

When you buy a new property, unless it already has a sitting tenant, you'll almost certainly have a void period to begin with. It will take a bit of time (perhaps a lot of time) to prepare it, market it, find a tenant, sign all the legal documents and get them moved in.

You need to be sure you can afford any mortgage on the property during this period (and any future void period) because even though you don't have a tenant paying you, the bank still wants its mortgage payment made on time each month.

A void period can be the difference between a profitable property and a loss-making property.

Using our example above, it would only take a void period of three months to pretty much wipe out any profit over the whole year.

As such, you need to be very careful when selecting a property and make sure there's a healthy rental market for the property you're thinking of buying.

How about flipping houses?

Although some people buy houses, do them up and then aim to sell them shortly after for a profit (so-called flipping), I don't think this really creates True Financial Freedom.

Don't get me wrong, if you're good at it, you could use the money you make to invest and create financial freedom. But developing houses in itself sounds like a job to me. It certainly is not Passive Income.

As such, you may wish to start a property development business, but you have to appreciate that you're creating yourself a job if you do so. It could be a job you love and are passionate about, which is great, but it's a job nonetheless. We won't talk about it anymore here but, again, there are loads of great books if you think this might be for you.

Investing in Everything Else to Gain Your Financial Freedom

Once I've spoken about Property Investments and the Stock Market, most people will say something like: "Yes, but how about [insert latest fad investment here – Bitcoin, Pokémon Trading Cards, Wine, Old Comic Books, etc.] – won't that help me to get rich quick?"

The simple answer is NO!

Don't touch this stuff with a barge pole.

There is always a next-big-thing investment. At the time of writing the best example is Bitcoin and other cryptocurrency taking the world by storm only a few months ago.

This is just the latest in a long, long line of fad investments that have been and gone over the years.

I could go on for hours about all of the different examples, but that would waste everyone's time. If you're serious about True Financial Freedom, you need to forget about all the other stuff out there. It's a waste of time and will probably cost you a lot of money.

By the time the Bitcoin story made the mainstream, it was already trading at over $8,000 per coin. Fast forward a few months and it had reached the heady heights of $20,000 per coin. At this point the bubble was in full swing. Bitcoin was all over the telly, people were talking about it in the pub. It was THE NEXT BIG THING!

Until it wasn't. In the few short months that followed, Bitcoin fell to $10,000, then to $8,000, then to $5,000 and at the time of writing it's trading at a lowly $3,000 per coin.

The people who got in early would've made a significant gain (even at the current price). These were the people who either took almost no risk (Bitcoin could be created very easily when it first came out) or who took a lot of risk (by buying into the whole Bitcoin concept before it had been proven). In either case it's more luck than judgement that has made them wealthy.

For most of us, by the time we hear about the next big thing, it'll be too late. Much too late.

Better to avoid these fads altogether and focus on the two investment tools that have always worked and always will work (not the latest tool that is working now).

Property and the Stock Market have been around for hundreds of years and have made countless generations of people wealthy without fail. Why would you want to do anything different? I certainly wouldn't.

Putting it all Into Action

Whichever investing option you choose (and you may well choose both of them – many of my clients do) you have to be aware that progress will be painfully slow at first – you may feel like giving up. But you must hold your ground. If you're investing in shares, there's a good chance you might not have that much to put away each month to begin with, but it's important you begin. The first £100,000 will always be the hardest and it probably seems impossible when you first start out but, over time, the snowball will begin to grow.

Let's use some examples to show us the impact of this snowball effect in action. For this illustration, we're going to assume that you're starting with £0 in the bank and you start saving £10,000 per year, earning a 7% return each year. At this pace (assuming you don't increase your £10,000 annual savings) you will have £100,000 after around 7.8 years – seems like quite a long time, huh!

Once you reach that first £100,000, though, the magic of compound interest starts to take over. If you continue to add £10,000 to your savings each year, the next £100,000 takes just 5.1 years, the third £100,000 3.7 years, and so on.

What's especially amazing is it takes just 6.3 years to go from £600,000 to £1 million. What this means is that once the snowball gets going, it takes less time to accumulate an additional £400,000 than it did the first £100,000. At this point, most of your return is just interest on existing savings.

OK, so we're probably getting a little carried away. The important thing at this point is to begin saving. It may be that you only have £25 or £50 a month to put away, but that's a great start. The key here is to begin.

If you're planning to purchase a rental property, there's a good chance you need to save some money in the first place even to fund the deposit if you plan to use a mortgage. Again, the important thing here is to just begin – even if the goal seems a long way off, it doesn't mean it's not worth trying.

Summing Up

In this chapter, we have learned about the very best tool to help you achieve True Financial Freedom: investments.

Investments come in all sorts of shapes and sizes, but you only need to understand and use two of them:

> The Stock Market is arguably the best wealth-building tool of all time.

> It has bad press, but only because the media loves to talk about when the market goes down, but never when it goes up.

> In reality, the Stock Market as a whole always goes up over time.

> Property is another good wealth-building tool.

> With a Property Investment you can use leverage (borrowing) to fund your investment, which can increase returns, but it also increases risk.

> You don't need to invest in any of the *next big things* – they almost always go wrong.

> Stick to property and the Stock Market – these wealth-building tools have worked for hundreds of years and continue to work today.

Which kind of investment would be right for you? Could you open an investment account today and get started?

1 www.cnbc.com/2017/06/19/heres-how-many-americans-have-nothing-at-all-in-savings.html
2 www.gurufocus.com/news/274000/the-stock-market-a-look-at-the-last-200-years
3 https://vantagepointtrading.com/whats-the-day-trading-success-rate-the-thorough-answer/
4 https://blogs.cfainstitute.org/investor/2018/12/21/analyst-forecasts-lessons-in-futility/
5 www.evidenceinvestor.com/active-will-continue-to-underperform-for-two-big-reasons/
6 https://ilcuk.org.uk/financial-advice-provides-47k-wealth-uplift-in-decade/

Resources

People to Follow

JL Collins
https://jlcollinsnh.com

Websites

Vanguard
www.vanguardinvestor.co.uk

Legal and General
www.legalandgeneral.com

Prudential
www.prudential.com/#invest

AJ Bell Youinvest
www.youinvest.co.uk

Summing Up – Everything!

This Summing Up section is a little different to the others because, my friend, we've reached the end of our journey together... or perhaps it's just the beginning?

Some believe True Financial Freedom comes to those who get lucky. Those for whom things just seem to fall into their lap. Some believe True Financial Freedom only comes to people who are special and it could never happen to someone like them.

There are people who've found True Financial Freedom by luck, but I can assure you they're the exception and not the rule.

The vast majority of people who reach The Hallowed Ground of True Financial Freedom do so not by accident, not because lady luck was on their side. They get here because they want to. They really, really, *really* want to!

That's what makes the difference.

If you ask people on the street if they'd like True Financial Freedom, almost everyone is going to say yes – who wouldn't?

If you ask the question 'are you willing to do what it takes to get there?' – that's where people start to stutter.

You see, there isn't that much that separates those who reach True Financial Freedom from those who don't. The only real difference is that those who get here have had the determination to make it happen. They've sacrificed, they've worked hard (super hard), they've dedicated themselves to the Journey and then one day they made it.

I believe everyone has the capacity to reach True Financial Freedom – you don't have to get lucky or be 'special'. You just have to want it badly enough and focus your energy on making it happen.

But the destination is only a part of what makes this trip so great. On the Journey, you'll probably discover things about yourself you never knew existed. You'll learn new skills, make new friends and contacts, perhaps start a business or even one day (dare I say it) change the world.

I've experienced all of this and more and perhaps, just maybe, in a tiny way, I've changed the world too.

When I committed to finding True Financial Freedom, I can assure you I was as normal and as average as the next guy. I don't have celebrity parents and I didn't have a viral video of a cat that gave me 10 million Facebook followers to start with. My Journey started from humble beginnings.

I started, first as an employee, using the tips and tricks in this book to leverage and maximise my work package. I used the money I saved as an employee to start a business, increasing my income further. I went through The Proving Ground – arguably one of the hardest times of my financial life. As my income increased, I started to invest – just a little at first – adding to my pot each month. I focused on increasing my income, while also building my Savings Rate as I went. Nothing that I've done is rocket science. It's all about taking small, simple steps, applied consistently and over time.

The irony is, having originally started on this Journey to escape work, I've fallen *more* in love with the work I do.

You see, it was never the work that was the problem. It was the organisations I was doing the work for and the financial stress I'd created for myself that were causing the problem.

Once I started my own business and created my own financial freedom, everything started to change. I now make more money than I ever dreamed possible and I have more fun doing it than should really be allowed.

I work incredibly hard because I *want to* – not because I *have to* – and I get to see more of my family, more of my friends, more of the people who matter most to me, and more of the world at the same time.

I get to see, hear, taste and experience things I never thought possible only a few years ago.

I LOVE my life. Every single day I'm grateful that I get to do this work, which fills me with meaning and purpose.

This book is part of that work.

I hope you've followed the steps in this book and if not, stop reading now and go back – you will thank me for it one day, I promise.

If you've followed the path laid down in this book, you should be starting to see progress in your own financial life, but progress is often slow to begin with.

What you've just read is the distillation of a nearly seven-year Journey for me. Most of the quantum leaps happened in year six and seven!

Give the process time. Enjoy the Journey, do the work and I promise you'll see results in your life too.

Those results might not be apparent in the next month. They might not be apparent in the next year. But if you commit to the process, if you do the work, if you refuse to give up, there will be a day, probably about 5–10 years from now, where you wake up and realise that you're Financially Free.

You'll realise you have created a life you can love. You will be able to escape your own 9–5 and do work that you really care about. You'll be able to feel the joy of ridding yourself of debt. You'll be able to do what you want to do, when you want to do it, with the people you want to be with. You'll be really, truly free.

If that dream becomes a reality for just one person as a result of this book, then I will consider it a job well done.

And, if you do manage to make it to the top of your own mountain, please drop me a line and tell me about the view. I would love to hear about it.

Here's to your Freedom!

Matthew Smith

About the Author

Matthew Smith is the Managing Director of Buckingham Gate Chartered Financial Planners – an award-winning Financial Planning practice in the heart of central London – and MillennialMutiny.com – a blog and knowledge site dedicated to helping Millennials achieve financial freedom.

With more than a decade of experience helping people at both ends of the wealth spectrum, he helps clients reach their financial goals through his work with some of the UK's wealthiest families, and those aspiring to be in that category.

Matthew holds a Master's (MSc) in Financial Planning & Business Management, is a Chartered Financial Planner, Chartered Wealth Manager, Certified Financial Planner and Trust & Estate Practitioner. He also holds various specialist qualifications in the field of investment management and personal finance.

His first book, *Efficient Estate Planning,* is regularly a top-10 Amazon bestseller in personal taxation and has helped thousands of families to plan their estates.

An award-winning personal finance expert, Matthew has featured on BBC Radio 5 Live and his writing has appeared in *The Times, The Telegraph* and *FT Adviser.*

Matthew's passion is helping people to enjoy their wealth and helping them to find freedom, whatever that means to them.

When not working in one of his many business ventures, you will find Matthew spending time with his wife and daughter in Essex or trying (in vain) to learn to play the guitar!

Also from **Springtime Books** 🕊
Bringing Your Book to Life

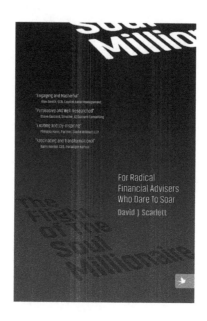

'Engaging and Masterful'

'Persuasive and Well Researched'

'Exciting and Joy-inspiring'

'Fascinating and transformational'

For Radical
Financial Advisers
Who Dare To Soar
David J Scarlett

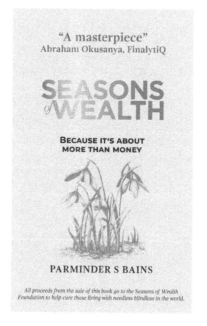

"A masterpiece"
Abraham Okusanya, FinalytiQ

SEASONS
of WEALTH

BECAUSE IT'S ABOUT
MORE THAN MONEY

PARMINDER S BAINS

*All proceeds from the sale of this book go to the Seasons of Wealth
Foundation to help cure those living with needless blindless in the world.*

Lightning Source UK Ltd.
Milton Keynes UK
UKHW022033270521
384488UK00006B/30